# The Enlightened Christian

A Psychological Interpretation of the Bible

Michael Roden

Copyright © 2015 by Michael Roden.

All rights reserved, including the right to reproduce this work in any form whatsoever, without permission in writing from the author or publisher, except for brief passages in connection to a review.

Infinite Passion Publishing Co.
Columbus, Ohio, USA 43147

www.infinitepassionpublishing.com
www.michaelroden.com

Library of Congress Cataloguing-in-Publication Data

Roden, Michael
  The enlightened christian: A psychological interpretation of the bible / Michael Roden

Summary: "An examination of the often-overlooked psychological nature of Christian metaphysics, theology and philosophy, showing how the Bible's conceptions are rooted in the capacity of human experience."

Includes Index

Library of Congress Control Number: 2015905478

1. Bible, N.T.--Theology. 2. Psychology and Religion.

ISBN 9780965299640
10 9 8 7 6 5 4 3 2 1
Printed on acid-free paper in the U.S.A.

*Bible Translations used:*

All Bible citations, unless otherwise indicated, are from:

*The Revised Standard Version,* copyright © 1946, 1957, 1971, by the Division of Christian Education of the National Council of Churches of Christ in the United States of America. Used by permission.

(Note: I use this version because of its more precise translation. The gender-specific language and the stress on the masculine are the product of an older way of speaking/thinking, and not any fault in the translation itself, which I believe is the most literal available. But in case there is any question, let me state clearly that I do not believe that God has a gender, being spirit, nor that God values patriarchy over any other element of human culture.)

Other versions used (when indicated) are:

*The New Revised Standard Version* (NRSV), copyright 1989 by the Division of Christian Education of the National Council of the Churches of Christ in the United States of America. Used by permission. All rights reserved.

*The King James Version* (KJV, also sometimes called the *Authorized Version,* AV). This version is in the public domain.

## ✻ Table of Contents ✻

✻ Introduction: The Bible and Ourselves ............................... 9

✻ 1. Demystifying Jesus ✻

    The Humanness of Christ ........................................ 17
    Selflessness and Universality ................................. 23
    Eternal Words ................................................. 29
    The Inner Living Word ......................................... 33

✻ 2. The Keys to Understanding ✻

    The Great Reversal ........................................... 37
    The Golden Rule .............................................. 41
    The Greatest Commandment ..................................... 43
    Forgiveness and the Unconscious .............................. 46

✻ 3. The Nature of God ✻

    God in Familial Terms ........................................ 53
    'God is Love' ................................................ 59
    Love or Fear ................................................. 63
    'I Have No Wrath' ............................................ 67

✻ 4. Belief And Transformation ✻

    Belief And Transformation .................................... 75
    'Your Faith Has Made You Whole' .............................. 78
    The Kingdom of Joy ........................................... 81
    The Gifts of God ............................................. 87

## ✽ 5. The Meaning of Life ✽

'You Search the Scriptures' (Eternal Life) .......................... 93
Original Life ............................................................. 99
Sonship ................................................................... 105

## ✽ 6. Spirit and Self ✽

The Spirit of Sonship .................................................. 110
The Spirit We Are ...................................................... 115
Be Still and Know ...................................................... 119

## ✽ 7. Salvation And The New Identity ✽

From a Great Height (The Fall from Original Being) ............ 124
Salvation and Return .................................................. 133
To Be Born Again ...................................................... 140

## ✽ 8. Raised As Children of God ✽

Resurrection as a Present Experience ............................... 145
The End of the World ................................................. 153
The Last Judgment .................................................... 160
The Image of Fire ..................................................... 168

## ✽ 9. On the Threshold ✽

The Devil and Satan ................................................... 177
Hell as a State of Mind ............................................... 184
The State of Heaven .................................................. 194

## ❋ 10. The Grandeur of Being ❋

Being Human .................................................. 205
Glorification .................................................. 211
'You Are The Light of the World' ............................ 217

## ❋ 11. From Metaphysics to Praxis ❋

Oneness ....................................................... 226
The Collective Christ ......................................... 231
Mutual Indwelling ............................................. 236
Predestined in Love ........................................... 239
The All-Inclusive King ........................................ 244

## ❋ 12. Living as a Child of God ❋
The Deepening of Religion .................................... 247
The Internalization of the Law and the Sacralizing of Life ..... 254
The Personal and Universal Symbolism of the Cross ........... 267
The Call to Freedom .......................................... 277

❋ Conclusion ..................................................... 285

*For now we see in a mirror dimly, but then face to face. Now I know in part; then I shall understand fully, even as I have been fully understood.*
          (1 Corinthians 13:12)

# Introduction:

# The Bible and Ourselves

The idea behind this book is very simple: The Bible makes more sense if interpreted *psychologically* rather than *conceptually*. That is because it becomes more personally significant. Mere intellectual concepts can be moved around like so much furniture in the mind, but psychological ideas are the real bedrock foundation upon which all else is built.

The Bible is full of psychological material. Too often, however, it is taken as having a metaphysical or theological meaning only—that is, a conceptual meaning—and its corresponding psychological meaning is missed. This is especially true for the biblical concepts with which we in the modern world have the most trouble such as the nature of miracles, Heaven and hell, and the end of the world.

It is not so much our modern psychological sophistication that renders us *better* able *now* to understand some of these ideas, for, after all, they were written with some degree of psychological understanding. But theirs was a much more *experiential* sense of psychological understanding, while ours had quickly latched onto the conceptual. The problem is that we in the modern world are distanced from what we know.

I do not adhere to any systematic theory, either in theology or psychology. What I want to do is let the words speak for themselves. To say that I interpret the Bible psychologically is to say that I seek to apply it to the *internal* self, the subjective sense of identity that we as human beings each possess. Simply put, I search the Bible in an effort to find out *who we really are* at the most basic and human of levels. Now of course this has ramifications for other things, such as relationships (even with God), and what it *means* that we exist.

I interpret "psychology" in its simplest and most classical sense to mean: "pertaining to the inner world of the *psyche*," where *psyche* means both mind and soul. It has no Freudian nor even Jungian connotations in the way I use the term, except insofar as both of those early modern psychologists were interested in the remarkable layers of depth they found in the human mind. They found veins of depth in classical philosophy and mythology and in Eastern religious traditions, but they seem largely to have missed the depth right under their noses: the depth that exists within the pages of the Bible.

This does not rule out theology. It is only because *we* have divorced the two that we think of theology and psychology as totally separate disciplines. (We might as well throw philosophy into this mix as well.) In fact, my point is that theology has much to gain by incorporating a more psychological understanding within itself. And psychology has much to gain by realizing it can work with religious and spiritual material on its own terms. We all have much to gain.

Theologically, too, I begin from a very simple starting point. We exist for a reason. This is all the faith one needs to start out on this journey. We do not know what this reason is, or how we got it. At first, we just *sense* that it is there, or we reason philosophically that it *must* be there.

The Bible itself is a collection of books all combined into one. Many different authors wrote it, and though they may differ conceptually in some areas, there is a remarkable unity in spite of its great diversity. Because it was written over many centuries by many different hands, one can detect trajectories of development among its ideas.

The Bible's 66 books (39 Hebrew or "Old Testament" and 27 Greek or "New Testament") are testament to human views of God along a timeline that ranges from approximately 3,000 years ago to roughly 2,000 years ago. Among its pages we can trace the development of views of God in one small society and culture from early monotheism to increasing psychological understanding.

Sociologically and anthropologically, the Bible can be studied as a library of variations on a theme: the relationship of humankind to itself and to what it conceives of as its God. Such approaches of study are all tied up in the Bible's overall meaning. They overlap with the psychological realm wherever they peer into the inner world of the human being: its motivations, its potentials, its sense of identity, its values, and basically all its thoughts and feelings.

The Bible speaks not only *to* us but also *about* us. Its revelation *includes* us. This is what makes it personally significant. As a human story, it is our story as well. Even that which is *divine* among its pages belongs to us. It is *our* divinity, as much as it is God's, insofar as we exist in relationship to it.

We tend to see the Bible only through our old, dusty and smudged theological lenses. We think we know what it means based on what others in the past have told us it means. We have not studied it sufficiently *for* ourselves because we have not studied it sufficiently in relation *to* ourselves. We did not see ourselves among its pages except perhaps in glimpses here and there. But no systematic attempt was made to piece all these glimpses together into one overarching picture that includes *the whole* of us and the Bible as well.

Differences among religions are primarily cultural, an *accident* of their geographic and historical birthplace. This affects the kind of philosophical backing the belief system will have, but in the end philosophy is philosophy, and its arguments are sound or not based on principles of logic and reason that really transcend cultural differences. And the psychology within and behind that philosophy in each major religion is more universal yet. It is in our psychology that we best see ourselves as similar in spite of culture. It is in our psychology that we see ourselves most as *human*.

The psychology behind the philosophy, which philosophy in turn stands behind the theology, is what makes the religion more human and more applicable to any human. It is in the psychological meaning therefore that we will find the most universal and generalizable meaning. We may have to wade through shallow waters to get to the depth, but the farther in we go, the more and more we shall find.

That is to say that our theology has become so very provincial, as if it were something we *own*, something attached to us but also detachable, like table manners might be. It is only loosely based on philosophy and so we hardly look for the logical and reasonable within it. We hardly expect to find logic and reason there, because we tend to think that belief *should* transcend these. But would not real belief, something we could really sink our mind and its choppers into, be as reasonable as possible lest it drive us away once we've seen through it? I mean, perhaps we really *were* given reason for a very valuable purpose, and for this reason alone, we might say that our theology should be *expected* to be reasonable.

This leads us to another definition: That which is most *human* in us is that which is most *given*, in the sense that we did not have to construct it from scratch so much as hone it, sharpen it. It was always there, though it lay dormant for so long a time. The good news is that it can always be removed from the toolbox and actually used.

It is by finding the things within ourselves that help us find our way that we find our own inner guide. We have external guides aplenty, but we remain lost if we do not have a capable inner guide. It seems as if it has been left entirely up to us to decide, to find, and to sharpen. It seems as if that, too, is part of what makes us *human*. All of this has been given to us. Responsibility is given in the same measure as freedom.

Perhaps it always was the case that each of us has already been given responsibility for developing our own individual theology, for discovering what makes most sense to us on a philosophical level and for uncovering what affects us or resonates with us most deeply on a psychological. And so our ability to experience various states of mind, another instrument we did not realize we owned, might be plugged in and given a whirl and used along with the reasoning capacity.

What we are trying to do, by not *starting* with the conceptual, is to ward off speculation for as long as we can while we find the truly human within us that will allow us to *extrapolate* rather than speculate as to the true nature of divinity. We will find that the Bible sees the divine level as transcending the human but not utterly superseding it; there is indeed an overlap, a bridge from one realm or state of being to another. It seems then that we *must* go through a stage of enhanced or honed humanity to get to divinity.

As much as a belief system is systematic it will also be *intuitive*, meaning that it will be sensed and adjudged as right or not for ourselves from within. The premises that underly our conclusions are, after all, as important as the conclusions themselves. There is a certain mystery as to how we come to any of this, so much so that theologians increasingly aver that belief, or to be more psychologically precise, the *will* to believe, is *given* to us. It is not really decided *by* us at all, but rather *for* us in some sense we do not yet quite understand.

There is still something of the preconceptual in even the most systematic system on earth. This is not to say only that it goes back to childhood for some of us, but that it seems to precede not only all the nurture we were born into but even our very nature. In other words, it *is* our very nature, but we still do not know this until near the end of the process wherein it will be made apparent to us. If successful, all things will come together at the point of culmination, and all the different levels that matter will be satisfied.

Yet another way of describing all of this from a macro-viewpoint is to say that, for the purposes of this study, we will be *bracketing* the theology as much as possible in order to avoid beginning with speculation and ending with speculation. That is, we will be setting it aside for the moment that we check to see if its deeper foundations at least match up with before they exceed our own. We will be checking it with what we learn about ourselves as we go.

It is by bracketing the theology that has attached itself to the Bible that we can better understand the raw data of its psychological and spiritual reports. We had allowed the theology to interfere with the psychological and experiential reality upon which such reports are based. Yet the experience *is* the thing. The theological and metaphysical concepts that have arisen on the basis of these reports often missed the experience that is at their heart, and which *precedes* even the belief let alone the theology.

We will be seeking the reader, the subject, the responder with depth of thought and feeling, even as we examine the Bible to find out about the thing itself. We hope to find a point of intersection at least, that compels us to go further in order to see if more points of intersection align to find a perfect trajectory: perfect for ourselves if not for others.

*The Enlightened Christian:*

*A Psychological Interpretation of the Bible*

# 1

# Demystifying Jesus

## The Humanness of Christ

How we think about Jesus tells us as much about ourselves as it does about him. Is he human or is he divine? This has been the question that has most concerned Christian theology from the start. And if he is both, in what proportion is he human and in which divine? All of this has implications for how we see *ourselves*, as I shall try to make clear.

Is he human in the same way that *we* are human? If so, then he is *fully* human. But is he divine in the same way that God is divine? Then he is *fully* divine. These are the two poles of our possibility, the two sides we must incorporate into a single and we hope consistent picture.

Each, we might say, is a frame of reference. Each is a way of seeing as well as being. For each would produce a world around itself, so to speak, a frame of context and reference for itself in which it might live and hope to thrive. The human side would build the world we have built, no doubt, while the divine side would add to the infinite increase of Heaven.

It is because they are so different, yet combined in the same individual, that we can say that both of these things happen at once, yet our awareness shifts from one to the other. In that way, the fullness of his humanity does not conflict with the fullness of his divinity. Rather, each is fully operational and existent within its separate sphere. He is, in a sense, the bridge between these two otherwise unbridgeable worlds and selves, simply by being.

*The same is true for each of us, according to Jesus' teaching.* This is what has been missed in all the furor about Jesus' nature. For the fact is that most by far of the teaching of Jesus has to do with *us*, not him. He himself was not as preoccupied with his dual nature as we tend to be. Instead, he was occupied with teaching us that we *ourselves* have a second nature. This was his mission: to have us see ourselves in much the same way he saw himself.

Theology has placed him on too high a pedestal to reach him. It tends to become all about him, and not at all about us. Yet why would he have bothered to teach at all if his teaching had nothing to do with us? And why would our own decision-making and the infinite power of our mind be emphasized to such a great extent in his teaching, if we ourselves were not important and indeed instrumental to the plan and process that God has willed for our eternal salvation?

These are the questions that will underlie our study. We are seeking *his* significance in order to find *our own*. Otherwise, however great we might see him, it would have little to nothing to do with us. Yet, as we have insisted and as we shall find, *his* teaching was more about us than it was about himself.

What Jesus' teaching says to me is that, though this other world, this divine context, is quite different from ordinary experience, it is fully accessible to us. In fact it was *meant* for us, so that it is not only fully accessible but, once accessed, will seem perfectly natural as well. This alone would *prove* that the human and divine do not conflict, if these two very different realities coincide in anyone. Jesus tells us they coincide specifically in us. The divine reality can seem as natural to us as the human already does, and in fact may eventually be seen as *more* natural.

We learn about Jesus and his bridging of the two natures by paying close attention to his own teaching on the matter, which has mainly to do with us. And so we learn about ourselves even as we learn about him. We learn about ourselves in an experiential and very personal way if we learn about ourselves *through* him.

This, I have explained in previous books, is how we follow him. This is how we see him as our great exemplar. We follow him all the way into divinity, a divinity he freely shares with all of us. This is what it means that any who partake can share in his life and even his Sonship.

This would mean that *we ourselves* are also bridges between the two worlds, and yet we have not known this remarkable fact about ourselves. How, then, could we have fully appreciated it about Jesus? Again, then, how we see ourselves has great implications for how we see Jesus, or at least for how constrictive or expansive our view of him might be.

We begin, however, with our shared humanity. This we already know we share, though we aren't fully aware of all the ramifications. No matter, we share *something*. And this something is enough to initiate the process.

Whatever else he was, he was a man, sharing all the characteristics of an ordinary human being. This is how he might have seemed to us had we seen him in passing. But he was an ordinary human being who taught about transcendent states of being, and taught most authoritatively, as if he knew exactly what he was talking about. He *experienced* them, he *lived* them, he had most likely taken the time to cultivate them or simply let them grow into his awareness. From there he attempted to describe and apply them to us for our benefit, in an effort to help us and all others like us.

The first thing we see when we look at the New Testament is an infancy narrative (in Matthew and also in Luke). Though these testify implicitly to his humanity, they are symbolic mainly of his divinity. They are beautifully poetic ways of bringing the two worlds together. But in our initial search for his humanness, we must look just beyond them.

In Matthew 4:1, for instance, we see that he was "tempted." In 4:2, we see that he could indeed become "hungry." In 4:17 he begins to preach and in 4:23 he heals. All the gospels agree that he submits to John the Baptist's form of baptism, and he may well have been part of the Baptist's circle of students before going off to teach on his own. None of this is as yet too superhuman, except perhaps the healing.

In Mark 2:16 we find that he is sitting and socializing, "eating with sinners and tax collectors." Religious authorities in the area are said to have criticized him for this. In Mark 3:21 we find that his family "went out to seize him, for people were saying, 'He is beside himself'" or that he was "possessed" (3:22). Evidently not even his own family knew what to make of him at times. For though he was human, he *also* was divine. That is, he knew himself to be something else entirely. He was aware of this side of himself, though whether he thought of it as his divinity or his divine side is subject to question. His expansive worldview may have seemed as natural to him as our constricted worldview seems to us.

We can further glean from the above passages that he did not allow himself to be subsumed by the socialization process. He did not think in the same categories as the world (even his family, even religion) tended to think. They had a hard time categorizing him and fully understanding him.

Yet he was not so different from us in many of his activities that we would not have recognized him. In Mark 4:38 we find that he slept. In Luke 19:41 we find that he wept. In Matt. 9:24 we see that people "laughed at him." In Matt. 19:14 we find that he loved and praised children. In Matt.11:5 we find that he cared for the sick and the poor. These are things that *any* of us either already do or might do.

His humanness, then, makes for a natural connection and grounding between him and us. He had some physical needs just as we have some physical needs, and perhaps emotional and psychological needs as well. The major difference between ourselves and him is how he experienced and thought of himself via his relationship with God and other humans. And yet, as we shall see throughout this book, this in particular is the very thing he sought to *share* with others.

He used many different kinds of symbols to describe what he was attempting to teach. "The kingdom of God" alone is described in dozens of different images, many of them everyday kinds of images (among them a mustard plant, a baker adding yeast to bread dough, a person finding coins or treasure). And then there are other images in the same class as the kingdom, though described in less earthly, more otherworldly terms: these range from being baptized with spirit or fire to being raised from the dead.

He seemed to know about heavenly or spiritual things and to teach about them with an authority that is rare among human beings. The Gospel of John's suggestion that he knew about these things from experience (3:11-12) seems a likely one. But as to whether he knew these things from the beginning of his earthly life or whether they developed in him, we cannot say with certainty.

We fail to understand him, however, when we place him on an unreachable level. For what he taught was how we, too, might see ourselves as otherworldly. Belief in him was belief in our own very human capacity for otherworldliness, for transcendence, for pure spirituality. Again, to believe in him was implicitly to believe in *ourselves* because of the nature of his teaching.

As evidence that Jesus did not think of himself as being fundamentally different than we ourselves are, consider the following statement:

> And Jesus said to him, 'Why do you call me good?
> No one is good but God alone.'
> (Mark 10:18)

This saying seems to go against the theological trend, begun very soon after his earthly existence, because it places Jesus on our level. Moreover, it has Jesus himself, for all his theological and spiritual authority, placing *himself* on our level, making *himself* one with us. It is likely that this saying goes back to the actual Jesus because it bucks the theological trend that was already in effect by the time the gospels were written, of distancing him from ourselves.

Jesus acts and teaches in the gospels with full spiritual authority. But such a saying as the above tells us that this is *not* because he was of a different order of being than we are. He does not even lay claim to be like God in this saying. The theology *about* Jesus seems to have leapt almost immediately to an incorrect conclusion about him, about God, and about ourselves, which has dominated Christian theology for nearly all its existence. It will take Jesus himself to break us free from this common complex of assumptions and place the emphasis back where it belongs: on the relationship between and among us, inclusive of our own relationship with God.

## Selflessness and Universality

As an example of our attempt to bracket our accumulated theology as we read the Bible, let us peer into the Gospel of John. The Gospel of John is known for its high Christology, meaning its tendency to portray Jesus as a divine figure, as "the Christ," and it is generally assumed that this high Christology comes at the expense of seeing Jesus as an ordinary human being. We will see in this section's passages, however, that John also emphasizes his humanness, providing a common starting-point from which we might share even his high Christology.

Take this statement of Jesus:

> I can do nothing on my own authority; as I hear, I judge; and my judgment is just, because I seek not my own will but the will of him who sent me.
> (John 5:30)

When Jesus says, "I can do nothing on my own authority," he is basically saying that even *he* had to overcome his old self to find his new self. It is this new sense of self that he speaks *from* when he utters his most lofty Christological statements. But here in this passage and in others in this Gospel, he is speaking from a more neutral place, and one that any one of his fellow human beings can apply to themselves.

When he says, "as I hear, I judge," he is basically saying that his judgment comes to him from beyond his ordinary self. But implicit in his saying this is the idea that anyone might do the same. If he himself does not decide one way or another, but instead waits on God to tell him what to do and how to decide, then anyone might do this.

Jesus himself had to overcome a false sense of self, and so he was able to show us by example how it is done. Or at least this is John's view of the situation. His Christology is not so high that it is out of human reach. It can be understood from the inside, by doing what he does, which was a theme of the Synoptic Gospels (Mark, Matthew and Luke) as well.

Here is a similar statement from the Johannine Jesus:

> For I have come down from heaven, not to do my own will, but the will of him who sent me.
> (John 6:38)

Here is John's high Christology in full display, yet in all its universality here wherein it speaks of Jesus as a universal being, it states that this Christology came about because of Jesus' decision to deny his false self. He, too, had two selves to choose from, two voices in his head, an angel and a devil on his shoulders, so that he had to find and to follow the one from God.

We are not demythologizing here so much as we are more carefully examining what Jesus is portrayed to have meant. Demythologization was an attempt to find the human Jesus by removing the supernatural element. This, to me, is based purely on presupposition before we find out the facts of the matter. Rather, what we are attempting is a kind of demystification, wherein we are setting the theology aside in order to better understand what was really said, both in a human sense and also in a supernatural sense. We are attempting to find out what is meant in both areas.

I do not discount John simply because his was a later Gospel, for John may be providing us with a valid glimpse into Jesus' own process and even into Jesus' self-consciousness. Someone in the Johannine community might have known Jesus from the inside, even if they did not know him personally. If so, this would make the Gospel and Letters of John extraordinarily helpful in exploring and being able to share Jesus' state of mind. In some areas John may be more helpful than the reportage done by the Synoptics, but we will begin with the latter because they may be more historically accurate, having been written closer to his time.

What is remarkable in these passages is that, even though he *knows* he came down from Heaven, Jesus realizes it had little to do his own individual will, except insofar as his aligned naturally with God's. In specifying that these are two different wills, Jesus is basically saying that we are all born into this world with two basic ways of seeing it and living in it. These two different ways of seeing correspond with two different ways of being, or two different identities from which we might choose: one that we have made (and are constantly making and remaking) for ourselves, and one that comes ultimately and directly from God. The one from God is our true will and our true self, the true will of our true self—and this was the case even for Jesus.

The Johannine Jesus reiterates over and over again that he neither speaks nor teaches on his "own authority" (Jn. 7:17; 12:49), that he does nothing on his "own authority" (Jn. 8:28), and that neither the words nor works he says and does are said or done on his "own authority" (Jn. 14:10). It is *always* God working through him. He says and does nothing on his own authority, nothing apart from God. For all his high Christology, then, John does not seem to assume that Jesus did not have similar earthly struggles to our own.

The Johannine Jesus describes further the major difference between these two selves from which we might choose:

> He who comes from above is above all; he who is of the earth belongs to the earth, and of the earth he speaks; he who comes from heaven is above all.
> (John 3:31)

We have here a self that "comes from above," or from Heaven, and one that comes from "the earth." The one that comes from Heaven belongs to Heaven and speaks of Heaven. It is "above all" in the sense that it transcends everything else. The self of the earth, the ordinary self, depends only on its physical senses, and cannot know anything from outside their rubric or domain. We shall see that this is consistent with Jesus' teaching in the Synoptics as well.

Here is another saying of the Johannine Jesus that upholds this interpretation:

> And Jesus cried out and said, 'He who believes in me, believes not in me but in him who sent me. And he who sees me sees him who sent me. I have come as light into the world, that whoever believes in me may not remain in darkness.'
> (John 12:44-46)

Remarkably for his high Christology, the Johannine Jesus is saying here that his denial of self, or denial of the false self, which obviously involved a kind of deconstruction or at least apophatism in regard to this false or lesser self, is the very thing that ultimately made him transparent to God. In a rather paradoxical turn of events, his selflessness was what led to his universality(!). His humanness, or more precisely his having to deal with his own humanness, was what granted him his air of divinity.

This is actually a new kind of Christology even for us, to the extent that we did not understand it before. And it came to us basically because we did not presume anything going in, but rather attempted to hear or read as if for the first time.

This internal shift from one self to another would have been quite difficult to explain particularly in that era, as well as in that cultural milieu, and so it is likely that Jesus showed it primarily by example. When he says, "the Father is in me and I am in the Father" (John 10:38), he is (besides speaking of a mutual closeness and intimacy) saying that he has chosen the self that is transparent to the Father, the self that comes directly from the Father, having willingly renounced or at least diminished his worldly self so that the latter would no longer block it out. This is why he can say, "I and the Father are one" (John 10:30) and also say, "the Father is greater than I" (John 14:28) without there being a cognitive dissonance in his mind.

The Johannine Jesus became the exemplar for choosing the transcendent self. His significance was that he was as human as they before he became transparent to God, which meant that he could be emulated. They would not be able fully to understand him until they followed him to this greatest extent, finding their own transcendent selves. They would understand on the basis of their shared *experience* with him, and so they would follow him from the inside.

This idea that universality arises from selflessness sheds light on the formula found in the Synoptic Gospels:

> For every one who exalts himself will be humbled,
> and he who humbles himself will be exalted.
> (Luke 14:11)

This saying seems to speak of two basic selves within each individual and of the inevitability of our ultimate decision between them, saying that by humbling one the other becomes exalted in our experience. Jesus himself is a great example of everyone's eventual re-identification with his or her own transcendent self.

**Eternal Words**

What we don't often realize about Jesus' teaching is that he is attempting to teach limitlessness to those who are already quite convinced they are limited. This would not be an easy task, particularly for his time period and historical place. It is even now for ours. He was attempting to describe an infinite and eternal reality to those who believed firmly that they were stuck in certain very mundane ways of seeing the world and their necessary place in it.

This different kind of reality that Jesus attempted to pass along is associated with concepts such as "eternity" or "the kingdom of God," or "the Holy Spirit." These are not just philosophical or theological concepts in his teaching, but instead descriptions of personal encounters *any* human being might have. Such concepts trickle down from the realm of abstraction into which theology has generally placed them when we look at them as potentially *lived* realities already existing as possibilities inside our minds.

And so when Jesus says such things as "earth will pass away, but my words will not pass away" (Matt. 24:35), he means that his teaching consists of an eternal reality that we as human beings can know. It can transform us from human beings back into spiritual beings, who have eternity just like his words. Eternal reality exists as a possibility within us It awaits only our choosing so that we might grow aware of it, and this is what his teaching is supposed to persuade us of.

Jesus' words are like instructions to this other reality, so that we ourselves might explore and map it out. They are instructions and affirmations both, confirmations from a spiritually authoritative source. This is why our praise of him is always for our own sake, because he does not *need* it. What he wants, and what he teaches that God desires, is to share eternal relationship and even *being* with him.

This is what he means when he describes his teaching as being like a solid foundation to us:

> Every one then who hears these words of mine and does them will be like a wise man who built his house upon the rock; and the rain fell, and the floods came, and the winds blew and beat upon that house, but it did not fall, because it had been founded on the rock.
> (Matt. 7:24-25)

Chaos is no match for what he's talking about. His words speak of a kind of reality that is not dependent on the world for its conditions. And notice that this eternal and quite stable reality of which he speaks is passed along simply in its hearing and in its doing. The hearing is for realization, while the doing is for application, for convincing ourselves and by extension all the world.

However otherworldly this may all seem at first blush, Jesus' message, he indicates himself, is simple enough for a child to understand:

> In that same hour he rejoiced in the Holy Spirit and said, 'I thank thee, Father, Lord of heaven and earth, that thou hast hidden these things from the wise and understanding and revealed them to babes; yea, Father, for such was thy gracious will.'
> (Luke 10:21)

However transformative and profound it may be, however different from the world, Jesus provides a realization that can be had by anyone. Its difference, then, is not in the sophistication with which it is expressed, but rather in the kind of life it opens us up to. The context of the above passage affirms this, for just before saying a child could understand, he is speaking of a kind of Heavenly reality that already exists in a kind of parallel universe to that of this world:

> Nevertheless do not rejoice in this, that the spirits are subject to you; but rejoice that your names are written in heaven.
> (Luke 10:20)

Joy is promised to be standing at the end of the process. But the realization is a gradual one because it is so different, involving "the spirits" to be "subject" to us and the realization that our true "names" are written in Heaven. All of this confirms that the eternal knowledge of which Jesus speaks is *inside* us as a potential experience of reality. It is not merely the kind of knowledge that we acquire conceptually. It goes beyond mere concepts because it is ultimately transformative of who we think we are.

Unlike children, unfortunately, we tend to complicate matters. In fact, it might be said that we almost *demand* obfuscation, so hard do we try to shield our eyes from the simple truth. We do this either by becoming lost in the weeds (hyper-detailed) or by dismissing the entire matter out of hand before we have properly examined it (hyper-critical). The main problem, if we might express it in modern language, is that we have allowed the socialization process to interpret "life" in a reductionistic way, whereas Jesus is trying to expand our definition of life to include what we have excluded.

This is what Jesus means when he says:

> I will utter what has been hidden since the foundation of the world.
> (Matt. 13:35)

He speaks here of having the role of revealing an underlying and foundational knowledge about life that the world itself tends to hide from us. We shall see further that Jesus speaks of a process involving our own uncovering or unearthing of such foundational knowledge, and of its bringing us the joy of true understanding.

We are the ones who will ultimately decide. Our freedom in this comes with great responsibility. We are asked only to give a fair hearing, first to determine whether it makes sense and then to apply it so this knowledge proves itself to us.

Once heard, the inner reality of eternity is sparked or activated, and then the words themselves make more sense. But the inner eternal reality was already there, pre-existing our realization of it, for it was implanted into our mind by God:

> He has made everything beautiful in its time; also *he has put eternity into man's mind*, yet so that he cannot find out what God has done from the beginning to the end.
> (Ecclesiastes 3:11, my italics)

Basically, God implanted eternity into our mind but we do not fully understand it. Because it is our own underlying, foundational reality, it is meant to be understood. For this, we need not earn it, or even acquire it, but simply open to it.

## The Inner Living Word

The only way that a human being can ever *know* about eternal reality is to experience firsthand said reality. To conceptualize about it from our ordinary human standpoint amounts to worlds of speculation. Psychology provides us with a more firm basis on which to build our theology.

The Word of God is more an experienced reality than a conceptual reality. The eternity of which it speaks is part of us, and so it is meant to be lived rather than merely conceptualized. Psychology must be involved then, as well as philosophy. The Word is meant to be taken inside ourselves (or recognized there) and *lived* like a potential reality that already exists within us:

> And we also thank God constantly for this, that when you received the word of God which you heard from us, you accepted it not as the word of men but as *what it really is, the word of God, which is at work in you believers.*
> (1 Thess. 2:13, my emphasis)

This passage from Paul is saying that the outer Word (the expressed message) in reality reflects an inner Word that each of us carries implicitly and unconsciously as a reality inside ourselves. From inside ourselves, this living Word is already at work in we who have believed in it or opened our minds to it. It is already operative, but we hold the key to our own realization of this fact. We are the ones who decide whether or not it lives and works *for* us, or whether it lives and works without our knowing.

We can trace this idea of an internal source of revelation back to Jeremiah in the Old Testament:

> But this is the covenant which I will make with the house of Israel after those days, says the LORD:
> *I will put my law within them, and*
> *I will write it upon their hearts;*
> and I will be their God,
> and they shall be my people.
> And no longer shall each man teach his neighbor and each his brother, saying, `Know the LORD,' for they shall all know me, from the least of them to the greatest, says the LORD; for I will forgive their iniquity, and I will remember their sin no more.
> (Jeremiah 31:33-34, my emphasis)

The prophet, in describing a more internal way of knowing God, describes a more *natural* way of knowing God. Even the law, which had always seemed external to the individual, codified and imposed from outside, will become known by the individual to reflect an internal reality, something existing within the human being. It will lead to a more direct knowledge of God, whereby we will know that He holds nothing against us.

Jeremiah is saying that we might think of the commandments as being evocative of a natural law within us. They are as much part of us as our natural identity is part of us, and in fact they flow from our inner beings even before we know ourselves as creations of God. The commandments at this stage in our moral development would become less commands and more ways of remembering our very present and very real relationship with God and by extension with his entire creation.

Jesus also spoke about fulfilling the law by *internalizing* the law, by seeing the law to be more about thought, value, and intention rather than by following some external code (e.g., Matt. 5:21-28). We will discuss his views on the law in a later chapter. For now we are specifically emphasizing the most clear statements in the Bible about a natural law which comes from within the human being.

For instance, Paul begins his exposition on the law by expressing a belief in a natural law, a natural moral sense in human beings:

> When Gentiles who have not the law do by nature what the law requires, they are a law to themselves, even though they do not have the law. They show that what the law requires is written on their hearts, while their conscience also bears witness and their conflicting thoughts accuse or perhaps excuse them.
> (Rom. 2:14-15)

This *internal* law is shared by everyone. It is built into us, part of the structure of our mind and heart. Those who follow this inbuilt law are "a law to themselves" and they "show that what the law requires is written on their hearts." Paul is describing here his belief in a natural way of abiding by the law that is innate to the human being.

The Word of God has the advantage of being both internal and objective to us at the same time. The two realms, inside and outside, subjective and objective, are brought together when we align our internal heart and mind with what we know of the objective law. Without this linkage and this internal connection, the objective law is merely external to us. Jesus calls this "tradition" and he contrasts it with the living and abiding Word of God:

> So, for the sake of your tradition, you have made void the word of God.
> 
> (Matt. 15:6)

Tradition *tries* to give us a sense of stability over time, but ultimately it cannot give us the sense of *certainty* that the heart can give us. This might seem to be backwards from how we usually think, for normally we think things that are institutionalized or established in the world are *more* certain than our individual thoughts and feelings. Yet *nothing* is more certain to a person than one's inner sense of being. Who we *think* we are is always primary. Everything else is secondary: all our actions and reactions follow logically from this core sense of identity, whose existence is only a product of mind and heart.

Jesus' parable about the Word being sown in different kinds of soil represents the stages of understanding the inner living Word (Matt. 13:19-23), culminating in our full experience of it:

> As for what was sown on good soil, this is he who hears the word and understands it; he indeed bears fruit, and yields, in one case a hundredfold, in another sixty, and in another thirty.
> 
> (Matt. 13:23)

The "good soil" into which the Word is implanted is our own mind, swept clean and purified to the extent that it can be open to reception, to "hear" and "understand" the spoken Word. The spoken Word, in other words, is meant to evoke the inner Word, the living Word. This is yet another of the ways in which Jesus describes how everything hinges on our subjective sense of reality.

# 2

# The Keys to Understanding

**The Great Reversal**

Jesus wanted to be known as a teacher (e.g., Mark 9:38; 10:17; Matt. 8:19; 10:24; 19:16; 22:36). He is said to have travelled all around Galilee (a region in northern Israel) "teaching in their synagogues and preaching the gospel of the kingdom and healing every disease and every infirmity among the people" (Matt. 4:23). His primary impetus seems to have been to help people both by teaching them and healing them. For now we will concentrate on his teaching which, due to his mastery over the inner world, holds the keys to our understanding of the psychology of the Bible.

Jesus' teaching centers mainly around what he called "the kingdom of God" (which Matthew calls "the kingdom of Heaven"). In Jesus' teaching this kingdom of God and Heaven is a reality that stands in contrast to the world, as an alternative reality than the world. We can live in either it seems, but not both at once. Hence the great importance Jesus seems to place on individual decision in his teaching and on reversing our thinking so as to align it with God rather than the world.

We begin with the Beatitudes, simply because they express the necessary great reversal in rather stark terms. They turn our usual valuation of the world on its head, pointing to a hidden dignity within people, whatever their apparent lowly circumstances:

> Blessed are the poor in spirit, for theirs
> is the kingdom of heaven.
> Blessed are those who mourn, for they shall
> be comforted.
> Blessed are the meek, for they shall inherit the
> earth.
> Blessed are those who hunger and thirst for
> righteousness, for they shall be satisfied.
> Blessed are the merciful, for they shall obtain mercy.
> Blessed are the pure in heart, for they shall see God.
> Blessed are the peacemakers, for they shall
> be called sons of God.
> (Matt. 5:3-9)

Here we find Jesus looking at the world the way a child of God or God himself/herself might look upon it. It is what we might call the divine point of view. In spite of the poverty, oppression, and great sadness we see from the world's point of view, there is a quiet and hidden dignity within people that cannot be ignored. The divine outlook focuses on this quiet internal dignity, and does not judge and make unnecessary comparisons quite like the world is accustomed to do.

This would represent a great reversal in our perception or way of seeing. It would change the world simply by changing our thinking about it and our valuation of it, and all of this simply by changing our focus. And so, for instance, instead of seeing people as poor, we see them as deserving of the kingdom of Heaven. These Beatitudes are in a sense an argument against reductionistic thinking and diminished judgment.

Consider this statement in particular:

Blessed are the pure in heart, for they shall see God.
(Matt. 5:8)

We can glean a number of things from such a statement. First, note that in order to "see God," one must in a sense become *like* God in being "pure in heart." There are some who are already like this, naturally we might say. Their thoughts and judgments are not about what they can get from other people, but rather involve what they can give. They do not seek to impose their self-interests on others, but instead they seek to find a common interest that joins people together.

If all our thoughts and feelings came from the divine place in ourselves, then we would have purity of intention, focus, and heart. We would be like God and we would see like God sees. Our motives would be entirely benevolent, entirely good without a hint of evil among them. They would be not only harmless but also helpful in every way.

In regard to 5:9, "Blessed are the peacemakers, for they shall be called sons of God," we sense that it is by joining our interests with others in some way that basic conflict is resolved. These are such simple statements, so concise, so easily memorable, yet so impactful, so rich in meaning. The idea that such peacemakers "shall be called sons of God," or will be identifiable as children of God, reveals that God, too, must have no inner conflict. This identification of people as "sons" or children of God will come to play a large and even predominant role in Jesus' teaching, as we shall later see.

What Jesus is teaching in the Beatitudes is that the world's point of view cannot determine the true worth of any person. It cannot penetrate that deeply. Societal or worldly standards will always be incomplete and insufficient to explain the true worth of the human being. The world itself will never see the real us, and would not know what to do with us if it did. There is something much greater going on behind the scenes. That inner being is all that really matters, and we will know this implicitly once we experience it.

The values of the world are reversed in these sayings. The same can be said of other sayings of Jesus, including: "many that are first will be last, and the last first" (Mark 10:31) and "he who is least among you all is the one who is great" (Luke 9:48). Jesus seems to have expected a great reversal in our perception as we began to accept the values of God over those of the world.

All these sayings suggest that a new world is available to us, and it costs only a change of mind. Those things we think are standard realities are really not so fixed; everything in this world is changeable, and not only that, it is generally the opposite of the real truth: God's truth.

If the meek were really to inherit the world (as in Matt. 5:5), how would they do so? It would be through a change of mind so complete that it would constitute a complete revaluation of values. This would help to underscore the great equality under God, not to mention the fact the idea that we might change the world just by changing our thinking about it. After all, we as human beings are those who make society, and so we can also change it just by changing our mind.

## The Golden Rule

> Jesus sums up his entire ethics in one sentence:
>
> So whatever you wish that men would do to you,
> do so to them;
> for this is the law and the prophets.
> (Matthew 7:12)

Note first that this idea is spoken of as a summing up of not only all the ethics, but also all the religion that came before. The phrase, "the law and the prophets" is a way of saying the entire Hebrew Bible, or what is often called the Old Testament, with the writings (Psalms, Proverbs, Job, etc.) being the third part. It seems incredible that such a simple statement could be said to capture the essence and all the intricacy and nuance of a religion. And yet here it is.

It is even more remarkable that such a summing-up of the essence of religion does not include the word "God." Now, of course, Jesus does speak of God in much of his teaching. But here all that is bracketed, so to speak, and the essence of religion is expressed in a purely human-relational way, as depending first and foremost upon the behavior of human beings to other human beings.

Whenever Jesus is asked to sum up his teaching, he does so on the basis of relationships. This casts religion and its ethics in very practical terms, focusing on who and what we see before us. Yet it also calls us to introspection, asking us to consider how we ourselves would like to be treated and directly associating this with how we treat other people.

A connection is established here between how we treat others and how we see ourselves. This is at once the most brilliant and the most simple of ethics, to connect how we treat others with how we see ourselves. The incentive for both is the same, so that self-interest joins up and connects with our interest in others. How we see ourselves and how we see others are essentially one and the same.

## The Greatest Commandment

Jesus was asked which, in his opinion, was the greatest commandment in the religious law:

> 'Teacher, which is the great commandment in the law?' And Jesus said to him, 'You shall love the Lord your God with all your heart, and with all your soul, and with all your mind. This is the great and first commandment. And a second is like it, You shall love your neighbor as yourself. On these two commandments depend all the law and the prophets.'
>
> (Matthew 22:36-40)

The first part of this two-fold great commandment comes directly from the Book of Deuteronomy (6:4) and involves loving God with one's entire being (with all one's "heart," "soul," and "mind"). To this Jesus adds a second part that involves loving one's neighbor as oneself. Therefore love is meant to apply to all beings: God, others, and even oneself.

Jesus indicates that these two commandments are the lynchpins of the entire scripture and all religion, using the phrase we had just seen in relation to the Golden Rule: "the law and the prophets." But whereas the Golden Rule was about *treating* one another as oneself, the Great Commandment is about *loving* others as oneself. There is still a behavioral component, but we have moved into the realm of depth of emotion and motivation.

Once again, a human being is viewed here not as an isolated unit, but instead as fully interconnected with others.

In fact, as with the Golden Rule, we are asked to view others *as* ourselves, suggesting that a metaphysical or "being" component also exists in these sayings. It is as if one were to think of others and therefore learn to see them as extensions of oneself. All sense of separation between and among beings is therefore erased. One is to think of oneself as belonging to a larger whole.

That love is the one law handed down by Jesus is verified elsewhere in the New Testament. Paul in his Epistles writes that love fulfills the law while it simultaneously sets us free from it:

> Owe no one anything, except to love one another; for he who loves his neighbor has fulfilled the law. The commandments, 'You shall not commit adultery, You shall not kill, You shall not steal, You shall not covet,' and any other commandment, are summed up in this sentence, 'You shall love your neighbor as yourself.' Love does no wrong to a neighbor; therefore love is the fulfilling of the law.
> (Romans 13:8-10)

He states the same thing even more succinctly elsewhere, saying simply:

> For the whole law is fulfilled in one word, 'You shall love your neighbor as yourself.'
> (Gal. 5:14)

Here and in the passage above, Paul seems to be quoting Jesus and elaborating on the teaching Jesus passed down to his students. The teaching itself is to love, even to the point of *identifying* with one's neighbors, of seeing oneself and one's own interests as being one and the same with these other people. For, as Paul says quite clearly and plainly, "love is the fulfilling of the law."

This is our call to "freedom," says Paul in Gal. 5:13. Love is at once freedom from the law and at the same time fulfillment of it. Ironically to live by love means freely to choose to become "servants of one another" (5:13). Such is the nature of love and such is our true, underlying nature that our true desire is to care for others in the same way that we care about ourselves.

The Evangelist John cites this same commandment, and the primacy of love in Jesus' teaching, so that we find in 1 John 3:23 similar instructions: "love one another, just as he has commanded us." The same is reiterated later:

> And this commandment we have from him, that he who loves God should love his brother also.
> (1 John 4:21)

Here we see that John connects the two parts of the Greatest Commandment from both directions—the love of others leading to love of God, and the love of God leading naturally to love of others. We will examine John's argument in more detail in the next chapter.

## Forgiveness and the Unconscious

In continuing our exploration of the primary themes of Jesus' teaching, which have to do with psychology and relationship, we turn next to forgiveness. The formula that Jesus uses to present forgiveness is a reciprocal one:

> if you forgive men their trespasses,
> your heavenly Father will forgive you.
> (Matthew 6:14)

We have seen a similar reciprocal relationship in Jesus' teaching of the Golden Rule (treat others as you wish to be treated) and the Great Commandment (love your neighbor as yourself). Here, though, the relationship is between ourselves and others *as well as* ourselves and God.

If we forgive others, then we will be forgiven by God. What does this mean, and what does it suggest? If we consider that God's nature, being eternal, is unchanging (i.e., that He is *always* merciful and loving), then it must be that our forgiveness of others leads to our own *realization* of this fact. We are not entering into a bargain with God so much as we are becoming like God in order to realize His point of view.

It is not uncommon for Jesus to teach that we must become like God in order to realize how God thinks and feels about us. It is a central feature of Jesus' teaching:

> You have heard that it was said, 'You shall love your neighbor and hate your enemy.' But I say to you, Love your enemies and pray for those who persecute you, so that you may be sons of your Fa-

ther who is in heaven; for he makes his sun rise on the evil and on the good, and sends rain on the just and on the unjust.
(Matt. 5:43-45)

But love your enemies, and do good, and lend, expecting nothing in return; and your reward will be great, and you will be sons of the Most High; for he is kind to the ungrateful and the selfish.
(Luke 6:35)

    This encouragement to become like God is one of the hidden keys to understanding his teaching, and yet—strangely—it was there in plain sight all along. We must have overlooked the connection previously because we had not believed such a connection between ourselves and God was possible. And we had not believed such a connection was possible because we had not thought highly enough of *ourselves* let alone others.

    In effect, Jesus is teaching us to know God *from the inside*: by sharing His inner Being. This is referred to in these passages as becoming "sons" or children of God. It is in some sense to share God's thought and emotion. In such a way we extend God's love for us to all others. And that which applies to love in these passages also applies to forgiveness.

    Nowadays it is a well-established psychological principle that we project thoughts and feelings what we don't like about ourselves onto others. This principle was in effect long before psychologists like Freud pointed it out just over a century ago. Freud himself learned it in part from listening to his Victorian-era patients and in part from his reading of classical literature (including the Bible, Homeric mythology, and classical poetry).

We do not normally think of Jesus as having taught about the unconscious, let alone unconscious guilt. Of course, the category of "the unconscious" did not yet exist in Jesus' day; there was no word for it. And so it was talked about in poetic images if it was talked about at all. But consider the following teaching of Jesus as pointing out how our own unconscious guilt obstructs clear perception of others:

> Why do you see the speck that is in your brother's eye, but do not notice the log that is in your own eye? Or how can you say to your brother, `Let me take the speck out of your eye,' when there is the log in your own eye? You hypocrite, first take the log out of your own eye, and then you will see clearly to take the speck out of your brother's eye.
> (Matt. 7:3-5)

Jesus is saying here that the real problem lies within ourselves, which can only mean our heart and mind, but we project it onto others in order to hide this fact from ourselves. What would we be trying to accomplish in so projecting? We would be warding off guilt, not simply mistakenness, by trying to keep this all unconscious. We would be trying to convince ourselves we did nothing wrong by blaming it on others, which means that the guilt must be too much for us (at least on some level).

It is this unconscious guilt that we try to pass around like a hot potato. Where does it come from? Even recent philosophical psychologists point to how it seems built into existence, which is why they called it "existential" guilt. It is free-floating in the sense that it has no apparent object. We don't know what we did wrong, but we are sure we did something—or at least our unconscious mind seems sure.

The fact that we (apparently) feel we cannot deal with guilt directly means that guilt is unnatural to us. The fact that we try to pawn it off on others, even unconsciously, *shows* this to be true. But Jesus tells us how to deal with the seemingly intractable problem of guilt in one fell swoop. The idea (as in Matt. 6:14) is to forgive those we've unnecessarily blamed, so that we might remember that in God's eyes, we are already forgiven. For it was the defense against guilt (i.e., projection) that kept it going by keeping it hidden.

Even though we keep it hidden, or unconscious, we still sense the guilt. Even though we think we've redirected it, it still has effects upon us. It is just that the guilt is now indirectly felt, as anxiety or depression, frustration or anger, or just a generally negative and hypercritical attitude toward others. We do not realize that by distancing them we are distancing our own basic guiltlessness.

Jesus seems to be talking about unconscious projection of guilt with the image of the log and the splinter, an image at once ingeniously simple and curiously absurd. The log in our own eye prevents us from seeing clearly, obviously, yet we do not realize it is there. And so we still try to peer around it to find the little mistakes others always seem to make. Yet from a more objective viewpoint we are simply ignoring the obvious (or what should be obvious): that we have our own problems to deal with.

Forgiveness, then, is a way of dealing with the underlying problem directly and at its root. It may not yet feel direct to us, but it is actually the most direct route. First, we reel in our projections, so as to deal with the problem within ourselves. And then we give that problem over to God, to be shone away forever in His light.

As we see others as being closer to God—whatever they do, however they believe—God draws nearer to us.

There would seem to be no relationship between the two, but Jesus assures us there is. In essence, their fate is ours as well. If they are condemned, we are condemned. On the other hand, if they are forgiven, so are we.

This means that all the problems we had seen in others had been our own problems all along. The following saying of Jesus seems to support this understanding:

> And if you had known what this means,
> `I desire mercy, and not sacrifice,'
> you would not have condemned the guiltless.
> (Matt. 12:7)

Jesus is citing Hosea 6:6, which reads:

> For I desire steadfast love and not sacrifice,
> the knowledge of God, rather than burnt offerings.

Jesus seems to be indicating here that even the ancient religious sacrificial system (common, as we now know, to nearly all the religions of the world) had inadvertently perpetuated this unconscious guilt. It therefore had not resolved the real problem. Our preoccupation with sacrifice had only *retained* the underlying guilt, driving it deeper into unconsciousness. It, too, had been a form of projection, specifically upon "the guiltless," or those we could otherwise have seen as innocent, which would have sparked our own deeper sense of innocence. Thus do we condemn those who might otherwise have helped us realize *our own* innocence before God.

This idea that *we* as human beings should forgive others seems to have been a radical message for his time and place, as evidenced by the reaction of the religious authorities who "began to question, saying, "Who is this that speaks blasphemies? Who can forgive sins but God only?" (Luke 5:21). Jesus answered them with a question of his own:

> 'Which is easier, to say, "Your sins are forgiven you," or to say, "Rise and walk"?
> But that you may know that the Son of man has authority on earth to forgive sins' — he said to the man who was paralyzed — 'I say to you, rise, take up your bed and go home.'
> (Luke 5:20-24)

Here we have a direct association between forgiveness and healing. It is by looking to forgive others that they are healed, which means that guilt (free-floating *un*-ease) had been a cause of *dis*-ease. Again, we carry this guilt around without realizing because we have already decided, by defensive habit, to "deal with it" or wish it away by projecting it onto others. Such projection, of course, is *not* dealing with the guilt directly, and so the guilt remains an active part of the unconscious mind, where it arises to affect us in distorted ways. The cover-up in many ways is worse than the crime, which may be the real reason we do not remember *either* nor their genesis.

In other words, it is by having kept our own guilt feelings hidden that they come to be seen as worse than they actually are. The simple act of bringing them into the light of conscious realization, then, is the way to undo their effects. This is why confession is good for the soul. By bringing our own perceived wrong-doing into conscious awareness, we find that it is actually much less severe than we had adjudged against ourselves. We worsened it by hiding it.

Via love and forgiveness we might project more positive thoughts and feelings as well. By discovering something to love in others, we are uncovering something to love about ourselves as well. And so, if we decline the unconscious impulse and habit to criticize or to judge, we will begin to feel better about ourselves as well.

Jesus also seems to be saying here that human beings have been given the authority to forgive others *for God*, to act in this sense as His representatives or proxies in the world. Such would be proactive forgiveness, or forgiveness prior to any kind of perceptible wrong-doing. Forgiveness here is transformative thought and vision. All forgiveness heals, even from a neutral state, even if there was no wrong-doing, transforming the world we see in the process by transforming our mind.

Note, too, that in this passage Jesus uses the phrase "Son of man" to mean *all* human beings. We will explore the further significance of this identification later. Suffice it to say that the core of Jesus' teaching, as we have examined thus far, has extensive implications for how we see all of God, ourselves, and others. It is meant to evoke transformation and the experience of a new reality where once it seemed only a broken one stood. Let us now turn to an examination of how our emphasis on Jesus' teaching clarifies the true nature of God and our true relationship with Him and with all creation.

# 3

# The Nature of God

**God in Familial Terms**

Jesus refers to God most often as "heavenly Father" (e.g., Matt. 5:16, 48; 6:14). He teaches his students to pray using the phrase "Our Father who art in heaven" (in Matt. 6:9-13; Luke 11:1-4). He teaches them to think of themselves as "sons" or children of this heavenly Father (Matt. 5:45). There is a highly personalized aspect to such language, of course. It is the language of *family* he uses to express their true relationship with a transcendent ("heavenly") Deity.

There is a paradox here, in that the phrase "heavenly Father" suggests both transcendence (through the use of the word "heavenly") and intimacy (through the use of the word "Father"). The word "heavenly" suggests that God is unknowable by human minds (because human minds can only speculate about Heaven), while the word "Father" suggests an intimate and firsthand knowledge.

Though God is transcendent, or inconceivable to the human mind, He is also intimately knowable and relatable. What this seems to mean, then, is that God, while seeming currently unknowable to the human mind, this same God is quite knowable when we know *ourselves* as His sons or daughters. It is then that we find that God, however transcendent He may currently seem, is infinitely relatable. God is both abstract, transcendent Being and knowable, relatable loving Parent.

To put this in other words, from the human point of view, which is necessarily limited in this world, the distance between the mind and God seems impassable. The gulf between them is too great; one is not like the Other. However, from God's vantage point, which Jesus is somehow in position to share with us, there is no gulf. Therefore we need to learn to see the relationship between us and God from *God's* viewpoint, rather than our own, if we are know the truth.

Jesus can see it from God's viewpoint because he has experienced closeness with God. He expresses this closeness in terms of a familial relationship of father and son. (It might just as well be mother and daughter, or any combination of the above, for again, the relationship is as transcendent of ordinary human categories as it is intimate.)

Jesus also expresses relationships among human beings in familial terms, teaching his students to think of other people as siblings or "brothers," as for instance in the following passage:

> So if you are offering your gift at the altar, and there remember that your brother has something against you, leave your gift there before the altar and go; first be reconciled to your brother, and then come and offer your gift.
> (Matt. 5:22-24)

The horizontal relationship here (between oneself and other human beings) must be rectified *before* the vertical relationship (with God) can be fully appreciated. Once again, we see in Jesus' teaching a direct association between our relationships with others and with God.

Though he uses familial terms to express it, the indication we get from Jesus' teaching is that our relationship with God is more important than even the closest family relationships here on earth. And so, although Jesus stresses the importance of fulfilling the law in making sure one's earthly parents are comfortable (Mark 7:10-12), for instance, the familial relationship for him seems to have extended far beyond the bounds of blood ties (Mark 3:31-35).

In Mark 3:35, Jesus extends the close, familial relationship to "whoever does the will of God," calling that person, even if unrelated by blood, "my brother, and sister, and mother." Thus it is simultaneously a close, familial relationship but also universal or applicable to *every* person.

Even when he seems to be speaking *against* being bound too tightly to family ties, as for instance in Matt. 19:29 ("And every one who has left houses or brothers or sisters or father or mother or children or lands, for my name's sake, will receive a hundredfold, and inherit eternal life"), the ideal still seems to be closeness and intimacy. It is just *extended* to people beyond one's original family unit. For Jesus, it seems, *everyone* was potentially part of a larger spiritual family with everyone else simply if they *wanted* to be.

Now, technically speaking, one does not *acquire* sonship so much as *realize* it, as if one has forgotten, as in the case of the prodigal son in Luke 15. The relationship was always there, the reality of it already existed, but it was not realized because it was not sufficiently appreciated. It had been forgotten along with the prodigal son's sense of his own worth and his remembrance of the true nature of his father. His problem was basically one of *amnesia*, forgetting both his identity and the reality of his loving father.

The prodigal son does not *become* a son of God so much as he *realizes and remembers* he is one. Therefore Jesus calls us to such remembrance by calling us to a change of mind about who we are:

> And call no man your father on earth,
> for you have one Father, who is in heaven.
> (Matt. 23:9)

Jesus teaches his students to think of God as their Heavenly Father, which means *ipso facto* they are His Heavenly children. That is, such a statement says as much about them as it does about God. Jesus advocates and encourages an entirely new way of thinking of oneself and all one's relationships, all the way up to and including the one we have with God.

In Jesus' view, in order to think of God as our Heavenly Father, we *must* think of ourselves as His Heavenly children. We can, should, and *must* (already) be spiritual like Him (John 4:23), merciful like Him (Luke 6:36), loving like Him (Matt. 5:44-45), and even perfect like Him:

> You, therefore, must be perfect,
> as your heavenly Father is perfect.
> (Matt. 5:48)

This is not something we aspire to be so much as it is a pre-existing truth that is hidden from ourselves. We cannot *will* ourselves to perfection like God's; either we are created perfect or we have no chance at perfection. We can will only to remember this fact. Our choice is simply in whether we will allow ourselves to realize it or not.

In the meantime, we *practice* being like God in our relationships with others. Practically speaking, this involves being merciful and loving towards them. We do this for our own sake as much as for theirs, for we are looking to know the true being and relationship of both at once. All of this is suggested in the passage we discussed in the last chapter about the need to become like God (Matt. 5:43-44).

We have mentioned Jesus' parable of the prodigal son in relation to how he squandered his rightful identity and inheritance by denying his true relationship with his father. In the parable, you will recall, the young son who squandered his share of the family fortune suffers from guilt and hardship. This leads him eventually to a repentant moment:

> I will arise and go to my father, and I will say to him, 'Father, I have sinned against heaven and before you; I am no longer worthy to be called your son; treat me as one of your hired servants.'
> (Luke 15:18-19)

The prodigal son believes he is underserving—"no longer worthy to be called your son." So deep is his regret that he is ready to undergo anything (even submit to being treated as a hired servant) just to be near his father again. But his deep-seated sense of unworthiness proves in the end to have been utterly unnecessary *except* that it urged him to return. As he is approaching his former home with trepidation in his heart, he quickly finds out the joyful news that his father was not thinking in the same way whatsoever:

> And he arose and came to his father. But while he was yet at a distance, his father saw him and had

compassion, and ran and embraced him and kissed him.

(Luke 15:20)

The son's guilt and reservations were neither shared nor reinforced by the father. The entire intervening nightmare had all been a product of the son's mind. All his father *ever* really cared about was having his son back, due to the great love he had for him, as evidenced by his dropping everything to run and embrace his son. The essential relationship between them, as father and son, *has never changed* in the father's mind. The father cared more about his son's present well-being than the gamut of his past indiscretions. He is focused solely on the joy of their reunion, saying, "my son was dead, and is alive again; he was lost, and is found" (Luke 15:24).

## 'God is Love'

The love of God is described throughout the Old Testament as being "steadfast" (e.g., Gen. 39:21; Exod. 15:13; 1 Kgs. 8:23; Ps. 13:5), meaning it is constant and unchanging, like a parent's love for her children. It does not matter what they do, they will always remain her children and she will always love them, always think of them as part of her.

Jesus saw God just this way. He stressed how God is "kind to the ungrateful and the selfish" (Luke 6:35), not that he encouraged selfishness, but was able easily to overlook it. Jesus indicated over and over how he came "not to call the righteous, but sinners" (Matt. 9:13), and seemed to demonstrate how God needed literally everyone to be God. God was in the whole—in the part as well, but even more so in the whole which comprised all the parts together in itself.

God is righteous and just precisely *because* He is so thoroughly loving that no one escapes His notice. He sees the good in everything, and everything to Him shines like a reflection of Him. To say that He is omniscient, or "all-knowing," is to say that He knows all life intimately, as Himself. Only the good could possibly come from such a Being.

The First Letter of John (or 1 John) takes this idea to its ultimate conclusion. So loving is God that He is *defined* by love, even *identified* with love. *All* love is of Him, also, in the sense that not even the smallest act or thought of love escapes His notice.

"God *is* love" this Letter declares, specifically in two places in chapter 4 (verses 8 and 16). There is no real difference between the two. God is simply love "perfected" (4:18). This is the perfect way to think of Him if we want to get a good sense of His/Her all-encompassing and universal nature. Love is this God's pure intention because love is what gives this God perfect joy.

The idea that "God is love" is perfect in its simplicity, its succinctness, and its concision. There is nothing within this declaration that is untrue, nothing sketchy, nothing dodgy. It is as pure a statement of belief and of *being* as anyone can have, as any child can understand, as any person can "do." A child, in fact, throws himself full-force into things in his excitement; this is how God is with His/Her love. It depends on nothing we do; it is simply there, to be accepted, as fully and freely as it is given, or not yet accepted.

For who could ever fully turn away from such love, if once it were known, if once it were felt? Once experienced, it would be everything to that person, longed for, hoped for and expected again and again. It would never leave their mind. It would be impossible to forget. This is how the God of love thinks of *all* His children. Being love, He could not be otherwise.

Let us take each statement of "God is love" in its turn. The first one argues that, ethically speaking, human beings should love one another because *all* love is from God:

> Beloved, let us love one another; for love is of God,
> and he who loves is born of God and knows God.
> He who does not love does not know God;
> for God is love.
>                                    (1 John 4:7-8)

Here the idea that God is love is revealed to us *through* our love of others. And so love is the thing we do to realize who God is from the inside. Such an idea parallels Jesus' teaching that love makes us like God, or children of God.

Those who love already know God, and from the inside, the only place He can really be known. They are in His Mind. They are doing what He does. They are His children, and they know exactly who they are, in the same way God knows Himself.

It is the loving part of ourselves, the source of pure love within us, that is most like God. John's argument, simple yet profound, is that because love is "of God," our own love allows us to know that we are "born of God," and exactly *how* we are born of God. Our own love of others makes us like God. Love literally transforms us, causing us to think like God, therefore to know God from within.

The selflessness of all-consuming love leads to a new self, which is actually the most ancient and original part of ourselves. This is our identity as children of God. Because God is love, *we* are also love. As we come more and more to love like Him, we increasingly realize who *we* most eternally and essentially are.

The second instance of the direct statement, "God is love," occurs in the same chapter:

> God is love, and he who abides in love abides in God, and God abides in him.
> (1 John 4:16)

Here we have the idea of God being love associated with a kind of *mutual indwelling* of God in us and we in Him. This suggests that love is in some sense the taking of another being inside one's mind and heart. This is why, when we love, as for instance our children, we think of those we love as extensions of ourselves. They abide in our mind and we in theirs if there is a mutual bond of love between us. Once it is felt, that bond of love is always there.

If the love of God for us began at the moment of our creation, then we have, ever since our original creation, *always existed* in the Mind of God. Furthermore, we must already be worthy, perfect, holy if we exist forever in the Mind of God. We are indeed these things, on a deep and fundamental level, at the core and essence of our being. It is only on a more surface level that we believe we are unworthy, or alone, alienated, estranged, and lacking the love of God. The lack of love or the denial of love is but a mask covering the all-consuming nature of the great love that exists within us and *as* us.

There is nothing we can do to *make* ourselves worthy. But what we *can* do is find the part that is *already* worthy and identify with that. There is nothing we can do to make ourselves worthy, but that also means there is nothing we can do to make ourselves *un*worthy. To know God is to know that it is impossible to change our true and eternal status as beloved children of God. We can only *delude* ourselves that this has been done, and that we are *not* His beloved children.

For Paul, too, *nothing* can "separate us from the love of God" (Rom. 8:39). This is just a simple fact. For once we have felt even a small ray of such great love, we *know* this to be true. If God does indeed love us, then *nothing* can keep us out of His Mind. And it really was just illusion that kept us feeling so removed.

**Love or Fear**

The First Letter of John goes on to explain how God is love by contrasting love with its opposite on the emotional spectrum, fear. Ordinarily we would think of hatred as being the opposite of love, but hatred, like anger, is a secondary emotion. There is another emotion behind both hatred and anger, and that emotion is always fear. This is well attested in modern cognitive psychology, which considers anger a secondary emotion to the depression that lurks beneath.

John points out the total contrast between love and fear, saying:

> There is no fear in love, but perfect love casts out fear. For fear has to do with punishment, and he who fears is not perfected in love.
> (1 John 4:18)

There is much about this verse to unpack. First note the complete and utter dichotomy between love and fear. They are polar opposites, each of which "casts out" the other. They cannot co-exist in the same mind if one "casts out" the other. The presence of either will drive the other out of mind. Fear, which includes all guilt, all anger, all hatred, all thought of punishment, and all evil, is the absence of love.

John in this letter denies that God thinks in terms of punishment whatsoever. For, as he says and reiterates, God *is* love. And if God is love, then He can have no fear whatsoever and therefore no thought of punishment. Note that just as love was the source of God's omniscience and full knowledge of our inner beings, it is also the source of His omnipotence.

John is attempting to describe the thoroughgoing internal consistency of God. This is the steadfastness of God's love, emphasized again and again in the Old Testament, brought to its ultimate and logical conclusion. The idea of punishment, sometimes mistakenly attributed to God, cannot exist as a thought in His Mind because His love is perfect.

Metaphysically speaking, there can be no opposite in His Mind. God is fully Himself, always and forever. Therefore what we once saw as punishment cannot be punishment. That was only our interpretation based on fear. Because God is fully and whole-Heartedly love, He does not think in terms of punishment at all. That would be contrary to His perfect nature as love.

The idea of punishment is declared here to be a human rather than a Divine idea. It is misattributed if we think of it as coming from in any way from God. It can only have been generated by beings who seek to hide their joy from themselves. It comes from a diminished perspective, not even fully human, rather than a Divine perspective.

Whereas we as creations of God might alternate between the poles of love and fear, God cannot do so. This is precisely John's revelation, that there is no darkness in Him:

> This is the message we have heard from him
> and proclaim to you, that God is light
> and in him is no darkness at all.
> (1 John 1:5)

God might be thought of as pure light, just as He is pure love. This is why just one dark thought among His thoughts would diminish His perfection or our own, Furthermore, His omniscience and His omnipotence as well as His joy all depend on His perfect love. Just one thought which was not based on pure love would make Him *not Himself*, and it is impossible that God be not Himself. This reinforces the ancient Hebrew idea that "God is one," adding single-mindedness and singleness of purpose to the ways in which God is one.

The one difference is that He gave His creation choice, and this in fact is why He created them. Apparently He felt that love involved beings with minds of their own, that it should take two rather than one, but that the two could feel and know themselves to be one based on the mutual love between them. Though He Himself could not be without love, His creation could at least believe they were without love, though there would of course be no conceivably good or sensible reason for them to so decide.

Anything other than love is incomplete. It does not contain the fullness of joy and so it can result only in suffering. Not being complete in itself and in its love, it can only diminish. It can see very little of what is available to see, tragically, only because it does not appreciate what is already always there. It becomes lost in its own self-made and much-reduced world of delusion.

To sum up the argument so far, fear, being foreign to God, has kept us distant from Him. We cannot imagine how He thinks in terms of total love if we have just a trace of a thought contrary to it in our minds. This would always be a lack and diminishment of what is always forever true, and so it would be unsatisfying and so produce suffering.

Fortunately, there is a part of us that does love perfectly, naturally and consistently and fully like God. It therefore knows God fully. This is the part that is born "of God." It is the true us, long hidden by our loveless thoughts.

All the foregoing would seem to shed new light on Jesus' saying:

> So have no fear of them; for nothing is covered that will not be revealed, or hidden that will not be known.
>
> (Matt. 10:26)

It is because love is more fundamental than fear that it will remain long after fear is gone. And so the full and ultimate revelation of truth—the truth of ourselves and of God—will always be entirely joyous. Otherwise it would be incomplete, and would leave us unsatisfied.

Love, being "of God," has an eternal foundation. It will always be, even if the reduced world around it were to fall away. Jesus is saying that there is a process *already underway* whereby this "hidden" or unconscious foundational reality that we share with God is being brought to light, brought into full awareness. We need only to trust the process of increasingly clear revelation of the fullness of truth, enough to allow it to prove itself to us.

## 'I Have No Wrath'

In the Book of Isaiah (27:4), God is portrayed as saying: "I have no wrath." This would mean of course that He has no rage, no anger. Such a statement ("I have no wrath") dovetails perfectly with John's argument that God does not think in terms of punishment because God, being perfect love, can have no fear. Having no fear, God has no *use* for either punishment or anger. Therefore neither anger nor fear nor punishment *exist* for God.

We have spoken of anger and punishment as spin-offs of fear, dependent on fear for their existence. Without fear, there can be no anger. One would be fully possessed of a cool head. And what exactly would God have to fear? What does He, who *creates* His own reality, possibly have to fear from the reality He creates?

Here is one way, then, that God's thoughts are higher than our thoughts, as the prophet writes:

> For my thoughts are not your thoughts,
> neither are your ways my ways, says the LORD.
> For as the heavens are higher than the earth,
> so are my ways higher than your ways
> and my thoughts than your thoughts.
> (Isaiah 55:8-9)

And here is why God seems incomprehensible to us: we are limited and he is not. Yet Jesus, as we shall see in the next chapter, speaks of our power as being unlimited like God's. And so, our limitation must have been self-imposed rather than God-imposed. God did not create our limits.

On earth, we must contend with a number of limitations, not the least of which is a limit on knowledge—a limit to how much we can know. We are prone to fear in large part because of these limitations and, being prone to fear, we are prone to anger and guilt as well. Anger would not befit a truly Supreme Being, and therefore precludes knowledge of God. Anger is one of our self-imposed limitations on knowledge, keeping us from knowing God as we might otherwise know Him.

As John said, fear drives out love, and so therefore does anger, which springs from fear. Neither fear nor anger can co-exist with love. They can only alternate in our minds, therefore, which gives us our seemingly natural and characteristic ambivalence. God does not share such ambivalence, and so it is something that we ourselves created for we ourselves.

Any blot of fear or anger would be a blight on the perfect light and purity of the mind. We must therefore gain some control over them, and more than a semblance of control: we need to eradicate them from our minds. They do not befit us as children of God. This is essentially what Jesus teaches when he says:

> You have heard that it was said to the men of old, 'You shall not kill; and whoever kills shall be liable to judgment.' But I say to you that every one who is angry with his brother shall be liable to judgment.
> (Matt. 5:21-22)

Jesus is advocating a change—as in a total transformation—in mind, not only a change of behavior. Murder is spoken of here as an extreme form of the real underlying problem, which is anger. This is a very psychological argument Jesus is making: that we need to pinpoint the underlying thought and feeling *behind* the behavior. And as Jesus indicates (in 5:20), it is a way of ensuring that our righteousness exceeds mere behavioral regulation, which is not foolproof, and instead goes straight to the heart of the problematic thought and feeling that produces the behavior in the first place.

Psychologically speaking, anger *does* make one feel that one is "liable to judgment." It produces the conditions under which guilt seems natural and begins to thrive. Even our so-called righteous anger is merely guilt's insidious way of entering our mind, because anger *always* results in guilt however hidden we may keep it from ourselves. And this guilt turns into (or reinforces) a diminished sense of being and thinking.

The vicious cycle continues back to fear—a free-floating, anxious fear—for guilt always comes with fear of punishment or at least reprisal. We project this free-floating fear onto God, thinking He is after us, but nothing could be farther from the truth. It is then that we unconsciously feel the need to judge, in part to stave off our own judgment and in part to deny our guilt and fear. Yet this judgment only produces more guilt and fear, and a much-diminished way of viewing both the world and ourselves. And of course this leads to a reduced view of God, whereby we assume that He is angry at us and is coming after us, when it is by love alone that He draws us to Himself.

This passage therefore suggests that all thought and fear of judgment is generated by the anger we have allowed into our minds. When we are angry and therefore judgmental, we are setting ourselves up for judgment, simply by having allowed any thought or seed of judgment to enter our mind. This is why anger would be so highly illogical for God, because it is for us as well.

Jesus continually argues from the position that what is unnatural for God is unnatural for us. On the other hand, what is *natural* to God is also natural to us. This is why, ultimately, we should think of ourselves as being God's children, who are like Him.

There is a correspondence between our own most natural way of thinking and God's way of thinking. If we could come to know *our own* natural way of thinking, we could know God's, and if we could know God's, we would know our own. Jesus makes such an argument when he talks of our own natural sense of being good to our children:

> Or what man of you, if his son asks him for bread, will give him a stone? Or if he asks for a fish, will give him a serpent? If you then, who are evil, know how to give good gifts to your children, how much more will your Father who is in heaven give good things to those who ask him!
> (Matt. 7:9-11)

The case is made here that what is good for us is even more so for God. If we in our diminished way of thinking know enough to treat our children well, at least at times, God knows this ever more thoroughly and consistently. For this reason, we can come to know God even as we come to know ourselves. We can instead safely and rightly extrapolate onto God a more consistent and perfect version of our own (albeit feeble) sense of natural goodness. As we attain consistency in this, we will be coming to know ourselves and God as well.

In this sense, then, our thoughts *are* like God's thoughts, and this is how we learn of God's thoughts: by finding and exercising our own natural thoughts. The difference would be that God's thoughts are more consistent and pure or perfect. As 1 John had argued, God is light and there is no darkness in Him. There is nothing about Him that is not perfect. Otherwise we would not logically see Him as God.

Isaiah expresses the relationship between God and the human being as one of reason and gentle persuasion:

> 'Come now, let us reason together,'
> says the LORD:
> 'though your sins are like scarlet,
> they shall be as white as snow;
> though they are red like crimson,
> they shall become like wool.'
> (Isaiah 1:18)

God, in this passage, is portrayed as working through our capacity to *reason* to persuade us of our underlying innocence. Guilt, we have seen, had been a byproduct of anger, which was a byproduct of fear. The guilt itself resulted in the unconscious impulse to judge, which led to unconscious fear of reprisal. Fear itself was produced by an initial turning away from love, so that even it depends on love for its existence.

God, being love, wipes this all away. The cycle never gets rolling, and so it seems as if it never existed. This is how blotted out our sins shall be, how clean our heart, how carefree our mind. What, then, shall we judge? Where has fear taken off to when we decide only to love?

Though we have not dared to look at the matter too deeply, we tend to assume we are basically evil because of the presence of unconscious guilt. We do not realize that it is a free-floating guilt, malleable in the sense that it can be shaped and reshaped to apply to anything. We apply this free-floating or ontological guilt to specific instances of what we call "sins" and, as we have seen in regard to Jesus' teaching on forgiveness, we tend to apply it to others rather than to ourselves. Looking thus outward rather than inward, we judge, and when we judge, we fear the judgment that we think will befall us from outside. We should instead have looked inside first, found nothing to judge, and then projected *this* onto others.

This passage encourages us to reason through the sins we think we have wrought, including those we harbor deep in the recesses of our mind, with the superior premises of God. Once we look at them in the light of day, the passage implies, we will realize they are nowhere near as unforgivable as we once had believed. They are in fact illusions of fear's making.

The passage suggests that God already knows that our sins do not exist as we *think* they exist, but it is only by mustering the courage to face them that *we* realize what He already knows. Obviously, then, God respects our minds and our beings enough to allow us to reason our way back to Him. The very fact that He seeks to reason with us suggests this.

God *knows* who we are—but we in our current state of mind do not. We will not know ourselves *or* God until we know ourselves in the same way God knows us. But to know both we need first to know the difference: that "the anger of man does not work the righteousness of God" (James 1:20). That is, our own thoughts of anger, projected onto Him as well as others, have distorted our perception of both.

> You are a God ready to forgive, gracious and merciful, slow to anger and abounding in steadfast love, and You did not forsake them.
> (Nehemiah 9:17)

Reason tells us that His slowness to anger is as infinite as He is. That is, it *never* comes, despite our fears to the contrary. His love, being steadfast and casting out any thought of fear or guilt, does not allow anger to rise in Him. This is what the ancients who tended to see God more anthropomorphically, more like their mistaken notions of themselves, missed. For in making Him to be like ordinary men, they imagined a God who was as conflicted and ambivalent as they, forgetting that their diminished thoughts were not His thoughts.

God is forever ready to forgive, but in truth He never really *needs* to forgive. From His point of view, there *is* nothing to forgive. (We have seen this already in the parable of the prodigal son.) After all, His children who turned away from Him, no doubt out of sorely illogical thinking, could only hurt themselves—not Him. They may in their distorted way of thinking have harbored the deep-seated belief that they have hurt God, but that, of course, would be impossible. His concern therefore would be only that they have hurt *themselves* by thinking this way.

Therefore God seeks to persuade His beloved children to return to Him. As we have seen in the quote from Isaiah above, He is not averse to using logic and reason in order to persuade them. The following account tells us how Moses used reason to quell his own anger:

> When Moses was angry with Dathan and Abiram he did nothing against them in anger, but controlled his anger by reason. For, as I have said, the temperate mind is able to get the better of the emotions, to correct some, and to render others powerless. Why else did Jacob, our most wise father, censure the households of Simeon and Levi for their irrational slaughter of the entire tribe of the Shechemites, saying,'Cursed be their anger'? For if reason could not control anger, he would not have spoken thus.
> (4 Macc. 2:17-20)

The ideal, of course, is to deal with anger through enhanced reason before it ever has a chance to arise, as this would be akin to thinking like God. It is by thinking of anger (along with guilt and sin) as utterly pointless, "powerless," and even absurd that we come closest to thinking like God. It is not so much that it needs to be *controlled* as it needs to be completely *re-thought*. If we realized that anger reinforced unconscious guilt and fear, for instance, would we really *want* to engage in it? Would we allow it to remain as a perpetual cloud over ourselves if we were fully aware that is what it was? Would we engage in it at all if we knew how it affects and alienates *ourselves* more than anyone else?

Ultimately one learns to trust one's inner guidance, and to see it everywhere. Until then we have the good advice: "do not let the sun go down on your anger" (Eph. 4:26), which reminds us not to carry anger as a burden from one day into the next. We might reason from this that it would be better not to carry this burden even into the next *moment*. The very next moment could be a transformative one, if we were not locked into our self-wrought and self-limiting position.

# 4

# Belief And Transformation

**Belief and Transformation**

For Jesus, belief was inherently and immediately effective. It carried with it the power to make things happen, the (actually infinite) power of mind. Thus:

> All things are possible to him who believes.
> (Mark 9:23)

Belief is transformative. It has the capacity to change things that we had convinced ourselves were unchangeable. Indeed, it was only our having convinced ourselves that had made it so. That is, belief's power can be used for good or ill, to our benefit or our detriment, and we had been using it for the latter by having convinced ourselves we were limited, diminished, unworthy. The truth, as expressed in the Bible, is that we are none of these things, but rather, we are much more powerful than we ever could have imagined.

We do not realize how much our belief in limitation has limited us. We have thought ourselves into ruts, but they were *our* ruts and so we loved them. We did not stop to think that we might have loved ourselves just as much, if not more, in spite of these ruts, or without these ruts. And so we did not allow ourselves to consider that the ruts themselves had only been products of our thought, not realities in themselves. Therefore they were subject to change.

Let us consider for a moment how great is our tendency to limit ourselves, and how effectively this is done just by our thinking. Our ideas about life itself are shaped and fixed for us very early on by the world, starting with our caretakers, and then solidified through years of schooling, peer and family pressure, and further socialization, reinforcement upon reinforcement from the outside, until the picture presented to us seems to be the only reality. Thus we limit ourselves before we begin.

This in itself would have proven the mind's great power, if we had reasoned it through. The way we have convinced ourselves of limitation is actually quite incredible. It involved the denial of all evidence to the contrary, which was summarily overlooked in favor of what we wanted to believe. Yet we never asked ourselves why we wanted to believe in such impotence, for we fooled ourselves into thinking it had been imposed upon us from outside.

Jesus argues, with characteristic memorable imagery, that all of this can be changed simply with a change in our way of thinking:

> Truly, I say to you, whoever says to this mountain, `Be taken up and cast into the sea,' and does not doubt in his heart, but believes that what he says will come to pass, it will be done for him.
> (Mark 11:23)

According to this passage, belief comes first, and then perception follows as reinforcement. We have had it the wrong way around, believing that perception influences what we think (and are *able* to think). We have misused the power of belief to set parameters around our mind rather than using it to free the mind from the strictures of the past. If we simply *realized* we were only limiting ourselves by our way of thinking, and that we could have changed this simply by changing our mind, then we certainly would already have changed it.

For Jesus, *any* limitation on the power of mind was unnatural. The mind is powerful because God, who created it, is powerful. It is in fact limitless. And yet we have used it to establish and never to question the limitations we have, with the great power of our mind, imposed upon ourselves.

By teaching us to believe in the power of our mind, Jesus teaches us to believe in *ourselves* as well as God, who created us with such transformative and creative power of mind. It is a reality and power, long lost to us and yet proven in various ways each day, that he is seeking to restore to our minds. Thus does Jesus consistently encourage belief in the power of *our own* mind: "Go; be it done for you as you have believed" (Matt 8:13).

## 'Your Faith Has Made You Whole'

When Jesus healed, he did so in cooperation with the faith of the person he healed. The persons being healed not only participated in their own healing, they *effected* it. The passages make it sound as if Jesus merely acted as facilitator for the person's own faith. And so, for instance, he told the woman who had secretly touched the hem of his garment:

> 'Daughter, be of good comfort;
> *thy faith* hath made thee whole.'
> (Luke 8:48, KJV, my italics)

In that instance he had not even known that she had reached out to touch him, and so the healing really was accomplished by *her own* faith. The act of touching his garment was not merely a sign of her faith, but it was the actual creative force to which Jesus attributes the healing.

He said at another healing, "According to your faith be it done to you" (Matt. 9:29). This faith changed things (in this instance restoring sight to two blind men), revealing the power of the mind to change what seemed very much like fixed reality. This belief in the power of their faith (and mind) is at the same time belief in God, who gave them such power. Moreover, their faith was in a benevolent God, a loving God, and a God who cared deeply and infinitely for them.

Jesus evidently inspired faith in those who saw him, but he subsequently praised the strength of *their* devotion. It was simply because *they* had truly believed it was possible to be healed that they *were* healed. His certainty inspired their faith, which was followed up by their own certainty. Their trust in Jesus to help them was by proxy a trust both in God *and in themselves* (at least according to Jesus' stated interpretation of it). He was basically telling them that his physical presence was not required nor even responsible for their healing. It was their faith, the power of their belief and of their mind, that was responsible.

Just the slightest bit of faith—enough to *want* to question supposed certainties and realities—is enough to start the process of real transformation rolling. Faith is openness, and openness comes from asking. To have faith is to make oneself open-minded by asking about the nature of divine reality rather than assuming upfront that we know. Jesus speaks of the certainty that can come with asking:

> Ask, and it will be given you; seek, and you will find; knock, and it will be opened to you. For every one who asks receives, and he who seeks finds, and to him who knocks it will be opened.
> (Matt. 7:7-8)

It is important that we ask. The truth is there for us to find, but it is hidden from our eyes by our presuppositions. Asking takes us beyond our presuppositions, opening our minds to a much higher and more all-encompassing truth. Faith is a reasonable bracketing of our own presuppositions until we *know* the utter and unbelievable goodness of God. Even a mustard-seed-sized amount of faith, Jesus says (Matt. 17:20), is enough to carry one through the entire process to actual knowledge because we do not know *what* we are looking for until it proves itself to us. By the time it proves itself fully to us, or simply appears to us in all its glory, it will have become reality and knowledge rather than simply faith and openness.

At any point in the process, however, we may need to borrow someone's faith to get us over the bumps. Early Christians therefore sometimes called upon the faith *of* Jesus (see Gal. 2:16, 3:22; Rom. 3:22; Phil. 3:9). Similarly, the Hebrew Bible had sometimes spoken of the faith *of* God in humanity, or of God's own "faithfulness" to us as a source of personal faith. Here the faithfulness of God is associated with His "steadfast love":

> The steadfast love of the LORD never ceases,
> his mercies never come to an end;
> they are new every morning;
> great is thy faithfulness.
> (Lamentations 3:22-23)

The real truth is that God has faith in humanity rather than the other way around. For all we do is ask and open, and therefore receive, of God's actual goodness. To read this passage as such is actually to appreciate God all the more. Even in spite of our darkness, which is mere ignorance of what really and eternally *is*, God Himself seeks to speak to us, continually and in myriad ways. His enthusiasm cannot be contained. Were our eyes open to it, we could see in the mere fact that we exist the steadfastness of God, the continual outpouring of His love. As long as we exist, and subjectively speaking we always do, there is not only hope and faith but also good reason for our brokenness to be healed.

What I mean by this last line is that God sees in wholes; He sees us in our full context with His Own reality, in full relationship, as well as in the reality of us *in context* with *all* our brothers and sisters. He *knows* us to be well beyond what we currently know ourselves to be.

## The Kingdom of Joy

> The kingdom of heaven is like treasure hidden in a field, which a man found and covered up; then in his joy he goes and sells all that he has and buys that field.
>
> (Matt. 13:44)

What if we were to think of the kingdom of Heaven as something more akin to a rich inner life rather than a place or destination? For one thing, it would become more immediate to us, more easily accessible, and less mysterious. It would be within our own realm of possibility, yet it would always be experienced actuality rather than mere possibility, an actuality that we can know, even now, through the great joy associated with it.

It is "hidden" in the sense that we are unaware of it until we open to its possibility, which becomes its actuality. It is hidden in the sense that it is buried, and note *who* it was buried *by* in this parable: it was buried or made unconscious by *us*. The way we think has hidden it from our thoughts, and yet it could be the central organizing principle of our thoughts if we let it be.

The kingdom of Heaven is associated with our own greatest desire. Thus we might think of it generally as what we *most want*—at least until we know what it is we truly want. This means that it is most *natural* to us, most innate to us, and most inherent in us.

We have been too externally-focused and oriented to see it, for it begins with us. Only as we find it first in ourselves can it be seen and appreciated in the world. It is up to us to uncover it simply because we are the ones who had covered it up. As we find that our natural joy and desire rests in it, we will become more and more motivated to find it, until we realize that we best find it by letting it out from where it is hidden (deep within our mind and heart).

The kingdom of joy begins within ourselves and then overspreads to all the world:

> With what can we compare the kingdom of God, or what parable shall we use for it? It is like a grain of mustard seed, which, when sown upon the ground, is the smallest of all the seeds on earth; yet when it is sown it grows up and becomes the greatest of all shrubs, and puts forth large branches, so that the birds of the air can make nests in its shade.
> (Mark 4:30-32)

It begins small, perhaps as immeasurably small as an idea is small, but once it is planted in awareness it begins to grow. Compared to how small and seemingly insignificant it once was, we might say it grows infinitely larger, so much so that it becomes established as a comforting and protective reality. And yet it all began with the smallest seed of openness within ourselves.

In order to find the kingdom, we might begin by asking ourselves what we most desire, what it is that would make us continually happy. If the kingdom is our greatest desire, the one for which we'd give up all else gladly if we had to, then we need only to *ask ourselves* what it is, what that might be. It can't be anything in the world itself because, alas!, all those things are temporary and never last. Also, often, once we achieve them, we throw them back into the ocean as too small, still not enough for us.

In such a way we gather evidence *from ourselves* as to the meaning and revelation of the Bible. Revealed knowledge is simply uncovered knowledge. The truth is both within ourselves and also from beyond ourselves, in the sense that it comes from beyond the way we ordinarily think and yet presents us with a world of open possibility.

What if all our trouble is part and parcel of what seems to be our ordinary, limited way of thinking? When we are troubled, which is too often even if just once, then at that time what we want most of all is simply peace of mind. When we are confused, we most want to know, to understand. When we feel oppressed, we most want freedom from all that troubles us, all that imposes itself upon our natural happiness

When we feel stuck and mired, we want to find just one opening, one way of ease, one natural way to a sense of unlimited freedom. We want to think and live creatively, to participate in life to the fullest, and we want to do this in cooperation with all who might help us in this endeavor. We want our world, the context and reality in which we live, to harmonize with our internal reality and match our inmost desire.

The kingdom is spoken in these parables may begin as one thing but it becomes a state of mind that includes all things. It is an internal reality that comes to include all things within itself, a state of mind that results in a new, more holistic way of perceiving the world. It may seem, when it is small and hidden, to be one thing, one possibility among many, but as it grows in our awareness, we begin to realize how it encompasses and includes all things and all beings.

For God, it could be no other way. He sees in wholes, or teaches us to see in wholes, because He *knows* in wholes. Each thing is seen in its glorious context with all other things. This is how all things come to contribute to an overall joy:

> The kingdom of heaven is like a merchant in search of fine pearls, who, on finding one pearl of great value, went and sold all that he had and bought it.
> (Matt. 13:45-46)

In this parable, too, we find a process of search and discovery, of working toward our greatest desire by learning just *how much* we desire it. The process might be described as a kind of whittling down of the mass of all desires into the one true desire that outshines them all yet includes all the passion thereof. It is a kind of contraction and expansion, a focusing and magnification of desire until that one desire is all we have, all we need, and all we really want to know. At that point, all things come to express that same desire.

Another way of stating this is that once we gain some awareness of the true desire of our heart, all else would automatically become lesser desires and would naturally fall away. As these lesser values undergo this process of fading, their gleam snuffing out though once they shone so brightly, the original desire grows that much greater to take their place. Each of the lesser ones, then, had served to hide the greatest one from our awareness, and yet in the end even their feeble strength proves helpful in spurring our discovery of greatness.

Jesus indicates that "the heart" (the seat of being and also of value and desire) within us has been impaired by our having valued wrongly (Matt. 15:13-20). Once our heart was corrupted, we were corrupted, and we began to value wrongly, carelessly in fact. We sought for things that glistened rather than for things that truly shone, things that were never meant to last and therefore were never intended to bring us everlasting joy.

Jesus cites Isaiah's lament that our false values have distorted our perception:

> For this people's heart has grown dull,
> and their ears are heavy of hearing,
> and their eyes they have closed,
> lest they should perceive with their eyes,
> and hear with their ears,
> and understand with their heart,
> and turn for me to heal them.
> (Matt. 13:15)

This is saying that we do not know our own true heart, do not recognize our own greatest good. How can we when we have let our heart grow dull with lesser values? How now can we even conceive of greatness at all, or true grandeur, when we live within a hall of mirrors showing only dim and distorted reflections of our greatest desire? How, also, can we find what we really want if we do not come preprogrammed with what we really want?

Yet we are strangely compelled to seek out these lesser and ultimately unsatisfying desires, and so God Himself decided to use them toward our benefit. We go through them *so that* they might fall away and leave only our greatest desire in their wake. In this sense we are selling them off to a higher bidder, and this higher bidder happens to be within us; it is our own greatest desire. It is our true and natural self.

But note that in this passage we need only to "turn" to God for help and healing in order to receive this help and healing. Thus it is a simple change of mind, a mere "turn" in fact, that begins the process of real understanding. We only need to flutter our eyes to perceive something new, only to open the door of our mind just a crack to understand at a deeper level. This simple act of turning toward the kingdom of God within is as easy and natural as going after what we most desire. Once we realize how much we actually do want to know this part of ourselves, no effort seems too great to expend; it becomes easy and natural to work to get it, or simply to let it come to us.

## The Gifts of God

The gifts of God have already been given, but they remain unopened. We open them simply by valuing them, or by discovering the great value they already hold. Until then, they are invisible to us. But once they do become visible, once they are appreciated for what they are, they can be seen literally anywhere and everywhere.

The first of God's gifts, which of course contains all the rest, is *life itself*. As Paul says, "the free gift of God is eternal life" (Rom. 6:23). If it is truly free, of course, then nothing need be done for us to *have* this eternal life. It is already ours. Yet we can fool ourselves into thinking it is not there, and the world seems in one regard to be a temptation to do exactly this. In the other regard the world is a place where we come to learn of this eternal life by experiencing it, which we do simply by learning to appreciate it.

To *have* eternal life means to have life in ourselves—even in the same way that God has life in Himself, for "as the Father has life in himself, so has he granted the Son also to have life in himself" (John 5:26). He has granted all of us to have a similar life in ourself as He has in Himself. God's life is vast, of course, being infinite, and it includes us, yet it is still *His* life. Ours is much the same. It is much more expansive and connected than we currently think it is, but it is still *ours*. It belongs to us and makes us who we are, even though it extends out from us to encompass God and every other living thing.

In a sense, what we need is for our *sense* of identity to begin to match up with the *eternal reality* of our identity. And this is why we are encouraged by Jesus to believe in *our own* eternal identity, mainly so that we can begin to accept it as being *truly ours*. Without this sense of eternal identity, a person "has no root in himself, but endures for a while" and eventually "falls away" (Matt. 13:21). We shall examine this teaching on eternal life further when we look into the Meaning of Life in the next chapter.

All the rest of the gifts of God stem from this original gift of eternal life. These gifts include joy, as we saw in the last section in Jesus' parables in Matt. 13:44-46, and also a sense of deep and abiding love. Eternal peace is another aspect of the same gift of life. This is a sense of peace that does not waver, does not change, but remains constant in the mind. If we knew the eternal constancy of life, we would know this peace as well, for the peace would be natural to the life. Jesus said as much when he said:

> Would that even today you knew the things that make for peace! But now they are hid from your eyes.
> (Luke 19:42)

Once again, the reason the gifts of life and life itself are not recognized as such is because they are "hid" from our eyes. They are not apparent to our physical senses. They require some extrapolation and some reasoning to be appreciated for what they are. But mainly they require a growing openness so that they might take up residence among our thoughts and experiences.

If just once we could experience eternal peace, we would begin to appreciate eternal life. For peace is an essential part of this life, as is love and as is joy, which we have seen in previous chapters. The power of mind is another necessary aspect of eternal life. Once we recognize the great power we have at our disposal, our own great value comes into view.

The true gifts given by God, the eternal gifts, are those that accompany eternal life, but they like this life are indeed hidden from our eyes. And so there are another set of gifts that lead toward this realization and awareness of the eternal gifts. These are the gifts of salvation, not eternal in themselves but leading toward *awareness* of eternal life. The first of these, in the Pauline tradition, is the gift of faith:

> For by grace you have been saved through faith; and this is not your own doing, it is the gift of God.
> (Ephesians 2:8)

To say that faith is a gift of God is to say that we are *provided* with the faith we need. We depend on God even for this, just as we depend on Him for our life. Neither our faith nor our life are our "own doing," but both are gifts, faith leading toward awareness of the original gift of life.

We have seen that Jesus healed by evoking faith in those he met. He established healing as a gift of salvation, a gift he associates here with forgiveness:

> But Jesus, knowing their thoughts, said, 'Why do you think evil in your hearts? For which is easier, to say, "Your sins are forgiven," or to say, "Rise and walk"? But that you may know that the Son of man has authority on earth to forgive sins'—he then said to the paralytic—'Rise, take up your bed and go home.' And he rose and went home. When the crowds saw it, they were afraid, and they glorified God, who had given such authority to men.
> (Matt. 9:4-8)

Here the phrase "the Son of man" clearly refers to all of humankind for it is paralleled with "men," meaning all humankind. And so it is clear that the authority to forgive sins was given to every human being, and the power to heal accompanies it; in fact, Jesus makes them seem like one and the same. Matthew makes sure to mention that it is God "who had given such authority" (to forgive and to heal) to all humankind. It is something we can do for one another, in a sense just by respecting and appreciating their being, which ultimately will allow us to remember and appreciate our own eternal being.

Among the gifts of salvation, then, we have faith, forgiveness, and healing, which are meant to bring awareness of the original gift of eternal life, the reality behind them. These gifts of salvation help us to change our mind about the very nature of reality. They allow for the light of the eternal to begin to shine from within the temporary. Once again, as our mind changes, so does everything change.

Furthermore, we have access to a divine Guide that helps to orchestrate all the gifts of salvation toward the recognition of eternity. We shall examine later how the Holy Spirit is meant to lead us back to our original eternal life, the truth of ourselves, of God, and of every relationship. The Holy Spirit is said to remind us of all that Jesus taught, like a superpersonal memory that comes from beyond our ordinary self. It comes, in a sense, both from God and from our eternal self, the same eternal self to which it leads.

Paul declares that it is the same Spirit in each of us that evokes in people the entire variety of God's salvific gifts. He says that the gifts, though manifesting differently in each individual, are meant to draw us together and reveal our oneness and interconnection:

> For as in one body we have many members, and all the members do not have the same function, so we, though many, are one body in Christ, and individually members one of another. Having gifts that differ according to the grace given to us, let us use them: if prophecy, in proportion to our faith; if service, in our serving; he who teaches, in his teaching; he who exhorts, in his exhortation; he who contributes, in liberality; he who gives aid, with zeal; he who does acts of mercy, with cheerfulness.
> (Rom. 12:4-8)

It is by seeing all these various gifts of salvation working together among people that we realize how the same Spirit leads us all. The paradox is that, as we discern the Spirit working individually and differently in each person (whether it be in "serving" or helping or merely acting mercifully towards others), we begin to gain a broad perspective on the Spirit's working. *Every* act of kindness—even if it does not involve us directly—therefore becomes a gift to *us*. This changes our view of the world as a whole, whereby ultimately we come to see all things working for the good, and every being including ourselves as being instrumental and essential to the common good.

The gifts of God are eternal in the sense that they are "irrevocable," says Paul (Rom. 11:29). They cannot be removed from us, but *only* given to us. God's original gifts granted us eternal life, complete with joy, love, and peace. These are fully and freely ours, awaiting only our acceptance and awareness of them. They are our divine inheritance. All the gifts associated with eternal life are also eternal in the sense that do not depend on time. They have been given in eternity, where God abides. That is why they are ours already: God does not wait on time, nor does He withhold for a second that which would bring us our greatest happiness.

# 5

# The Meaning of Life

## You Search the Scriptures (Eternal Life)

We tend to think of eternity as endless time going forward, progressing like an arrow from past to future. But what if eternity were actually more the present moment that lies between them? What if eternity were more timelessness than endless time? What if it were closer to the sense of timelessness one gets, for instance, when when one loses all sense of time in the rapture of a beautiful aspect of nature or the sublimity of a great philosophical idea?

We might have it any moment, then. At any moment, particularly in the most spontaneous and immediate of moments, we might experience something of our eternal life: the true sense of *being* granted to us by an eternal God. One might have a sense of losing oneself in that moment, but what is gained is so much more. It is a greater, expanded sense of being that one gains when one loses one's old self in something greater.

Eternity in such cases would be more a *suspension* of ordinary time rather than endless time. It would be more timelessness than it would have anything to do with time. Therefore the experience of eternal life could happen at any time, and the possibility would exist that we would be able to *choose* such an experience. We have already seen that there are indications in the Bible that eternity is built into the structure of our mind:

> He has made everything beautiful in its time;
> also he has put eternity into man's mind.
> (Eccles. 3:11)

From a psychological standpoint, eternity, if built into the mind, is not something we need to *achieve* so much as *realize*. To realize it is to allow it to emerge from unconsciousness, where it was relegated for whatever reason, and allow it thereby to prove itself to us. It is to allow it to rise to conscious awareness from wherever in our mind it had been hidden.

This process need not be fearful, but is often experienced as such simply because when we allow this eternal structure of our mind to arise, everything that we've held in unconsciousness rises along with it. Yet this, too, is a process, happening over time, and so it can usually be dealt with without fear at some point or another. The eternity in our mind is not something to fear. It is something we treasure with the whole of our being. The question is: are we going to treasure it consciously or continue unconsciously?

We have spoken of eternal life as the original gift of God. It has already been given, but there is something that blocks our realization of it. The myth of the fall from a higher state of being is trying to tell us that realization of this eternal life has been blocked by our own doing, our own decision, and our own way of thinking.

The Bible indicates that the experience of eternity will seem familiar, even here on earth. Here is one example:

> The eternal God is your dwelling place,
> and underneath are the everlasting arms.
> (Deuteronomy 33:27)

We feel more at home with eternity because it is our truth. At the very least, it was intended to be our truth. And if it was intended to be our truth, then it is still in God's Mind the truth about ourselves. And so He calls us back to this, and to Him, and to His everlasting care and support.

For now we straddle two worlds, we dwell in two places, both in God and in the world, but our true dwelling is the eternal one.

> For thus says the high and lofty One
> who inhabits eternity, whose name is Holy:
> 'I dwell in the high and holy place,
> and also with him who is of a contrite
> and humble spirit,
> to revive the spirit of the humble,
> and to revive the heart of the contrite.'
> (Isaiah 57:15)

The irony is that we must re-enter and remember such greatness with a humble spirit, a humbling of the old self so that the new might come. Our own eternal sense of being is blocked by our temporary and temporal sense of existence. We have to de-identify with the existent so as to re-experience the being, if we want to know the eternal truth about ourselves.

We are beings of eternal mind who delude themselves that they are creatures whose entire lifespan is encompassed by the relatively few years we spend on earth. Yet even this was an act of mind, and it can be changed by an act of mind that reverses the situation and places us back in the driver's seat where we belong. Our environment need not control us unless we hand over control to it.

The more eternal the mind, the more fitting a dwelling-place for the Supreme Being. And the more we will find we are like that Being. If God wants relationship, in other words, then He wants it with beings who are, like Himself, eternal.

When asked about the process of inheriting eternal life, Jesus associated it with his teaching about love's centrality and primacy in our life:

> And behold, a lawyer stood up to put him to the test, saying, 'Teacher, what shall I do to inherit eternal life?' He said to him, 'What is written in the law? How do you read?' And he answered, 'You shall love the Lord your God with all your heart, and with all your soul, and with all your strength, and with all your mind; and your neighbor as yourself.' And he said to him, 'You have answered right; do this, and you will live.'
> (Luke 10:25-28)

Here Jesus is asked directly what one must do to attain the state of eternal life. And Jesus answers that person with a restatement of the Great Commandment (to love God with one's entire being and one's neighbor as oneself). Love, then, in both of these senses must be eternal. The love we give here on earth contains the greatness of self and the eternity of being that accompanies us into timelessness.

Note that to "inherit eternal life" means basically that we will be like God. In other words, the part of us that loves like God is the part that is eternal. It is by loving that we will learn of our own eternal being.

Additionally in the Synoptics, Jesus speaks about eternal life as being inherited from God in Matt. 19:29. He speaks of it in terms of the mythological final judgment in Matt. 25:46. In Luke 16:9, he speaks intriguingly of "eternal habitations" in relation to ourselves.

The highly experiential and psychological Gospel of John expands on this subject. There Jesus speaks of himself as a kind of conduit for eternal life in 4:14: "the water that I shall give him will become in him a spring of water welling up to eternal life." Think of this inflowing water as increasing experience with the ultimate culmination and realization being one of our own eternal life and being.

Jesus speaks further in that Gospel of a person's being able to bypass both judgment and death by accepting eternal life in the immediate present:

> Truly, truly, I say to you, he who hears my word and believes him who sent me, has eternal life; he does not come into judgment, but has passed from death to life.
> (John 4:24)

Note that he is speaking in the present tense here, and so there must be a way of knowing "eternal life" with sufficient certainty and clarity that death is no longer feared nor experienced as such. We will examine this overcoming of both death and judgment in further detail later on.

Jesus speaks of eternal life as being evidenced by the scriptures but not to be found in the scriptures alone:

> You search the scriptures, because you think that in them you have eternal life;
> and it is they that bear witness to me;

> yet you refuse to come to me that you may have life.
>
> (John 5:39-40)

For the Johannine Jesus, eternal life comes from a teacher who has experienced and is adept at sharing his or her experience of eternal life. In such a way a teacher hands his own certainty and the reason for his certainty to his students, so that they might taste and see for themselves. Jesus also says that the scripture will retroactively "bear witness" to the eternal life he means to share with us.

Eternal life is the focus of much of Jesus' teaching in the Gospel of John (e.g., 3:16-17; 4:36; 6:27, 40, 47, 54; 12:25). Those to whom he imparts this eternal life, he says, "shall never perish, and no one shall snatch them out of my hand" (John 10:28). This passage seems to be saying that he will continue to guide them as long as they need him because they will learn directly from him, who learned it directly from God.

God's will for human beings is simply that they return to and acknowledge their own eternal life. This is God's will for us just as it was for Jesus himself (John 12:50). Eternal life is simply the transcendent greatness we hold in ourselves but have yet to acknowledge. Jesus' suggestions for remedying this situation, as we have seen, include forgiving, loving, and treating others as ourselves. These are all ways of realizing or growing increasingly aware of this eternal truth about *all beings*, including God, others, and ourselves.

**Original Life**

In the Gospel of John, Jesus says in reference to his own teaching:

> It is the spirit that gives life, the flesh is of no avail; the words that I have spoken to you are spirit and life.
> (John 6:63)

We think of life as being bound up with the flesh, but in so doing, we neglect the spirit. Jesus is saying that it should really be the other way around: that we should overlook the flesh, or think of it as being only the surface, the tip of the iceberg, so that we might realize our true depth of being. He is looking at life from an eternal perspective, seeing it in an entirely new context and therefore seeing an entirely new life.

To say that "the flesh is of no avail" is to say that the body does not influence let alone determine who we really are on an eternal level. The flesh is contingent or dependent upon the inner spiritual being, which is first, or should come before the body in our thinking and identification as to who we are. In other words, the body should not be the primary determinant of our identity. Only the spirit and eternal mind at the center of our being are deserving of this role. All of this is another way of saying that our true life is eternal.

Note that it is *not* that the flesh is evil, nor inherently sinful; it is just that it has nothing to do with the *magnitude* of who we really are. Its sinfulness, in effect, lies in its failure to match up to our true greatness. (Sin is here both a missing of the mark in archery terms, as well as an absence of good and therefore to some degree an incompletion.) Our surface reality has no bearing on our true life as given to us by God because the latter is so much greater. This is why we are not *bound* to anything temporary or limited if we do not choose to be.

If the body represents the farthest extent of our vision, then we will come to believe that we live and die with the body. If we identify too much with it, we will not be able to see past it to the vast and eternal inner world that lies just beneath its surface. The body then becomes a trap for our minds, a means of limiting ourselves when it could instead have been a means for learning of liberation.

Jesus is saying here that life does not begin with the body, but rather with the spirit. Life should be thought of as eternal. He emphasizes the dichotomy between them here in terms of our point of origin (or, where we ultimately come from):

> That which is born of the flesh is flesh, and that which is born of the Spirit is spirit.
> (John 3:6)

Here are two natures, quite distinct, this flesh and spirit, for each retains the characteristics of its origin. They are contrasted here because they are opposites, resulting in opposite world-views and self-views. So thorough is the changeover that one's point of origin, or where one thinks one comes from, is also changed.

Whichever we accept as our point of origin is that which spins the world around us, or interprets it for us. Each interpretation is a fundamentally different view of both world and self. This is why only one or the other can be our true point of origin. Flesh and spirit are ultimately too different to be combined and fully integrated. What is flesh is flesh and will always remain flesh, while what is born of the Spirit *is* spirit and will always remain so. This means that *we*, once reborn of the Spirit, are in a position to know ourselves as essentially and purely spiritual beings.

All things return to their origin, remaining true to their origin. Paul expresses this fact as well when he calls Jesus the new Adam, forerunner of an entirely different *kind* of life. Jesus is called the Adam of the true spiritual creation:

> The first man was from the earth, a man of dust; the second man is from heaven. As was the man of dust, so are those who are of the dust; and as is the man of heaven, so are those who are of heaven. Just as we have borne the image of the man of dust, we shall also bear the image of the man of heaven. I tell you this, brethren: flesh and blood cannot inherit the kingdom of God, nor does the perishable inherit the imperishable.
> (1 Cor. 15:47-50)

Paul describes here *two different creations*, seemingly running along parallel tracks, resulting in two different kinds of beings, one of dust (physical matter, or matter describable by way of physics) and one of spirit and mind. We as human beings are able to think of ourselves as either one or the other. From Paul's viewpoint, Adam and Jesus are representative of these distinct possibilities within our mind, as to whom we shall be. We may identify with *either* the "man of dust" or "the man of heaven" in a primary sense; our entire interpretation of world and self will vary accordingly.

When Paul says that "flesh and blood cannot inherit the kingdom of God," he is saying that our normal thoughts cannot hold our spiritual thoughts. Our normal thoughts are all based around form, which is inherently lifeless, and quite intertwined with it, or they are based around spirit, which holds the key to eternal life. For the spiritual mind knows itself to be eternal; all we need to do is identify with it to know what it knows.

We "inherit" or assume the characteristics of the being of spirit simply by believing in its reality and then realizing it. Such deep-seated belief, we might say, drives us to know it and therefore compels us to find it. Jesus gives us a clear point of reference, Paul is saying, because *he* had chosen the spirit as his identification, which therefore succeeded or took precedence over the physical world as its point of origin. Eventually we come to "bear the image" of whichever of the two natures we have chosen as our point of origin and our identification.

Belief, therefore, is not the end, but only the beginning. As in 2 Cor. 3:18, those who had begun with mere belief are now "being changed into his likeness from one degree of glory to another." Thus belief always involves transformation, even of the fundamental nature of our being. Those who believe this is so are basically being returned to their own original state of being, the original state of purely spiritual creation, and yet this process of return is occurring over time. Consequently, our destination will be the same as our origin.

Paul is speaking of a process of transformation already underway whereby believers over time are being changed into the likeness of Christ, which name represents the eternal being of Heaven present at the origination of everything. They are "being changed into his [Christ's] likeness."

Colossians picks up this theme of Jesus as model of what we shall eventually be, saying: "He is the image of the invisible God, the first-born of all creation" (1:15). Physically speaking, of course, many were born before him, and so the physical world is obviously not being discussed here. Nor is time being factored in by this use of the term "first-born." Rather, Jesus is first because he became fully aware of what is eternally true of each of us. Believers follow him into a similar transformation of themselves, until, as Paul had said: "Now you are the body of Christ and individually members of it" in 1 Cor. 12:27. We will explore this idea of sharing the collective spiritual being of Christ in a later chapter.

Jesus therefore begins the process of the restoration of the original creation (created in God's own image and likeness as in Genesis 1:26-27). It is a process that must remain incomplete until every last being has decided for its truth and reality, each in his or her own individual way, a way best suited to each. And this process is already well underway. For the original creation is already being restored—and will be made known to itself through us.

As essential members of the true, original spiritual creation, ultimately we will know ourselves as Christ knew himself: as sons or children of God, beings who were intended to be like God. John arrived at a similar point of view:

> But to all who received him, who believed in his name, he gave power to become children of God; who were born, not of blood nor of the will of the flesh nor of the will of man, but of God.
> (John 1:12-13)

Again we see here the language of origination, and the idea that there is an eternal life that parallels yet precedes this earthly life that we think of as everything to us. In other words, the being that God created *as spirit*, like God in being eternal, carved out of God Himself, remains like God and does not share our physical orientation. This being that God created entirely as spirit remains with us because it *is* us, even as we go about our lives unaware of this essential fact. The reason we remain unaware of this other life is simply because our true point of origin has been obscured.

## Sonship

We have examined the following passage before, but let us highlight here how Jesus tells his listeners that, by loving others, they will know themselves to be sons (or children) of the Most High because they will be like God:

> But love your enemies, and do good, and lend,
> expecting nothing in return;
> and your reward will be great,
> and *you will be sons of the Most High*;
> for he is kind to the ungrateful and the selfish.
> Be merciful, even as your Father is merciful.
>       (Luke 6:35-36, my italics)

It is specifically through loving like God that human beings will know themselves *to be* beings of God. Such eternal identification comes by gradual identification with the part of us that loves. It is in this way that the loving and Godlike part becomes conscious of itself, through our mere acceptance of love like this.

To become "sons of the Most High" is to come to know ourselves as divine beings in our own right, created by God and therefore similar to God. Note that God is characterized here as being "kind" to all, even to those with perceptible flaws ("the ungrateful and the selfish"), and as being infinitely "merciful," always willing to start from a clean slate. To be like God, then, is to be likewise kind to all and infinitely loving, and this also happens to be true of our true selves.

Sonship here is spoken of as a "reward," though of course it would be the *realization* of sonship that is the reward.

Sonship itself is, as a characteristic, already given to us. It is simply a fact about our being, but a fact which draws out our eternal likeness with all other beings. To know we are sons or children of God is to know we are never alone.

Sonship, then, is not an exclusive to Jesus. It is a universal characteristic of God's creation, making it all similar and alike in spite of what might otherwise seem its great and grand diversity. In fact this essential trait or characteristic is what holds it all together as one whole reality. Jesus teaches that, as God's fellow sons or children, we should expect good things from God (Matt. 7:9). He encourages us to think of ourselves as sons or children who are, like God, utterly "free" (Matt. 17:26). Jesus describes them further here, saying:

> they cannot die any more,
> because they are equal to the angels
> and are sons of God,
> being sons of the resurrection.
> (Luke 20:36)

This theme of sonship is expressed clearly and repeatedly in both the Johannine and Pauline writings. We begin with John, in whose first letter we find the following direct statement:

> See what love the Father has given us, that we should be called children of God; and so we are.
> (1 John 3:1)

It was of great significance to the early scribes that human beings were now able to call themselves children of God. It was as if the phrase took on a new significance with Jesus. Far from being just a metaphor, it became their reality. It was, further, a reality that actually preceded their entry into the world, just as it had for Jesus himself. It was a spiritual reality that came down to them ultimately from their original life with God in Heaven.

For John, the promise of eternal life (1 John 2:25) awaits only our realization:

> Beloved, we are God's children now;
> it does not yet appear what we shall be,
> but we know that when he appears we shall be
> like him, for we shall see him as he is.
> (1 John 3:2)

John says that we already *are* God's children, whether we know it or not. This fact is not yet apparent to us because it must be our free choice to identify with it. Surface reality cannot picture it except perhaps in the highly spiritual being to which we devote ourselves. For John, of course, this paragon and exemplar of spiritual reality is Jesus, and John basically speaks of following him all the way to the sharing of sonship and and even his divine nature through the sharing of his universal love.

Paul quotes the prophet Hosea, saying, "they will be called 'sons of the living God'" (Romans 9:26), revealing how far back this tradition of sonship actually goes and also how universalized it has become with Jesus. No longer does sonship apply only to kings, such as David or the Roman Emperor. With Jesus, it comes to belong to everyone and will be known to all who choose to accept it as their reality. Though it is the highest state of being, it is also the most democratic.

Paul indicates that sonship is the purpose of all creation, saying:

> the creation waits with eager longing for the revealing of the sons of God; for the creation was subjected to futility, not of its own will but by the will of him who subjected it in hope; because the creation itself will be set free from its bondage to decay and obtain the glorious liberty of the children of God. We know that the whole creation has been groaning in travail together until now; and not only the creation, but we ourselves, who have the first fruits of the Spirit, groan inwardly as we wait for adoption as sons, the redemption of our bodies.
>
> (Romans 8:19-23)

Note that this "adoption as sons" is more a state of total identification and freedom than it is a qualification of the sonship itself. It is more the culminating experience (and "redemption of our bodies") than it is a modification of the sonship. All of creation, in other words, will achieve this culminating experience of sonship as its rightful due. It will ultimately be a revelation to all creation about the reality and "glorious liberty of the children of God."

Creation had suffered and groaned precisely because it had not known this underlying fact about itself, though deep within it must have sensed it. It had not seen fully through the illusory appearance of decay and death to reach the more foundational reality of sonship. This foundational reality is also the highest reality we can conceive for ourselves.

Paul states further that: "in Christ Jesus you are all sons of God, through faith" (Gal. 3:26). Again, we are already sons of God, but this reality is not fully known and experienced by us. It is the Spirit that reminds us of our sonship: "And because you are sons, God has sent the Spirit of his Son into our hearts, crying, 'Abba! Father!'" (Gal. 4:5-6).

As we shall see in the next chapter, the Spirit is instrumental to our realization of sonship. Paul reiterates that the Spirit was sent by God specifically for this purpose of revealing our true identity as sons or children of God: "all who are led by the Spirit of God are sons of God" (Romans 8:14).

# 6

# Spirit and Self

### The Spirit of Sonship

We have seen that the realization of sonship was a major aspect of New Testament teaching, underlying its morality as well as its metaphysics. To know oneself as a child of God was the stated goal of Jesus' teaching and the reason for his injunctions to love, forgive, and to treat others as ourselves. We shall find in the next chapter that it is part and parcel of what it means to be saved: to find this Divine Image, this sonship, within ourselves. In this section, we will examine specifically the Holy Spirit's role in reminding us that we ourselves are composed of spirit, being beloved children of God, and we will touch on how Spirit-led prayer is also meant to return us to this realization.

At his baptism, "the Spirit of God" is said to have descended on Jesus in the form of a dove swooping down from Heaven (Matt. 3:16). More precisely, this is Jesus' vision of the situation; this is what he saw, this was his experience. And what he heard confirmed his sonship to God: "This is my beloved Son, with whom I am well pleased" (3:17). And so, the Holy Spirit has always been associated with sonship.

The Spirit has other functions as well, but they are all related to this primary function of helping us remember our sonship, or the realization that we are children of God in the same way that Jesus was Son of God. This is the Spirit's overarching function, the one that unifies and integrates them all. It is the one to which all the others lead, the hub from which each derives its ultimate meaning.

In the middle of Matthew's Gospel, Jesus is said to have been filled by the Spirit of God while sitting in synagogue, and this is associated with his universal function, extending beyond his own people, a broadening of his message to include all people, and a fulfillment of this prophecy from Isaiah:

> 'Behold, my servant whom I have chosen,
> my beloved with whom my soul is well pleased.
> I will put my Spirit upon him,
> and he shall proclaim justice to the Gentiles.'
> (Matt. 12:18)

The language harkens back to Jesus' baptism (e.g., "well pleased"), to the revelation of Jesus' Sonship, his own role in the Divine Being. His service expands here to include everyone, from whatever religion or culture, because his mission is to "proclaim justice," which is equal to everyone.

The Spirit is spoken of as the source of Jesus' significant power and this power is associated with the coming kingdom of God (Matt. 12:28). But Jesus' great power is evidently not meant to be reserved for Jesus alone, because early in his ministry Jesus is said to baptize his followers in the Spirit (Matt. 3:11), and towards the end he encourages his followers to baptize others with the very same Spirit (Matt. 28:19). This bestowal of the Spirit is also the bestowal of sonship, because of the Spirit's role of bestowing realization of sonship.

Jesus teaches his students that the Spirit would remain close to them—so close in fact that it would speak for God *through* them (Matt. 10:19-20). In this sense the Spirit is the Father's Voice speaking through them almost in an unconscious sense so that they might hear and learn from their own unconscious selves (while at the same time from God) how to deal with even pressing situations in the world.

The Spirit is therefore a trusted advisor of sorts, a confidante with whom we can share even our secret thoughts. Thus in John's Gospel the Spirit is called a "Counselor:"

> And I will pray the Father, and he will give you another Counselor, to be with you for ever, even the Spirit of truth, whom the world cannot receive, because it neither sees him nor knows him; you know him, for he dwells with you, and will be in you.
> (John 14:16-17)

So close is the Spirit to them that it will be located specifically inside them (i.e., in their mind). The world would not see or know it, but they themselves would experience this "Spirit of truth" which would guide them "into all the truth":

> When the Spirit of truth comes, he will guide you into all the truth; for he will not speak on his own authority, but whatever he hears he will speak, and he will declare to you the things that are to come. He will glorify me, for he will take what is mine and declare it to you.
> (John 16:13-14)

Again, the Spirit speaks for the Father. But here it also makes one transparent to the Father, and therefore represents the Father's Voice within the individual. In this way, too, it bestows a sense of Sonship upon the individual. And this is what it means when Jesus says: "he will take what is mine and declare it to you." The Spirit (personalized here as a "he") would bestow upon them the same sense of Sonship, the same close relationship with their Father, that Jesus himself enjoyed and by which he was empowered.

This association of the Spirit with Sonship is especially clear in Paul:

> For all who are led by the Spirit of God are sons of God.
> (Romans 8:14)

It is the Spirit's function to reveal to those who let it guide them that they are indeed "sons of God." It leads them ultimately to this realization. Therefore the Holy Spirit is called "the Spirit of sonship" (Ro. 8:15).

It is the Spirit that allows us to understand the thoughts of God, among which are our true selves, for:

> no one comprehends the thoughts of God except the Spirit of God. Now we have received not the spirit of the world, but the Spirit which is from God, that we might understand the gifts bestowed on us by God.
> (1 Cor. 2:11-12)

With the help and guidance of the Spirit, we human beings can comprehend "the thoughts of God," among which thoughts is our own eternal life as His children, a gift from

God, understood through the Spirit to be our sonship. Paul describes the Spirit as "a guarantee" of our own immortality (2 Cor. 5:5), a taste of the eternal sonship promised us. The Spirit, being *experienced* as an eternal presence within, prepares us for the *experience* of our own internal presence and eternal being. Furthermore, the Holy Spirit is described in Ephesians 1:13-14 as "the guarantee of our inheritance until we acquire possession of it," which "inheritance," too, is our own true spiritual nature we are being led to remember. We inherit our own true nature directly and naturally from God, but we receive confirmation of this fact through the Spirit.

In bringing realization of sonship, or the fact that we are truly children of God, the Spirit provides us with knowledge of the suffusion of God's love into our hearts:

> God's love has been poured into our hearts through
> the Holy Spirit which has been given to us.
> (Romans 5:5)

And so, again, it is by loving like God that we realize our true nature as God's beloved and eternal children, who shine like eternal suns, like Him radiating total love.

## The Spirit We Are

The Holy Spirit, then, was sent to convince us of our own true spiritual nature. The comprehensive, all-encompassing truth to which the Spirit leads, then, is *our own* truth. We are taught indirectly, gradually, and symbolically until we can know directly. But the overarching goal is to know *ourselves* as spiritual beings.

Because "God is spirit" and *we* in our true nature are spirit, it is by knowing our own nature as spirit that we come to know *God*, according to Jesus:

> God is spirit, and those who worship him must worship in spirit and truth.
> (John 4:24)

God, says Jesus here, is purely spirit. And so, we must know ourselves as spirit if we are to know Him. Knowing ourselves as spirit would be knowing the eternal "truth" about ourselves. Once again, the truth is that God is less like us human beings, and we are in actuality more like Him.

As we learn to identify with our own spiritual nature, we come to know God increasingly well. As we come to know our true selves more and more completely, in other words, we come to know God who created us and who still wants relationship with us.

What it means to know ourselves as spirit is to know that, behind our physicality lies our core essence of spirit and mind. This is, in fact, our true essence, the true nature of ourselves, which renders the physical part of our nature to be merely the surface, the playing out of what is inside.

When Jesus says to his students: "you are not of the world" (John 15:19), he is telling them that their true nature cannot be confined or limited to the world they see. They are spirit, as God is spirit. When Jesus says: "I will utter what has been hidden since the foundation of the world" (Matthew 13:35), he is speaking of our own reality as well as God's, both of which precede or pre-exist the world.

What we think of as reality, then, is not the entire picture. In fact, it often serves to distract from the true and more comprehensive picture. We need to expand our conception of reality until it becomes clear to us that we had *no idea* what it was—it is so infinitely greater than we had thought. Sometimes this occurs to us naturally, in a moment wherein things seem suddenly transcendent, but most often we are led to such revelation gradually by realizing in specific situations that appearances alone do not show the entire picture. We get either an *experience* or a *sense* that there is something more. And this "something more" is either full or partial realization of the hidden truth about *both* God and ourselves.

Paul affirms that the Spirit is able to penetrate the interior reality (what we would call the "consciousness" or subjective reality) of God. But because we ourselves are spirit, or have "spirit" and "being" within us, we can know the interior depths of God by learning of our own inner depths:

> For the Spirit searches everything, even the depths of God. For what knows a person's thoughts except the spirit of the being which is in him?
> (1 Cor. 2:10-11)

This ability to know "even the depths of God," is "revealed to us through the Spirit." Moreover, our own spirit, "the spirit of the being" within us, works with *the* Spirit, the

Holy Spirit, to fathom the depths of not only our own being but also the Being of God. In fact, God gave us a spiritual nature like His own for just this reason: so that we may have direct knowledge of Him and remain forever in communion with Him. Note that "the spirit of the being which is in [us]" is the part that knows our true thoughts. This is our true being, which we have called our original being, our sonship, and our true spiritual nature.

Paul says that "our old self" (Romans 6:6) yearns to know its liberation. It has already felt the great and gnawing need to transcend itself. It has groaned under the weight of the masks it wore, the burdens it bore, the artifice to which it eventually assimilated itself. It was an unconscious weight we carried simply because we had not allowed ourselves to realize the full extent of what we were doing to ourselves—how, in effect, we were *denying* ourselves. Therefore this "old self" had been an unconscious cause of our frustration.

The old self was unconscious both of the burden it bore and the burden it placed upon others. It lived and moved and had its being in unconsciousness, going through the motions without knowing what it did. Because it was frustrated, but did not realize how much or why it was frustrated, it simply projected its frustration onto others in a feeble and ultimately unsuccessful attempt to deflect it from itself.

We could have lifted the both burdens we bore and those we imposed on others with just the touch of one of our fingers (Luke 11:46). We could have released them and ourselves at the very same time. The newly emergent self, eternal and pre-existent, had at its fingertips the power of God but we (as the old self) did not realize.

Paul uses another image in order to affirm that how we already see ourselves in the world is only a faint and fuzzy image of who we really are:

> For now we see in a mirror dimly, but then face to face. Now I know in part; then I shall understand fully, even as I have been fully understood.
> (1 Cor. 13:12)

As mirrors in those days were made of pounded and polished brass, the physical image would have seemed distorted, much like a funhouse mirror. But that is how we had known ourselves before, as through "a mirror dimly," that is, with only partial understanding. To know only in part distorts the whole picture. It is only the complete spiritual knowledge of our own emergent spiritual being that allows us to "understand [ourselves] fully."

## Be Still and Know

There exists within us an inexhaustible peace. Once we decide to sink into it, we never reach the end. It is a stillness, an unmoving still point within that does not change with the ever-changing surface of things. It does not change even as moods change, as one thought or feeling skips to the next, nor even as the world turns all around us. It is the one "set" thing in this world, the one stable thing in all our experience, in all our lives.

It is here, we are told, in this deep inner stillness that we find God. He abides in utter peace, and that utter peace abides within ourselves, from whence it beckons us to approach the sacred ground of all being, including our own. It is the old self that leaves its sandals behind, while the new self hears and follows the Word of God directly from His Most Holy Mouth. The new self walks *always* on holy ground.

Jesus refers to an inner chamber, like a secret room inside ourselves where we encounter God in utter stillness:

> But when you pray, go into your room and shut the door and pray to your Father who is in secret; and your Father who sees in secret will reward you.
> (Matt. 6:6)

This innermost chamber exists as far away from the world as it possibly can, and yet it is behind just one door. It is not far at all to go, to be in a place and space so different from the world. Though it begins in emptiness and in stillness from constant chatter, it ends in joy and a sense of fullness so great that it must overflow to all beings, to receive as they choose.

God is encountered within the heart and mind of the individual. In the innermost part of ourselves, far from the world, secret even to ourselves, is where we will find Him. The reward is that we will find exactly what we lost along the way: we find our own selves there. In this very same emptiness we find total fulfillment.

We seek only the stillness and emptiness in which we might know Him. Therefore we follow the advisement of the Psalmist, who says simply:

> Be still, and know that I am God.
> (Ps. 46:10)

The more still we are, the more is revealed. In inverse proportion to how we experience the world, we experience the utter completion of God, the dynamic Mind of God whereby each thought lives, having a life of its own. Therefore nothing is empty, but every corner, every nook and cranny full, and we can find no empty chamber any longer.

All we truly want is revealed in this moment. It is not that God is qualitatively different from everything, as He seemed from our worldly perspective, but rather He *is* everything because everything finds its true existence in Him. And so all things might be approached even as He is approached, sandal-less, almost sideways, yet in each thing He draws us ever closer until full communion is achieved.

He reveals Himself to us in silence so palpable that it can be heard, stillness so ethereal that it can be felt. It is through the initial boredom of empty spaces and times, through such mundaneness, such ho-hum everydayness in fact that we become most transfixed by divine beauty.

We become, as it were, a blank slate on which God writes His holy Word, yet we find when we get there that it is already inscribed. The Word is fulfilled, the original promise kept, in just the space of our own existence. He did not leave us, nor did He sentence us to the perdition of alienation. How can He have when we live and move and have our being in His most sacred and fully extended Heart and Mind?

We had tried so hard to find such utter stillness that all being exists within it! It was a task made more difficult than it need have been simply because we had no idea what we were looking for, and what truly would fulfill us. Hence the need for the emptiness and stillness of that moment to find the incredibly eternal and infinite life inherent in all things.

Paradoxically, it is from what seems to be emptiness to the world that fullness arises:

> The whole earth is at rest and quiet;
> they break forth into singing.
> (Isa. 14:7)

From the most complete "rest and quiet" does the selfless joy of "singing" break forth. And in that selfless joy is found universality and the deeply-felt connection with every part of reality. Just a moment ago the world was full of cares, but then we realized we wanted nothing of it, and then we realized we wanted for nothing. And for one bright and shining moment, all searching was finally done. The culmination of all things, and the clearest exposition of how they all work together, is found to be an experience within us.

Therefore:

> Better is a handful of quietness than two hands full
> of toil and a striving after wind.
> (Eccles. 4:6)

That which we thought we wanted was not what we really wanted. Therefore it was "a striving after wind," ultimately meaningless, and the cares we heaped upon our minds by so striving after nothing are similarly stilled.

Whatever we strove for in the past, we really strove for "the peace of God, which passes all understanding" (Phil. 4:7). But we find that, because it passes all understanding, we have to let it come naturally to us. Such peace comes naturally or not at all; we have to learn how to let it happen of its own accord. It is through a kind of paradoxical intention that we sink into it, and let it overflow us. We want it, but not knowing what it is before we realize we have it, we have to let it rush in like the wind. We can only throw open our windows, and wait but a moment.

The practice of prayer is the practice of *being*. It is the sweeping out of the inner space to reveal "the hidden person of the heart with the imperishable jewel of a gentle and quiet spirit, which in God's sight is very precious" (1 Pet. 3:4). Notice that what is uncovered is spoken of as an inner and hidden *person*: "the hidden person of the heart." For what is evoked in this practice of emptiness is our true being, the same as the true being of all, arising from out of the depths of inner silence.

The complete fullness of our God-given eternal being can only arise of itself, from the stillness; it cannot be bought or sold, cannot be constructed, cannot be drafted or planned. The stillness reminds us that all is done, already completed, and we realize that we did not know this because we had chosen instead lack and incompletion.

So now, as we open our eyes, we look at the world as if for the first time. We see in it all those things we missed before. We expect them and they appear. Had we known what we would find, we would not have delayed. We would have run to them and would have begun to realize that, wherever it is we roam and wander, we walk on holy ground. Whatever our glance lights upon, we hear within it: "Behold, I make all things new" (Revelation 21:5), and we know that vision has followed our moment of contemplation.

Overall, we have learned from our moment of prayer and the emptiness that led to such fullness that it was by turning toward Him ever so slightly that all things are done, and done for us. Thus is it written, inscribed now on our experience:

> Draw near to God and he will draw near to you.
> (James 4:8)

# 7

# Salvation And The New Identity

**From a Great Height**

**(The Fall from Original Being)**

Human beings, according to the first creation story in Genesis 1, were created in the image of God:

> So God created man in his own image, in the image of God he created him.
> (Genesis 1:27)

They were created to be like God. Humanity is the culmination of all creation and its crown, so to speak. They are, as originally created, the closest thing in this world to God.

The second creation story in Genesis chapters 2-3 is meant to tell the story as to how this Godlike creation, humankind, fell from its original Godlike status. It is in this story that we find the myth of Adam and Eve, and how this original pair somewhat naively fell away from their original perfect state. In this second story, we find that humankind is created first, whereas in the first story it was the culmination. In either case, humankind is the closest part of all creation to God. In this second story, we read that:

> God formed man of dust from the ground, and breathed into his nostrils the breath of life; and man became a living being.
> (Gen. 2:7)

God's own breath and life is what animates the human being. Though its form is comprised of dust, its internal reality is all God. It is the breath and life of God within him which makes of man "a living being."

It is in chapter 3 that the downfall occurs. This chapter seeks to answer the question of what happened to the creation of humankind that caused it to fall from its original Godlike status. It begins, as does many a folktale with which early humans sought to place themselves in the universe, with the introduction of an animal antagonist, "the serpent," which immediately begins to question the original couple (Gen. 3:1).

One might think of this serpent figure as rather like the coyote or trickster figure of some native American myths. The serpent is never in the Genesis account equated with Satan or the devil; this was a later association. Seen clinically in fact, we might think of the serpent as more a projection of the thoughts of the original couple, a figure on which blame might be projected for their own wayward (though still naive) thoughts.

By the time they meet this serpent figure, the original couple are already confused. And so we would have to trace the onset of humanity's fall from grace and Godlikeness to before it met the serpent, or certainly before it ever began to talk to them. Thus we might place the origin of the actual fall back to when it fell into a "deep sleep" in Gen. 2:21.

I say this because the serpent immediately begins to lie to them, and they fall for it hook, line and sinker. Specifically, in Gen. 3:4-5 the serpent attributes the couple's own jealousy and envy onto God, telling them that God feared their becoming "like God" when in fact He had already created them like Himself and had breathed His own life into them. The couple is already inclined to give credence to the serpent's lies, which would render the serpent more a mouthpiece for their own stray thoughts rather than the true instigator of their fall.

Another indication that the serpent is a projection of the original couple lies in the fact that the original couple uses it as a scapegoat to escape their own responsibility for the diminished nature of their thinking: "The serpent beguiled me, and I ate" (Gen. 3:13). Such an interpretation has the advantage of giving the couple full responsibility for their fallen thoughts.

Even in its folktale form, the story of Adam and Eve is entirely psychological, representing their reduced way of thinking, the *forgetting* of their original beatific state. At some point, this original couple falls into a state of amnesia wherein they forget and/or deny their original identities and accept what turn out to be lesser, much diminished identifications instead. The entire story is an early attempt at explaining how human beings think the way they do, when in fact they could have thought so much more highly about themselves. It is an attempt to explain what seems to be our natural inclination toward reductionistic thinking.

It is possible, in other words, that the only thing that *really* changed about the original couple was their minds and their way of thinking about themselves and God. Their eternal, perfect, and Godlike state may still the same as it ever was. Yet somehow, for some strange reason, this original couple decided to forego all this and to forget it.

This would mean that their original Godlike state of being remains somewhere in their minds, but it has become unconscious to them. Now it seems to be happening from outside them, when in reality it is all a product of their own way of thinking. If this is so, then the real nature of the problem and the corresponding real solution await their own simple recognition.

In other words, nothing really changed except in their minds. Eternal life, by definition and in all actuality, is still eternal life. However, humankind has placed itself in a position where it no longer realizes this fact because it has forgotten its own original nature. That is basically what the myth of Adam and Eve is attempting to tell us.

The problematic nature of existence is what is emphasized in the Adam and Eve narrative. It is found in the fact of death (2:17; 3:19), the sense of aloneness (2:18), all suffering (3:16), all struggle (3:17), and all conflict (3:15). These are the things that must be explained, philosophically speaking, if we are to conceive of life as originally having been "very good" as in Gen. 1:31, or like God, as in 1:27. Certainly at some time or another, suffering and death, struggle and alienation interfere with what might otherwise be "a good life." They are more like shocks to our system. Yet these things seem sewn into the very nature of existence; they seem inescapable.

Death seems built into existence (as does suffering, as does conflict, etc.), and this produces an inescapable philosophical problem, an existential situation and a contradiction in terms if the opposite of life is inherent in life. Both creation stories make clear that God had made the original creation to be perfect, and had provided it with all its wants and needs (e.g., 1:29). Therefore the only change possible was to step down from original completion to some measure of incompletion, from perfection to some degree of imperfection. It had to be a *lessening*, a *diminishment*, of creation because this is the only direction it could have changed if it was indeed perfect, whole, and complete to begin with.

The serpent represents a projection of Adam and Eve's already-diminished way of thinking. Therefore by the time "the eyes of both were opened, and they knew they were naked" (Gen. 3:7), which nakedness suggests alienation and estrangement from God, they had already begun to think along these lines. They had already posited themselves as distinct from God, far from the creation that was carved out of the same perfection as God. They must already have fallen from their previous and perfect state of being, even before this decisive moment of the fall, or else they would not have *believed* the serpent when it told them "your eyes will be opened, and you will be like God, knowing good and evil" (Gen. 3:5). They must have already lost knowledge of themselves as perfect.

In the beginning, God had mingled with the original creation. He was, in effect, one of them. The story says that God was present in the garden ("walking in the garden in the cool of the day" in Gen. 3:8). It must have been fear that induced Adam and Eve to want to hide from God "among the trees of the garden" (3:8). The real problem seems to be that they thought themselves to be utterly distinct and separate from God, for how could they have sought to hide?

They were estranged from God but also from their own true selves. This is the only way they could have felt guilty in the first place. And it is this existential guilt that produced their fear and their desire to hide. But all of this—the guilt, the fear, the hiding—comes from the initial estrangement or sense of separation and alienation between themselves and God. They must first have conceived or thought of themselves as already being apart from Him, and He from them.

This was the real fall: the notion that there was some distance between themselves and God. And they brought it with them to the encounter with the serpent, and the eating of the fruit of "the tree of the knowledge of good and evil" (Gen. 2:17). Their fall was part and parcel of the idea of separation, and their exile from Heaven was their pre-made choice. Even the command, the prohibition, not to eat of the fruit of a certain tree, would have been part of their dream of separation.

Where could they hide from God? There would be no place to hide in Heaven. They would have to venture out, to make a world, a new context to hide in. And so they built a world around themselves, a world in which they could hide from the presence of God and from themselves as spiritual beings.

The very fact that they could be tempted in the first place implies lack, meaning they had forgotten they were already complete like God. There could have been no temptation had they known this and been secure in their own perfect being, as given and willed by God. The "knowledge of good and evil" (Gen. 2:9), then, *must* have been a *lesser* knowledge than their original *complete* knowledge of pure good. Being a *limitation* on the original perfect knowledge, this "knowledge" based on duality and opposition would have cemented this sense of lack into their awareness, thus covering over their real awareness and hiding it from them, driving it into unconsciousness, replacing it with a temporary but seemingly fixed state of lack and incompletion.

The story is, remarkably, an early pictorial representation of our own existential situation, our own sense of estrangement from perfection. Here is the source of our "guilt" and all our "shame." It is the source of envy and the estrangement that presupposes it. Such "guilt" is existential, meaning that it comes from how we think about ourselves.

Adam and Eve fell away from perfection only in their minds. Reality itself did not fall because God did not follow them into the deep woods. In the Mind of God, reality was still what He made of it, and they were still His perfect creations. His love has only one boundary, one limit: it cannot be mixed with what is *not* love. Thus does it remain pure.

This is why evil can only have been an *absence* of good, born of the void, having no real substance of its own. It could only have been a lessening, a decrease in perfection, which is why it had to be separated from perfection, for the protection of both perfection and the original couple.

Neither Adam and Eve's nor our own original knowledge had consisted of opposites of any kind, of which "good and evil" is a representation, for with such dualities part of reality would have opposed itself. But once the first dichotomy has been introduced (in the story, "good and evil"), it multiplies quickly: other basic oppositions quickly follow, most notably life and death. Just as evil is a mere void, the seeming absence of good, so is death the seeming absence of life. And all of it would forever only be at best mere appearance, some degree of that original thought of imperfection, intending to deceive (i.e., hallucination, illusion).

The prohibition not to eat of that tree of the knowledge of good and evil makes sense only as a limit on how far we could limit ourselves, a limit on how much we can diminish ourselves and our state of being in our mind. The truth about us must always shine through, in some way, in some situations at least. Our original dignity as beings of God must still exist, if only in nascent form, even if we ourselves do not realize it about ourselves. (This is why, to get it back, we must generally see it in others first before we can believe it about ourselves.)

If the original split is illusory, then so are all its supposed consequences, including our being condemned to a life of "toil" and struggle (3:14, 17), all of our "enmity" or conflict with one another (3:15), all our "pain" and suffering (3:16). We need only trace them back to their supposed foundations to find out that they have *no real foundation* in God. They cannot therefore pertain to our original selves as created by Him in perfection. That is not to say that all of these aftereffects do not appear very real to us; only that they have *no basis* in God's nor our own reality. They were all *added* to the original creation which could only have had the effect of *subtracting* from its original completion.

One of the more immediate effects of the fall is that, after hiding out, the original couple immediately began to blame one another:

> The man said, 'The woman whom thou gavest to be with me, she gave me fruit of the tree, and I ate.'
> Then the LORD God said to the woman, 'What is this that you have done?' The woman said, 'The serpent beguiled me, and I ate.'
> (Gen. 3:12-13)

Note that *God Himself* does not quite understand what they have done ("What is this that you have done?"). This is a sign that, thankfully, He retained His sanity and did not follow them into the wilderness of illusion. God did not forget His own perfect nature, but they had, and so they sought to hide, compounding their problem by hiding away from their former reality (God's and their own).

When they hid, they hid so well that they forgot the true nature of not only the problem, but also of reality itself. Furthermore, they forgot not only their own reality but also

God's. Now they had both feet firmly planted in illusion, their every step taking them a little deeper into the wilderness. But still they had a haunting sense that they were not where they were *supposed* to be. The reality at their core was still there of course, implanted in their hearts by the Eternal Mind of God. But even this slight sense of imperfection was enough to keep them in a world of illusion rather than reality.

The Garden according to this interpretation *is* their mind, but fully aligned with God's Mind. Where else or what else would it be, and still be eternal? The wilderness into which they wandered, on the other hand, was made up entirely of their own thoughts, without God's. God could not go there. It was an illusory place in their mind where they thought hiding from God was even *conceivable*. More mistaken than evil, they had naively, without knowing the full consequences of their actions, bitten off more than they could ever hope to chew.

In reality, meanwhile, the original Garden is all there is. It must exist all around them, but they cannot see it now. They themselves were still the breath of God (Gen. 2:7) and living souls (*Ibid.*), but they could not know this now. Yet the original knowledge is still there and it can still be evoked, remembered, recognized at any fully present moment.

God's purpose in creating free beings like Himself, with free and independent will, was to love them and have real relationship with them. (Nothing else makes sense.) He created them *by* loving them, and so love was their essence from the beginning. This means that their self would be found in relationship, and that love must always accompany them. The context or reality into which they were born must therefore be as eternal as they, or else they will sense deep within themselves that something is missing.

## Salvation and Return

For the ancient Israelites, salvation always involved some kind of *return*: a return to freedom from slavery in Egypt, a return home from their long exiles in the foreign lands of Assyria and then Babylon, a return to the paradisiacal Garden of Eden, a return to more faithful days, a return to God and to their true selves. Therefore we have Isaiah saying: "In returning and rest you shall be saved; in quietness and trust shall be your strength" (Isaiah 30:15). The great return was an often-used metaphor and motif in the Hebrew Bible.

There is a tendency throughout the Bible to view everything as returning to its point of origin. And so we see early in Genesis that while dust eventually returns to dust (Gen. 3:19), and the body to the ground from which it sprang, the God-breathed part of ourselves (Gen. 2:7) would return also to its ultimate Source: It would fold back into the Infinite Being of God.

The Psalmist arrives at the conclusion that it is a return of God's presence in our earthly lives that ultimately saves:

> Restore us, O God; let thy face shine,
> that we may be saved!
> (Ps. 80:3)

Notice that to realize God's presence is to be restored to our natural state and therefore *saved*. If contemplation of God's presence has the power to save us, then it must have been the state and thought of *separation* from God that we needed saving *from*. In our original state of being, we had only to:

> Look to him, and be radiant;
> so your faces shall never be ashamed.
> 
> (Ps. 34:5)

It was natural for God to pervade our thoughts in our original state of being. We have just seen that shame, or thinking we are anything less than we really are, was one of the consequences of the fall, and the fall was a result of the forgetting of our original state of being. It is by re-including God amongst our thoughts that we return to our original and "radiant" state of being.

The prophet Isaiah emphasizes the great joy that accompanies this return to God:

> And the ransomed of the LORD shall return,
> and come to Zion with singing;
> everlasting joy shall be upon their heads;
> they shall obtain joy and gladness,
> and sorrow and sighing shall flee away.
> 
> (Isa. 35:10)

And so we see the theme of return associated with great joy. By the time of the Second Isaiah it is associated also with forgiveness of sins and guilt, and this becomes an immediate and present-tense experience:

> I have swept away your transgressions like a cloud,
> and your sins like mist;
> return to me, for I have redeemed you.
> 
> (Isa. 44:22)

A great internalization of salvation can be seen developing in the Book of Isaiah as it goes along. Here, the sticking-point is identified as *guilt*. It is guilt that keeps us away from from God, God's presence, and our true selves. Therefore it is guilt that keeps us away from being saved. By the time of the third Isaiah, return and therefore salvation depend not only on right behavior but also right thinking (Isa. 55:7), which includes seeing God as ultimately all-merciful, saying, "he will abundantly pardon" (Isa. 55:7).

Jeremiah speaks similarly of the change in the human heart as being most significant—our return to God will be like opening to a new heart inside ourselves:

> I will give them a heart to know that I am the Lord;
> and they shall be my people and I will be their God,
> for they shall return to me with their whole heart.
> (Jeremiah 24:7)

Salvation here as elsewhere in the Hebrew Bible involves seeing ourselves differently, which is described as accompanying a return to God in some whole-hearted fashion. It makes sense that our return to God will also be a return to our true selves because these are the selves God gave us.

Similarly, in Jesus' teaching, when the prodigal son returns to his father in the story, he expects to be treated poorly (out of guilt and shame), but instead, once the son makes his way back home, his father accepts him with a joyous embrace and with celebration (Luke 15:11-32). The son receives his former identity back upon his return, and immediately restored are all the psychological effects of love, joy, and peace which accompany return. But it is specifically through loving and forgiving others, according to Jesus, that we will be *like* our Father in Heaven (and therefore be saved), as we have seen earlier.

To be saved may seem like being picked off the heap, because we generally have reached our lowest point when we most want salvation. And it is only when we most *want* salvation that we will do everything in our power to *seek and to find* the salvation held out to us. It is only as we ask with our whole hearts, and therefore fully congruently, that we are ready to receive with our full hearts.

Paul tries out a number of metaphors for thinking about salvation, but in the end he lands on *reconciliation*, a return of full relationship with God:

> All this is from God, who through Christ reconciled us to himself and gave us *the ministry of reconciliation*; that is, in Christ God was *reconciling the world to himself*, not counting their trespasses against them, and entrusting to us *the message of reconciliation*. So we are ambassadors for Christ, God making his appeal through us. We beseech you on behalf of Christ, be *reconciled* to God.
> (2 Cor. 5:18-20, my italics)

God's plan is, then, "to reconcile to himself all things, whether on earth or in heaven"(Col. 1:20). Human beings, for Paul, are meant also to be God's ambassadors in fulfilling this plan. The reconciliation includes us, of course, if it includes all things. Moreover, it *must* include *all* beings, if it is to be whole, if it is to be be a reconciliation with "all things." With such passages as this, Paul achieves the spirit of universalism we had seen in nascent form in the Book of Isaiah.

The theme of return and reconciliation suggests that we have been there before, so to speak. That is to say, salvation is more a reversal of course than it is a new arrival. What this means is that the state of Heaven will not be new to us, but will actually be quite familiar. It will be accompanied by joy and singing. The problem is that we have *forgotten*, rather than that we never knew. Such an interpretation makes salvation much easier, as if we need not reinvent the wheel, nor even enter unfamiliar territory to get there.

And this interpretation makes more sense when it comes to our conception of a rational God, a God for whom reason and persuasion are instruments of return. That is, God did not create beings who had to *strive* for their salvation. He created beings who were already saved, which means that He gave them everything right up front and from the beginning. Salvation, like eternal life, is in Paul's words "a free gift." And, logically speaking, if we did not initially and originally *need* salvation, then once our minds changed and we *did* need it, it was there for us in a form we could understand.

Because we have forgotten what it is like, this original state seems to have been relegated to some primordial past and some long-forgotten memory. In reality, it belongs to a different *kind* of time altogether, one that is based, paradoxically, on a recurrent moment of timelessness, an ever- or omni-presence. Sacred time is often conceived as cyclical, which, brought to its logical conclusion, is the recurrrence of an eternally present moment. Time would not have been needed in our original state, because salvation would not have been needed, and also because there was, we have just seen, no growing old, no decay or deterioration, and no death.

You might glean from the foregoing that the physical reality, *our* physical reality, is therefore not as significant to our original state of being as is our internal reality (which would include our cognitive, affective, volitional and spiritual realities). It exists for salvific purposes, but it does not represent our true state of being. That is, we employ this current physical reality for the larger purpose of real and deeply felt cognitive and affective salvation, but in the end we realize it is nowhere near who we really are.

This is what it means, I think, that Adam and Eve found themselves suddenly to be "naked" as a result of the fall. They saw themselves suddenly *as* physical entities, rather than as spiritual beings *with* bodies. They began to *identify* too exclusively with the physical body that seems always to be growing old and which, to all appearances, seems likely to meet its end in death. They forgot that there was anything else, let alone something so transcendentally "more" that it would totally outshine their turned-feeble sense of reality.

Sin, for Jesus, was newly interpreted: rather than a set of behaviors that did not live up to God, it became an entire state of mind and being that did not live up to God. Sin, in effect, was any diminished *thought* of being, whether in ourselves or someone else. It was the product of having convinced ourselves, through our own thoughts actions, and reactions, that we were *less than* what God created us to be. It was *this* "sin" of thinking ourselves to be *less than* we really and eternally are that was and is the cause of all our existential guilt. It is not as if we truly *are* less than God created us to be, after all, but that we *think* we are that is the problem.

The entire problem is that we have actually succeeded in convincing ourselves of our own insignificance, using the great power of our mind for self-limiting and reality-diminishing purposes, purposes not worthy of the truth of ourselves. It is only these misbegotten purposes, steeped in false-self-interest, routinely and mindlessly followed in the world, that perpetuate this sense of unworth and this strange need to reduce ourselves to nothingness.

According to this interpretation, the "punishment" (or simply, ill effect) is part of the "sin" itself, not something added by God afterward. It is therefore not something that should be feared as if it awaited in the future; we are experiencing both hell and purgation even now. It is an immediate consequence, and it is not so much punishment as it is *consequence*. The sense of diminishment of our own being *is* the hell we are *nearly* trapped in. It is all around us, which means there *seems* to be no escape. The very idea of guilt diminishes us, and though we may think we are free of it, at any given moment, as long as we project it onto others we retain it for ourselves, caught in its muck as if in a smothering quicksand.

The entirety of what we are to be saved *from*, therefore, is inside ourselves. It is our way of thinking, or more specifically identifying, that needs to change. And yet our new way of thinking already awaits, also inside ourselves, as a possibility and potential at least of universally salvific proportions. The entire cosmic battle takes place in the arena of our minds.

Salvation is associated with the themes of return, restoration, and reconciliation that run throughout the Bible. That which is most Godlike within ourselves will return to God, while that which is illusion will return to illusion. Sin was both the diminished being and the fear and guilt that proceeded from that. It was its own punishment basically, but none of this came from the God of love. It must have been our own thought, our own idea, that led us to conceive of such a thing. This was more than the breaking of a few laws or societal rules or norms; it was instead the active choosing of a lesser state of being. Or at least that was the illusion we fell into—as with Adam and Eve, without full awareness of what we were doing to ourselves. It is simply by seeing through this grand illusion that the truth returns to take its rightful place in our minds.

## To Be Born Again

Jesus spoke of a new life so thoroughly different from the old that he called it being "born anew":

> Truly, truly, I say to you,
> unless one is born anew,
> he cannot see the kingdom of God.
> (John 3:3)

Jesus states that one must become *a new being* in order to "see the kingdom of God." In other words, only a new being can see the new reality characterized here as "the kingdom of God." What this means is that one sees the world according to how one sees oneself. It is possible to see a new world because it is possible to identify with a new self.

One cannot force this new identity, which is why it is spoken of as being "born." However, it is something that happens to us as a result of our decision and therefore according to the power of our mind. The decision itself is a great one, so great that it results not only in a new self but also a new world, or context for this self.

All of this can happen at any time, even now. However different and new this rebirth is, it is not physical. One need not actually be born again in a *physical* sense in order to be born again in a cognitive and spiritual sense, as Jesus explains to Nicodemus, who is described as "a man of the Pharisees" (John 3:1). Nicodemus tries to understand this all too literally, too concretely, as evidenced by his asking: "How can a man be born when he is old? Can he enter a second time into his mother's womb and be born?" (John 3:4).

Jesus responds to him with this:

> That which is born of the flesh is flesh, and that which is born of the Spirit is spirit.
> (John 3:6)

"Flesh" and "spirit" in this saying obviously represent two basic ways of being, two very different realities and *experiences* of reality each with its own very different point of origin. Each of these realities is associated with its very own way of being, just as each of the two ways of being is associated with its own reality. We might therefore say that each of these two ways of being results in two very different ways of seeing. Each way of being comes complete with its own reality, inhabits its own world, sets its own context around it.

We think of being born as an accident, as something beyond our own choice. Perhaps our parents had something to do with setting the stage, but not even they chose exactly who would enter the world at their behest. And so, being born is something that "just happens," although Jesus is saying that there is more to it than this. At least in regard to the new birth, the rebirth, Jesus suggests there is an element of personal choice involved.

Jesus explains further what it means to be born anew:

> Do not marvel that I said to you,
> 'You must be born anew.' The wind blows where it wills, and you hear the sound of it, but you do not know whence it comes or whither it goes; so it is with every one who is born of the Spirit.
> (John 3:7-8)

This all seems somewhat cryptic, but let us see if we can parse it out. Jesus is explaining how being born anew is like the wind blowing freely, wherever it "wills." The new and nascent being seems very much to have a mind of its own. It is free, and perhaps as spontaneous the wind. It is as free, we could say, as our mind is free, as the Spirit is free.

We "hear the sound of it," that is, we sense the effects of this new being within us, we feel it, we know it is there, but we do not immediately know the full extent of where it comes from. Its true point of origin comes from well beyond what we thought our own point of origin was, which means we have to re-assess ourselves and reevaluate everything if we are to understand it.

The wind may be invisible, but we can see its effects. We know it is there, even if we do not know where it comes from or where it ultimately goes. The same is true of the Spirit and the new life associated with it. We can experience its effects and thereby know it is there even if we cannot see it with the naked eye nor trace its true origin.

Nicodemus asks again about being reborn by spirit: "How can this be?" Jesus responds by pointing to *his own* experience and new perception:

> Truly, truly, I say to you, we speak of what we know, and bear witness to what we have seen;
> but you do not receive our testimony. If I have told you earthly things and you do not believe, how can you believe if I tell you heavenly things?
> (John 3:10-12)

Jesus is simply saying that his (and his school's) knowledge of God is based on experience, not conceptualization. Heaven, he suggests here, is a state of mind. It is a new state of being with a new context around itself. Altogether it is a new reality that begins with one's experience. We will explore this idea of Heaven in more detail a bit later. Suffice it to say for now that the understanding of "heavenly things" does not come from outside those things, as is true of conceptual worldly knowledge. We do not stand apart from such knowledge, either earthly or Heavenly, but we are part of it and it is part of us.

Jesus continues to Nicodemus:

> No one has ascended into heaven but he who descended from heaven, the Son of man. And as Moses lifted up the serpent in the wilderness, so must the Son of man be lifted up, that whoever believes in him may have eternal life.
> (John 3:13-15)

Here we have a kind of parable whereby the phrase "Son of man" seems generalized from Jesus onto all humankind ("whoever believes"). And it seems a hard and fast rule that only the part of ourselves that came originally from Heaven will be able to rise to Heaven. There *must* therefore be something within us that originated in Heaven.

To believe in Jesus is at the same time to believe in that higher part of ourselves, characterized here as "eternal life," for it is Jesus who teaches about it, identifies with it, and teaches us to identify with it. To believe it to be true of Jesus is to believe it to be true of ourselves. Again, to believe in him is to believe *more* in ourselves.

If there were not something within us that originally came from Heaven, then the reality and experience of Heaven would continue to elude us. But to believe that there is something of and from Heaven *in Jesus* is to begin to open our minds to the possibility of utterly new experience in ourselves as well. Hence the importance of seeing Jesus as human, and not too far beyond our own potential way of being.

Let us end here with Peter's statement of rebirth:

> Having purified your souls by your obedience to the truth for a sincere love of the brethren, love one another earnestly from the heart. *You have been born anew*, not of perishable seed but of imperishable, through the living and abiding word of God.
> (1 Peter 1:22-23, my italics)

An earnest and sincere love is what purifies and draws us close to the truth that we are eternal beings. Peter, like the Johannine Jesus, speaks of this as being "born anew." Furthermore, he speaks as if it has *already happened*, because indeed it *has* even if we do not always realize it. We are only now growing into it, and growing into its understanding which comes by experience of it. Even though it begins as "the truth," generalized and objective, it becomes our own truth, experienced as such and subjective.

This "imperishable" seed is the thought of our true identity, the essential truth of ourselves, which is, as Peter says at the beginning of his letter, "imperishable, undefiled, and unfading, kept in heaven for you" (1 Peter 1:4). It is the eternal thought of ourselves, kept safe and unfading in spite of the fading world. He speaks of this new identity as being "kept" for us until we are ready to accept it (or re-identify with it). In other words, *it already is* who we are to God, and we are playing catch up. According to Peter, the life we were originally given by God still exists, kept safe in Heaven for us, waiting for us simply to waken to it and reclaim it.

# 8

# Raised As Children of God

**Resurrection as a Present Experience**

Throughout this book we have argued that Christian metaphysics are best and most reasonably to be understood in terms of psychological experience. In the next couple of chapters, we will severely put this thesis to a test as we examine the most metaphysical concepts surrounding Christianity, including the ideas of resurrection, the end of the world, and the *psychological states* of hell and Heaven. This is not to say that these ideas cannot be conceived of as metaphysical concepts, but that that is *all* they can be as metaphysical concepts. They make more sense if interpreted as psychological and experiential realities.

For instance, "the resurrection" begins as something specific to Jesus but it ends as a general reality. From there, it has gotten bogged down in speculation most of the time, stuck in the conceptual way of thinking rather than being allowed to show itself for what it is. Yet concepts can take us only so far, because events that happen outside ourselves, including objective thinking, are never fully understood unless we participate in them in some way. We shall see that there is sound biblical basis for believing this to be true, for seeing the idea of resurrection as a very present and immediate type of psychological experience. If it were not, after all, we would not be able fully to understand it.

On a metaphysical level, the idea of resurrection conveys some event that will supposedly happen to us at some point in the future. But on a psychological level, the resurrection is a potentiality currently within our range of experience. It is more *potentiality* than *eventuality*, more a thing known to experience than a thing that may one day happen to us. Therefore it can be understood in the here and now, and we need not wait for a fuller understanding.

To best understand the resurrection as a psychological experience, we must first seek to share how Jesus thought of death. Very simply put, *death* to Jesus was *nothing*. It had no reality *at all* from God's perspective, and so it should have no reality from our own. What we see as death or interpret as death is therefore *no such thing*. The finality of it is all appearance, and deceptive appearance at that. Only God's perspective is always true; ours is subject to illusion and delusion, deceptive appearance and thinking—but this need not be.

Jesus seems to treat death as if it were an *illusion*, a trick of perception. He seems to *know*, somehow, that life is not dependent on the body (Luke 12:22) and that death could affect neither him (Matt. 16:18) nor those who followed him (Matt. 16:28). He also seems *certain* that the little girl whose family was grief-stricken is not really dead but instead "sleeping" (Mark 5:39). In all these instances he does not accept death as fact, or reality, but treats it as if it were quite literally *nothing*.

We have seen that Jesus concerned himself first and foremost with *eternal* life, a life that does not depend on the body for its existence. Such eternal life would not be subject to death. Death would be quite literally nothing to it. Thus he stated that those who come to know their eternal life "will not taste death" (Matt. 16:28) and that they "will never see death" (John 8:51). Death will stop stalking them like a shadow once they see it for what it is in the light.

It is all a matter of perspective, and which we consider to be the basis of reality. There are basically two choices: we can either think with God or we can speculate by ourselves. If we think with God, then we share His eternal perspective, but if we think alone, we have only ourselves to fall back on. If we think with God, then eternal reality will be paramount, and therefore the basis of *all* reality, whereas if we think only by ourselves, we will "judge by appearances" rather than with "right judgment" (John 7:24).

To be frank, we must admit we have *no idea* what happens to the seemingly once-living being at the point where it seems no longer to exist. We can see only what our two eyes show us. Insofar as they are limited, therefore, so are our thoughts. We are as limited as our perceptual apparatuses. We can see past them only with something that has a greater, more comprehensive reality than they, only with something that does not know death and cannot experience it: the eternal mind, soul or being within ourselves.

If such a thing does not exist, then we will never know what death is or what lies behind it. But we could never be completely satisfied *not* to know. There is something within us that strives for certainty, that wants and needs to know, and is anxious and insecure in itself until it *does* know, with certainty. The only way to know with certainty, we have seen again and again, is to know through firsthand experience more psychological than strictly conceptual.

The Gospel of John understands Jesus as speaking of resurrection and deathlessness as a personal experience, beginning here and now, in the present. Thus he says:

> Truly, truly, I say to you, he who hears my word and believes him who sent me, has eternal life; he does not come into judgment, but has passed from death to life.
>
> (John 5:24)

There is a way to pass "from death to life" even while living in this world. Some in Jesus' circle had already done so in their minds. It all had to do with a change in thinking about life itself. If life is indeed "eternal," then death would quite literally be nothing. For one would seem to be the negation of the other. We will examine this passage later in regard to judgment.

To believe in eternal life is to disbelieve in death. To identify with eternal life in this world, to whatever extent we *can*, here and now, is to put death behind us. This is why Jesus could promise his students:

> Truly, truly, I say to you, if any one keeps my word, he will never see death.
>
> (John 8:51)

What we expect, in the back of our minds, concerning death, never comes. It was only a presumptive interpretation that, once changed in our mind, is changed forever. This is why resurrection must be an immediate experience, an experience we have in this life, in our present existence, because it is simply the belief, followed by the growing certainty, that life is eternal. Jesus, you will recall, in providing characteristics of the sons or children of God, includes deathlessness among them:

> they cannot die any more,

> because they are equal to the angels
> and are sons of God,
> being sons of the resurrection.
>
> (Luke 20:36)

Knowing themselves to be "sons of God" would change them fundamentally, according to this passage. They would come to know themselves to be "equal to the angels" in terms of having eternal life. *Knowing* themselves to be eternal, "they cannot die anymore."

All of this happens here and now, with a simple change of mind. Resurrection is simply re-identification with the eternal part of ourselves, and a corresponding de-emphasis on bodily identification. It is not that the body no longer exists, but it is no longer seen as the locus *or* focus of either life or reality. Identification rests instead on those aspects of the subjective self that might be thought of as eternal: mind, heart, soul, spirit, and simply life, internally-oriented states of being that do not depend on the body for their existence.

The freedom of the children of God is total, and so it must include the overcoming of *anything* finite, *any* limitation whatsoever, all the way up to and including death. Resurrection is utter liberation, total freedom from all finite thinking. It is an experience wherein at its culminating point one rises above the strictures and structures of the world, and can there truly declare independence from all of it.

Resurrection must happen *before* death because, again, death *never happens*. It was only a misinterpretation, and always from the outside. As such, it was born more of fear than anything else. It would certainly not be a product of love, in which case also death would not exist for God nor for any of God's creations. This is why those who know themselves to be children of love "cannot die anymore."

Jesus' resurrection, whereby he conquered death, happened in mind well before it happened in deed. It is the same with all of us, according to his teaching. His resurrection was meant specifically to be an example to all people that death is nothing but a fearful thought in our minds:

> Now is the judgment of this world, now shall the ruler of this world be cast out; and I, when I am lifted up from the earth, will draw all men to myself.
>
> (John 12:31-32)

The mere presence of a being on earth who does not believe in death or limitation of any kind can be considered a blessing for all the world. Everyone benefits, whether they believe in his words or not, whether they know him or not. Mind and being has a special connection that neither bodies nor physical senses can know.

Jesus says: "I ... will draw all men to myself." This of course means *all persons, all human beings*. There are no exclusions stated here. The Johannine Jesus intended to be universalized, to appeal to all the world. *All* are called, most likely then in various ways—perhaps as many ways as there are individuals. This would be the case if Jesus were speaking in the most logical and basic of terms, of universal experience and knowledge that anyone could understand.

What is death in the face of the call of God to all beings? It is precisely nothing; it has no reality anymore. All the reality it ever had was that which we ourselves had lent it. And what had we really known about it? We surrender our thoughts about it therefore to the One who truly knows.

Paul had also spoken of the resurrection as being a participatory event, and one that could be had in any present moment. Speaking from his own experience he finds agreement with Jesus that the necessary change of mind can indeed occur without death:

> Lo! I tell you a mystery. We shall not all sleep, but we shall all be changed, in a moment, in the twinkling of an eye, at the last trumpet.... For this perishable nature must put on the imperishable, and this mortal nature must put on immortality. When the perishable puts on the imperishable, and the mortal puts on immortality, then shall come to pass the saying that is written: 'Death is swallowed up in victory.'
> (1 Cor. 15:51, 53-54)

Paul speaks of a great change that will happen to believers *while they exist in this world*. This change will lead them to a conviction of deathlessness, of "immortality," and of resurrection. It is by recognizing one's own imperishability that one can be changed, here and now. Faith accepts it as true for oneself, while reason accepts it as true for all if an eternal God with eternal creations does indeed exist.

For Paul, Jesus' resurrection not only *signifies* our own resurrection, it also *effects* our resurrection or causes it to happen. The meaning of Jesus' resurrection is that it assures us of *our own*, and therefore of the eternity within *us*. It thereby has *already* transformed our idea of life by having transformed our experience of it:

> As Christ was raised from the dead by the glory of the Father, we too might walk in newness of life.
> (Rom. 6:4)

The resurrection of Jesus was intended as a means by which "we too might walk in newness of life." For us, because Jesus realized it first, "death no longer has dominion" (Rom. 6:9). It is spoken of as a past occurrence also in later Pauline tradition: God has *already* "raised us up with him" (Eph. 2:6) and "made us alive together with Christ" (2:5). Resurrection is simply a very different experience of reality wherein spirits, minds, eternal beings all can mix and intermingle as if they were already *one*. Of *all* of us it is therefore said that:

> the people who sat in darkness
> have seen a great light,
> and for those who sat in the region and shadow of death
> light has dawned.
> 
> (Matt. 4:16)

## The End of the World

We have seen that Jesus' resurrection signified for early Christians an immediate experience in which they would come to participate. There was a process underway whereby all people were being drawn into awareness of their own eternal state of being. So potent and overwhelming is this experience that it becomes a kind of enduring grand moment, as if everything had suddenly shown its true eternal nature. It is this *effect* of the resurrection experience (or experience of eternal life) that is referred to as "the end of the world."

When *we* are changed, *the entire world* seems to change. As the mind changes, so does perception of the world. This proves that perception is a result of our thinking, and specifically a result of interpretation. We see a much different world through a different state of mind. And so the world changes significantly in our perception: it seems to *end* and to change in the space of a moment. It does not end entirely, therefore, but changes so thoroughly that it is perceived differently.

With a simple change of mind, the world changes into something very different, with a very different point of origin. This is how the world can be changed and yet still await the fullness of its change: it is done individually first, and only later collectively. This is how we can think of ourselves as currently resurrected but awaiting a more general resurrection, how we can be reborn and the world along with us, yet still feeling the urge to explain this experience to others (whom now we love).

Jesus' teaching seems designed to enable us to share his vision, to see a "new world" (Matt. 19:28). It is only by seeing the world through different eyes, drained of self-interest but refilled with love and forgiveness, that the world will truly change, will indeed become for us a "new world." And just as the old world was constructed out of old interpretations of reality, so will the new world seem to rise out of a new interpretation. A new focus in particular can bring out things that had been hidden before, renewing their life so to speak. What was formerly background (unconscious, hidden) becomes foreground (and rises into consciousness). In this way, too, the "first will be last, and the last first" (Mark 10:31). This reversal and transformation of the world, again, is a function of how differently we see it.

We have seen that in Jesus' teaching, the coming of the kingdom is not some future event so much as it is an intensely present one. When the kingdom finally does appear to us, we are told, "of [this] kingdom there will be no end" (Luke 1:33). Yet we will see this kingdom, this new world, even here amid the temporariness of the old. The old is fading even now, or as Paul (1 Cor. 7:31) says, is "the form of this world is passing away." Yet what replaces it is immeasurably greater in "splendor" and also "permanent" (2 Cor. 3:11). Thus the world does not end immediately, but rather changes when seen in a new light: the light of eternal vision.

The so-called "end of the world" is therefore more a visionary transformation of the world in our experience than a true end. For what is eternal about the world never ends, and this includes our own sense of being, especially as it knows itself in and through its loving. The end is more a transforming vision that changes us and the world at the same time, or reveals the previously hidden and internal infinitude in both, previously hidden behind its form.

The change in the world, or its enfoldment into our own eternity, has already happened. The previous way we viewed the world was as if *we* depended on *it*, but now we realize how fully *it* depends on *us* and our interpretation. Nothing has really changed therefore except our minds. We realize that the world needed changed simply because *we* were seeing it wrongly. We actually take priority in the change. It is because of us, in tribute to us, *for* us that the transformation occurs.

This all goes to say that we will see a new world first, before our minds are lifted wholly into Heaven. There are stages to the process of re-engaging in eternity precisely because the transformation is so great. We will walk in newness of life, a raised and enhanced life, as we saw in the last section. This is not the final end of all things, but it is a figurative end in that it is a very significant change.

In the world, it seems, "most men's love [has grown] cold" (Matt. 24:12). "But," Jesus assures us, "he who endures to the end will be saved" (24:13). That is to say that the loving outcome is sure, more sure than the world itself had ever been. But it is precisely this temporary unlovingness that ends, giving way to a vision in which the world is flooded with love. From that point, it is *we ourselves* who will be able to judge in an eternal sense which things in the world truly measure up to the great love inside us. The world is fully changed for each of us with that awaiting final judgment, which aspect of it we will examine in more detail in the next section.

This throws new light on the idea that it is only when "the gospel of the kingdom" is preached "throughout the whole world" that "the end will come" (Matt. 24:14). It is only when the gospel is *understood* in a personal, psychologically-significant way that the transformation will happen for each. Note that it is specifically the "gospel *of the kingdom*" that must be taught everywhere before the end may come. This is because the kingdom does begin with us and it is meant *for* us, having been "prepared" for us since before "the foundation of the world:"

> Come, O blessed of my Father, inherit the kingdom prepared for you from the foundation of the world.
> (Matt. 25:34)

There is no one who does not fit this description, but there are plenty who do not believe they and others fit this description. All are blessed by the Father as a function of His having created them. All are therefore destined for greatness, both to know it and to *be* it. But this means that the part of us that does not believe this must change and in some sense be utterly forgotten, as if it never *really* existed, more like a hallucination than actual fact. This is what it means for our minds to be purged as if in fire, as we shall see at the end of this chapter.

Jesus made use of such contemporary imagery (derived in the intertestamental period largely from the highly dualistic, light/dark Persian Zoroastrianism) to declare, "the close of the age" (Matt. 24:3), a transition to a new era, a *renewal* and progression into a new epoch rather than a literal end of the world. One great year begins as another aeon ends. That the real (or initial) change is internal and psychological rather than external (i.e., an event in history) is also indicated by such sayings as:

> So, if they say to you, `Lo, he is in the wilderness,' do not go out; if they say, `Lo, he is in the inner rooms,' do not believe it. For as the lightning comes from the east and shines as far as the west, so will be the coming of the Son of man.
> (Matt. 24:26-27)

Hence "the coming of the Son of man," which accompanies the change (and which will be explored more fully in the next section, in relation to its role as judge or arbiter), is an actual phenomenon that must be *accepted* phenomenologically or through experience. We ourselves will be the Son of man, a step up from our being merely human. As we saw with the kingdom itself, it will not be so much an outward phenomenon as it is purely inward:

> Being asked by the Pharisees when the kingdom of God was coming, he answered them, 'The kingdom of God is not coming with signs to be observed; nor will they say, "Lo, here it is!" or "There!" for behold, the kingdom of God is in the midst of you.
> (Luke 17:20-21)

And so we see the progression from the kingdom coming near (Luke 10:9, 11), to coming upon (Luke 11:20), to being "in the midst of" or *within* you (Luke 17:21). These are the stages of the gradual revelation of the kingdom to the mind from within one's experience. It is the last step, the internalization of the entire process, that is emphasized in these passages.

In the Gospel of John, all of this is brought into the present tense primarily as if it were an *experiential* reality. Jesus states in that Gospel that "the hour is coming, *and now is*" when "the voice of the Son of God" will be heard by all—even those who seem to have died (John 5:25, my emphasis). It will be heard all the more as grow adept at *speaking* it.

Likewise Paul declares: "Behold, *now* is the acceptable time; behold, *now* is the day of salvation" (2 Cor. 6:2, my emphasis). The fullness of our realization awaits only the present experience of this very present and therefore internal reality that gradually begins to fill our sight as well, all in preparation of the culminating moment which can happen at any point in the process.

Eternity, being timeless and thus ever-present, is always experienced in the present. Therefore not only is the resurrection experienced as a present reality, as we have seen, but so is the end of the world (and the preparatory end of the age). We might think of it as a kind of paradigm shift that happens in each mind individually, and spreads from there to affect consensual, general reality. One of the primary themes in the teaching of Jesus, remember, is that it is the effects of our own change of mind that will prove to us how powerful is that mind. Our inward state of reality *can* and *must* change the outward, consensual reality just by our re-thinking it. The implicit message here is that we are creators along with our Father. Even in our roles as perceivers and interpreters we are always creating, making and ending worlds as we go.

Apocalyptic and eschatological (end-time) thinking sees everything in the context of this present moment, which is why its fantastic visions always seem more dream-like than historical events. They are in themselves symbolic of deeper realities. End-time, in effect, is time*less*, removed from ordinary time. This is what gives it its dream-like quality.

With each moment out of time, that is, with the experience of each timeless moment, paradoxically the thought of time is made *more* significant. Everything becomes more significant as it leads and accedes to the eternal. This is how we know that the attainment or realization of such timelessness is the true meaning of time. The fact that we *could* see it utterly differently tells us all we need to know about time. It depends on us rather than we on it. (The same can be said for the world, as we have discussed.) Our previous thoughts of time, world, and self had been ways of *not* noticing the rather glaring *obviousness* of the timeless and eternal present, and of the power of *our* mind to change what seemed before like a binding, constrictive, and very narrow slice of reality into an infinitely expansive, universalized conception of reality.

## The Last Judgment

The so-called Last Judgment is literally the last judgment that will ever be made by each of us, handled by us in our roles as Son, first of man (i.e., humankind) and then of God. It happens in the process of our final decision no longer to judge others, as we grow to understand them by hearing their personalized stories, that we find that we have no reason any longer to judge *ourselves*. The perceived *need* for judgment of any kind will be gone.

I say that we ourselves are the final judges because it is made clear in a couple of Jesus' Johannine sayings that *neither he nor the Father judges anyone*:

> The Father judges no one, but has given all judgment to the Son.
> (John 5:22)

The Father does not judge because He knows only pure good. He represents what seems to us only one side of reality, but which to Him is total completion. Anything else would be something less, and that something less, even intermixed with good as it is, is what is called "evil." Therefore evil is always by some degree an absence of good, a void in and of itself, having existence only by virtue of its inverse (and distorted) relationship to the good.

The last judgment will therefore be the last discernment between the good in us and its absence in us. The very concept suggests that the good is complete in itself, having no real opposite nor even any degrees in itself. What is good is completely and thoroughly good, like God.

And so we see that the Father, being pure good, does not judge. Judgment, says the passage above, thereby belongs to the Son, the Father's creation. Jesus is representative of this begotten Son but, as we have seen, he is not the only representative of it. We are all in some sense representatives of it insofar as we reflect the pure good that is God. We are all, collectively, the Son (as will be explained in more detail later).

Jesus himself says that he does not judge:

> I did not come to judge the world but to save the world.
> (John 12:47)

Judgment, then, if it belongs neither to the Father nor to His Son, must be *our own* responsibility. The last judgment is our own eventual decision for *only* the good, only completion and perfection. It will be entirely reasonable every step of the way as we learn to discern between pure good and its variations of admixture with evil. Again, anything other than pure good is not and cannot be the true good.

Paul speaks of our own capability for judgment as well, saying:

> Do you not know that the saints will judge the world?
> (1 Cor. 6:2)

But we need to heed Jesus' caution that what we seek to judge in others is what we unconsciously want to remove from ourselves. To evaluate others is therefore not the real focus; all such judgment is truly self-judgment.

Our conscience, we find as we slowly uncover it, is finely calibrated. It is in its natural state *extremely* sensitive to the absence of good, such as for example any lack of love, and it is through this kind of precise discernment that we eventually arrive at the pure good. The final judgment will be the final decision regarding the lack of love within ourselves, so that only the pure light of good might arise from us.

Recall that Jesus had taught that we would eventually find and be able to follow the highest standard: that of God Himself. There is in reality no other standard. All good exists because of Him and *only* pure good exists because of Him. *Everything else* is our own responsibility, so to speak. This is why we are the ones who must judge, and we judge *only* ourselves.

The Johannine Jesus is explicit in his teaching that we should not judge others, saying: "Judge not, and you will not be judged" (Luke 6:37). He is saying that we should seek not to judge others, so that we might know our own perfect innocence before God. He uses the same formula for judgment as he had for forgiveness, which was basically that if we refrained from judgment of others, and instead forgave them readily and at the blink of an eye, then we would realize how truly merciful and purely good the Father is. It is as we learn to see others as purely good that *we* realize pure goodness.

Recall that Jesus said that those who followed him into the eternal life of sonship would not only *not* be judged, they would *not* know death either:

> Truly, truly, I say to you, he who hears my word and believes him who sent me, has eternal life; he does not come into judgment, but has passed from death to life. Truly, truly, I say to you, the hour is coming, and now is, when the dead will hear the voice of the Son of God, and those who hear will live.
> (John 5:24-25)

Such neutralization of judgment in turn leads to a general resurrection of the dead, which designation includes all those who are not convinced of their own eternal life, when all those who "hear the voice of the Son of God ... will live." We had assumed that this meant hearing only Jesus, which is why we misunderstood such sayings, but ultimately we will hear how we echo him. We, all of us, are as much the Son as he is; we will know this about ourselves and about everyone else simultaneously. And when we do, we will have passed from judgment to non-judgment, from some degree of absence of good to pure good alone, and from death to life.

Paul makes a case for non-judgment using much the same concept as Jesus had: that when we judge others, we implicitly judge ourselves. The guilt we derive from judging others may not arrive immediately because it is hidden and arrives through circuitous routes:

> Therefore you have no excuse, O man, whoever you are, when you judge another; for in passing judgment upon him you condemn yourself, because you, the judge, are doing the very same things.... Do you suppose, O man, that when you judge those who do such things and yet do them yourself, you will escape the judgment of God?
> (Rom. 2:1, 3)

Thus Paul takes a position quite similar to Jesus': It is through the practice of *not* judging others that we ourselves escape the fear of judgment. Such fear is always our own doing, and has nothing to do with God. It is our responsibility, the product of our own misunderstanding. Such an idea confirms that, for Paul as for Jesus, *our ideas about others affect our own self-concept*. We and our brothers and sisters are connected in such a way that we cannot easily be separated. They are as much love as Christ is love, and Christ as much love as God is love, so that we ourselves have no choice and *want* no choice but to be love alongside them.

No matter how it might seem in this world, where the beings of God seem different, some for instance seeming to hold higher positions than others, and where some seem greater than others and others lesser, our conscience tells us that this is not truly the case. For the conscience does not let up until perfection is reached, and this process is only extended and intensified by our insistence upon exercising judgment in the world. Paul gives some very practical advice in this regard:

> Then let us no more pass judgment on one another, but rather decide never to put a stumbling block or hindrance in the way of a brother.
> (Rom. 14:13)

He speaks similarly elsewhere:

> Therefore do not pronounce judgment before the time, before the Lord comes, who will bring to light the things now hidden in darkness and will disclose the purposes of the heart. Then every man will receive his commendation from God.
> (1 Cor. 4:5)

Note that our own last judgment is associated here with realizing "the purposes of the heart" which had formerly been "hidden in darkness." This purpose of the heart would be our God-given impetus for pure good, and only good.

Once we realize this in ourselves and recognize only this *as* ourselves, then we will receive our "commendation from God," who knows *everything* but who knows *only* good. (Again, evil is only absence or distortion of good, and so it does not have existence in itself, and so it is not included in the complete and total knowledge of God.)

In the end, says Paul, "if we judged ourselves truly, we should not be judged" (1 Cor. 11:31). We have made mistakes, but only when we were not in our right mind. Once we begin the process of judging ourselves truly, we shall find this out about ourselves and at the same time we shall extend it to others as well. If we consider all the positives of *just one person*, then we would be forever in contemplation of this same goodness throughout the world, and in the process have no reason nor inclination to judge ourselves. If we are in a state of constant *commendation*, or appreciation, there will be neither room nor space for any kind of *condemnation*.

The Letter of James expresses this well in terms that apply both negatively and positively:

> For judgment is without mercy to one who has shown no mercy; yet mercy triumphs over judgment.
> (James 2:13)

This is how natural law works: the true measure of justice is already within us, part of us. It knows before we do if our actions and intentions are for good or ill, and rewards or convicts us accordingly, even *before* we do anything. Yet all the judgment we fear is that which we have heaped upon our own heads by judging or even inadvertently harming others in the past. Eventually we get to the point where we realize that to judge another *at all* is to judge them over-harshly. To criticize them is to experience hell. The calibration at that point has become extremely fine, the correspondence and association between self and other greater and greater until they seem most definitely and completely *one*. Loving another, this other becomes part of us, and it is thus that we begin *really* to know and to love ourselves.

This is why the perfection of our own capacity and ability to love is all we ever need to think about. It affects us as well as them, and when the process is complete we will end up exactly like God, as it was in the beginning:

> In this is love perfected with us, that we may have confidence for the day of judgment, because as he is so are we in this world.
> (1 John 4:17)

We have seen that Jesus taught his followers not to judge—so that they themselves would not live in fear of judgment. For consistency's sake, then, we might easily view the separation of the sheep from the goats (Matt. 24:32) or the wheat from the chaff (Matt. 3:12) or the weeds (Matt. 13:29-30) as a distinction, an evaluation, made *within ourselves*, primarily a distinguishing of the eternal and purely good part from the temporary part intermixed with void. This would be our own final judgment about the state of *ourselves*. According to this view, eventually only the good and complete part will continue, and for this the evil which is its absence must be forgotten for good. The good or eternal part of ourselves will and must go on; the temporary or evil *cannot* ultimately. That which *does* go on is our original, indomitable, eternal and loving self, the same that we can begin to know even now.

This suggests that all will eventually, inevitably be realized to be good, purely good without hint or trace of evil, which makes perfect sense if one considers where we as beings of God come from. The tradition we are studying in the Bible sees judgment and the end of the world primarily in psychological terms. This is why these concepts have been so little understood. Contrary to popular belief (in early Christianity as it is today), this tradition insists that God Himself does not judge, but rather such a function belongs to someone else, variously described as the "Son" of either man or God and also as ourselves. Just as imagery of the end of the world was used to see an entirely new world from within, these images of judgment are used to describe a phenomenological and entirely subjective experience of *the needlessness of judgment*.

The fact that judgment will one day be final, and therefore not continue into our new reality, is a good thing, and nothing to fear. The good part of each of us will and must continue, because eternal, while even the smallest traces of evil will be utterly forgotten—purified or, if this is impossible, consumed in fire. We are the ones who will judge this, by way of the natural conscience and discernment given to us, each for ourselves and in the end entirely for ourselves. We cannot properly judge others without knowing their true intentions, and we cannot know their true intentions without being inside their mind. *Only* we can judge, and the only being we can truly judge is *ourselves*. It *must*, therefore, be an entirely internal event.

## The Image of Fire

Much of the imagery employed in both Jewish and later Christian apocalyptic writing (such as the much-disputed "millennium" or "thousand years" of peace and true justice, which in numerological tradition signifies an infinite period) seems to have derived ultimately from Zoroastrian (ancient Persian) sources. The Zoroastrian influence was especially prominent in the intertestamental period because we see it suddenly pop up all over in the New Testament, whereas it is largely absent from the Old except, tellingly, in its latest book, Daniel.

In Zoroastrianism, basically, the world is clearly divided into two evenly-split halves each presided over by its own god, forces of pure good opposed by almost equally-matched forces of pure evil. This is indeed how it *seems* from an earthly point of view, prior to the final consummation. Zoroastrian apocalyptic mythology culminates in this final judgment and fiery purification which described the mythological final battle whereby the good, after long stretches of impasse or stalemate, ultimately prevails and the conflict is ended.

Apocalyptic is more fruitfully viewed as a literary and mythological (or highly symbolic) genre than as a real exposition of what is to come. We can see this by looking at the other examples of Jewish and Christian apocalyptic writing that also come down to us from the intertestamental period, besides the few tidbits that made it into the Bible. (There are many such apocalyptic books that, even though Christianized, did not make the canonical cut.) What they have in common is the use of certain stock images to impress upon our mind the sense of an entirely different, transcendent yet dreamlike reality. There are clues in the Book of Revelation that its outlandish imagery is meant to invoke a psychological transformation upon its hearers, such as trance or an experience of another reality (up to and including Heaven). Rather than reading like news of future events, we might more beneficially see them as news of culminating *inner* events, the end of a long process of internal conflict, symbolized by a cosmic battle, culminating in *internal* transformation. However we see these apocalyptic books and passages, we must admit that the world is described in them as a dream-scape rather than in ordinary, mundane terms.

By the time Jesus comes along, we can see that it had already become popular in and around Israel to think in such dream-like apocalyptic terms. And so apocalyptic imagery pops us occasionally in short sayings and parables, yet for the most part in the Synoptics it is confined to Chapters 24-25 of Matthew (which gives it the appearance of a tacked-on tract of sorts, originally not Christianized) and the Book of Revelation, which after much debate was finally included into the canon by the fourth century. We have seen instances whereby both Paul and John take this surrounding stock imagery and spiritualize or *psychologize* it, rendering it useful for describing purely internal experience.

Apocalyptic writing was a common literary genre of the time period, a way of expressing symbolically the dream-like states behind ordinary reality. And so we should see it as such, and not as a newspaper report of things to come. It was all about the trance: both the trance of the author and that trance evoked in reader and hearer.

As such, we can see that among the apocalyptic writings, the imagery is relatively standard, as if it were *expected* that such tracts or books be written in imagery reflecting a final monumental battle resulting in a fiery consummation. The similarities are often striking, though beyond the scope of this book. In Revelation as in other apocalyptic writings, the real action is one of spiritual forces even more so than earthly forces, representing the cosmology of good versus evil spirits that, in modern terms, is best referenced to an inner conflict. All of earthly life is representative of this underlying conflict, participating in it even without realizing (i.e., unconsciously). And so, even as it seems to play out outside us, it is in reality an internal conflict.

In a dualistic cosmology (such as the Zoroastrian) wherein good and evil forces are fairly evenly matched, the concepts of good and evil take on increased significance. And indeed they often *seem* counterbalanced in the world. But that is only because the weeds (which will be consumed by a fire or utterly forgotten) are seen to grow alongside the wheat for a while (Matt. 13:30). It is by seeing each purely for what it is—and in the case of evil, again, always as the absence of good, defined by what it is *not*—*in ourselves* that *we ourselves* are finally able to judge which is which.

And so it is actually a very good thing—for each of us and for all of us—that:

> Every plant which my heavenly Father has not planted will be rooted up.
> (Matt. 15:13)

It is that part that was not put there by God (nor by ourselves in our right mind) that must be rooted out. This means that everything that is left over will be completely and perfectly good, as it was in the beginning, and as it was forever intended to be. This is true of both ourselves and of everyone. Only the core of true good in each of us, however hidden it may seem, will continue on into eternity because only it *can* continue into eternity. Insofar as we identify with this part, therefore, we will be identifying with our eternal self.

The image of fire represents both the purification of our mind and the ultimate end of conflict. *Conflict itself* will be consumed by fire, or utterly forgotten, while the purest good that is within each of God's creations will return to predominance. *Duality itself* will be utterly forgotten.

Eventually our own mind will be purified, just as metal's impurities are, by fire, but natural law suggests that the fire is our own, though it begins as an almost-insignificant spark until it catches hold in us. At that point it grows inevitably until it consumes everything *but* the good and eternal, showing everything thereby to be either illusory, and coming up short, or real. Before we go on to describe this eschatological process, let us examine how the image of fire is used throughout scripture.

The image of fire plays a part in many of the early sightings of God. The angel of the Lord had appeared to Moses "in a flame of fire out of the midst of a bush," but this fire was not destructive, for "the bush was burning, yet it was not consumed" (Exodus 3:2). Obviously this fire of God was no ordinary fire. Later, as Moses was leading the Israelites through the wilderness, "the Lord went before them … by night in a pillar of fire to give them light" (Exodus 13:21). Here the *light-giving* function of fire is emphasized. We see later on that the prophet Elijah rode "a chariot of fire and horses of fire" when he "went up by a whirlwind into heaven" (2 Kings 2:11). Again, this is not a physical fire but an internal one; Moses and Elijah and those around them were blessed to see a light not of this world. This fire of God is not a fire of wrath; the fire that Moses and Elijah experienced was a manifestation of His glory.

The prophet Jeremiah declares that there is an internal fire burning in the heart:

> If I say, 'I will not mention him,
> or speak any more in his name,'
> there is in my heart as it were a burning fire
> shut up in my bones,
> and I am weary with holding it in,
> and I cannot.
> (Jeremiah 20:9)

In other words, it does no good to try to suppress this inner fire. It remains in our heart, and we can perceive it or not. This fire of the prophet comes from his calling; it is the fire of ardor, passion, and devotion for God, yet the prophet is not in control of it, for it comes from the deepest place within himself. Only as the prophet becomes "another man," or a new being, does he or she come into full control.

> Then the spirit of the LORD will come mightily upon you, and you shall prophesy with them *and be turned into another man.*
> (1 Samuel 10:6, my italics)

Jesus said: "I came to cast fire on the earth; and would that it were already kindled!" (Luke 12:49). This, too, is no destructive fire, but rather, it is ardor and passion for God. He declares a baptism of fire, saying "I have a baptism to be baptized with; and how I am constrained until it is accomplished!" (12:50). He seeks to spread this ardor and devotion until it covers the earth. This inner fire spread upon the earth would make us one, because, experienced by each, it is a fire that can be (and in reality already is) shared by all.

Jesus had told his disciples that "John baptized with water, but before many days you shall be baptized with the Holy Spirit" (Acts 1:5). Here, baptism with the Holy Spirit is set in opposition to baptism with water, suggesting that it will be with a kind of fire. And, indeed, on the day of Pentecost, the Holy Spirit came to the earliest Christians as "tongues as of fire, distributed and resting on each one of them. And they were all filled with the Holy Spirit..." (Acts 2:3-4). The Holy Spirit came to these earliest disciples like fire, to fill them with an ardent passion for infinity and zeal for truth, as well as to burn through their illusory self.

Jesus' apparent early mentor John the Baptist had said:

> I baptize you with water; ... he will baptize you with the Holy Spirit and with fire. His winnowing fork is in his hand, to clear his threshing floor, and to gather the wheat into his granary, but the chaff he will burn with unquenchable fire.
> (Luke 3:16-17)

The unquenchable fire is our ardor for God and for one another, as well as our laser-like focus on purest good or only good. The chaff that is burned in unquenchable fire is all that surrounds this but is *not* this. The chaff through which the unquenchable fire burns is the illusory self and its entire repertoire of illusions. Again, this is true of all of us, not only of some of us. The division is not between groups of people but rather, between the good *in us* and the extraneous illusion.

There is one foundation that is real, one cornerstone that will be left standing when the truth comes. Paul expresses it this way:

> For no other foundation can any one lay than that which is laid, which is Jesus Christ. Now if any one builds on the foundation with gold, silver, precious stones, wood, hay, straw—each man's work will become manifest; for the Day will disclose it, because it will be revealed with fire, and the fire will test what sort of work each one has done.
> (1 Corinthians 3:11-13)

All of our works—everything we do or think—will be tested in fire, but only that which contributes to and participates in the eternal reality will come out unfazed and unconsumed. The fire is meant to reveal the true essence of a thing, to disclose or bring to light its truth, unmixed and pure, and this is why the fire burns in us: to reveal our own pure being, *our* truth.

David says, "My heart became hot within me. As I mused the fire burned" (Psalms 39:3). It burns constantly, even unconsciously, until it burns through even time and space, leaving us only a moment out of time that will turn out to be eternal. Within the mind and heart this unquenchable fire already burns, a fire that cannot be quelled by anything in the world, anything that is not eternal.

Just as *Sheol* (or what later came to be translated "hell") is "never satisfied, and never satisfied are the eyes of man" (Proverbs 27:20), so, too, is the fire within us never satisfied. Proverbs lists and combines them:

> Sheol, the barren womb,
> the earth ever thirsty for water,
> and the fire which never says, 'Enough.'
> (Proverbs 30:16)

The only thing that can calm and finally quench the fire of the heart is the heart's true desire. We may pass through many ultimately unsatisfying desires before we realize that our search for satisfaction in the world, at least in the world's terms, is in vain. However, the love of God always stands at the end, however distant it may appear getting there.

This fire within us is our will to truth, because it is not satisfied by anything but truth—our own, God's, and others'. We can delude ourselves that we are satisfied with aspects of illusion, but we cannot truly be satisfied with anything less than complete truth. Jesus said that all that was hidden would be brought to light, that it is inevitable that all that is repressed or hidden from awareness will eventually come to light. This is what it means that the ardor of our desire for truth will eventually burn through all illusion to the true essence of ourselves and of all things, stopping only at the core of truth within all beings.

One by one our defenses we had built up *against* the truth are seen through, released, relinquished as unnecessary, to be burned up in the fire of forgetfulness. But only the works of darkness or delusion are burned. As Paul says: "he himself will be saved" (1 Corinthians 3:15). We ourselves, the truth in us and in every being, will prevail.

The world of illusion we had fortified around ourselves behind layers of defenses had not been true; it had been literally *nothing* in the face of the real. Yet God both surrounds us and fills us with *Himself*. "For I will be to her a wall of fire round about, says the Lord, and I will be the glory within her" (Zechariah 2:5). And so what is consumed is not us, never us, but only that which was most unlike the true us.

All that is not true to God is illusion, and will be returned to the nothingness from which it came. Whatever was based on a lie to begin with, whatever began in error, will not emerge from the fire as something true and real. The fire of ultimate truth will have burned away the surrounding illusion and left *only* eternal truth in its place.

The fire, then, is purgative and not punishing. Its worst aspect is also its best: the forgetting of illusion and of the mistaken thinking upon which illusion is based, leaving only truth in its wake. Our mistakes, which include our mistaken thoughts, must ultimately be erased or gradually deconstructed by the mind. Either of these outcomes is directed and facilitated by the Spirit. Our eternal minds and spirits are striving, ultimately, to know themselves, our truth.

# 9

# On the Threshold

**The Devil and Satan**

In this chapter, we will explore ideas that have been little understood in Christian doctrine: the devil, hell, Heaven, and predestination. These are misunderstood topics, in large part, because they are not fully worked out in the pages of the Bible, but are rather presented only in sketch form. Our vivid imaginations fleshed out for us the rest of the picture.

In the Hebrew Bible the term *Satan* is rarely used, but where it is used, it appears with the definite article ("*the* Satan," meaning "the Adversary"). "*The* Satan" refers, most often among its brief appearances, to a kind of prosecuting attorney in the divine court, as for instance standing up *against* Israel to David (1 Chr. 21:1) and striving to make a case against Job (1-2), as well as being accusatory also in Zechariah 3:1-2. That sums up the *only* references to "the Satan" in the Old Testament. The term describes a role or description and not a proper name. Moreover, *the* Satan is a bit figure, subordinate to God but within His council of advisors, not yet a full-fledged rival.

Therefore we have another case here, as with "the end of the world," of something developing between the time the two parts of the Bible were written, when Hellenistic and other surrounding mythological influence was strong. Tracing the development of the devil (sometimes named Satan, sometimes known by other names such as Mastema and Belial) in the extra-canonical apocalyptic books such as those of Enoch and Jubilees, one detects a strong Zoroastrian (Persian) dualistic influence that propels the chief demon (by whatever name) into a strong rival of God.

One of the non-apocalyptic intertestamental mentions of the devil emphasizes its function as bringer of death into the world by changing humankind's conception of itself:

> for God created man for incorruption,
> and made him in the image of his own eternity,
> but through the devil's envy death entered the world,
> and those who belong to his party experience it.
> (Wisdom 2:21-24)

The devil is seen here as inspiring "envy" and also the "experience" of "death" in human beings. We shall see that later Jesus speaks of death as the ruler of the world, equating the devil with death. Whether we think of it as devil or death, it remains only for a time because its days are numbered, which is basically what the apocalyptic literature is saying. This intertestamental saying also hints at Jesus' saying that there were some among those standing with him who would neither "see" nor "taste" or experience death (Luke 9:27). They will have already moved on in their minds, having identified with the eternal being within themselves, past any state where death could possibly reach them.

By the time of the New Testament, also, Satan had acquired a function as tempter of humankind with the things of the world, as evidenced by his role in Jesus' temptation in the wilderness (Mark 1:13). In Matthew's fleshing out of this temptation (4:1-11), we have Jesus equating "Satan" (4:10) with "the devil" (4:1), one of the few times the two terms meet and match up in the Bible.

In Matthew's account of the temptation of Jesus, we find that it is "the devil" who is in charge of "all the kingdoms of the world and the glory of them" (Matt. 4:8). They are his to give away (4:9). Thus Satan and the devil are equated here as spirits of worldliness, playing on humankind's distorted value system and specifically the acquisitive nature that rises from that. It is the part of ourselves that always seeks "to get," for itself alone, and so it doesn't care who it has to step on to get what it thinks it wants. Any bargain with it, however, is a bargain with death.

Still Jesus finds the Satan's tragic flaw:

> And if Satan has risen up against himself and is divided, he cannot stand, but is coming to an end.
> (Mark 3:26)

The Satan is in fact seen by Jesus as divided against itself, being a symbol or representation of all conflict. Psychologically speaking, this Satan would be the seed of conflict within our mind, even the point in our thinking where we turn against ourselves, blame ourselves, accuse ourselves, following its original accusatory role. This is fundamentally an irrational act for a being of God. Yet if this self-depreciation is hidden or repressed from awareness as this tendency usually is, then it automatically is projected as conflict with others and accusation of them.

Jesus, I believe, was merely accepting what had become popular mythology of the time period, using it symbolically as he used just about everything else. Thus Satan appears in one of the parables:

> And these are the ones along the path, where the word is sown; when they hear, Satan immediately comes and takes away the word which is sown in them.
> (Mark 4:15)

Here the Satan symbolizes the fleeting spirit of the world, wherein everything is temporary, too fast-paced and too disposable to last. It also appears in Jesus' teaching as taking "the side of men" rather than that of God (Mark 8:33). Exclusive to Luke, we have a Jesus saying whereby he says: "I saw Satan fall like lightning from heaven" (Luke 10:18), thereby prophesying the Adversary's demise, the final overcoming of any kind of accusation of the human being.

Satan is also spoken of as having "bound" a woman with illness (Luke 13:16) and as a "hindrance" (Matt. 16:23), both of these instances pointing up its limiting effect on human beings, its power to make them believe they are less worthy and less valuable, therefore more vulnerable, than they truly are.

We see from Jesus' teaching in John's Gospel that human beings can take on the misplaced character of the devil (13:2) and can in fact be identified with *being* "a devil" (6:70). "The devil" in such passages represents a state of mind that human beings have and *ordinarily* share in the world. Yet what is *ordinary* is not always *natural* to us, because the socialization process indoctrinates us to believe certain things are ordinary and certain things are not.

Perhaps surprisingly, Jesus refers to a ruler of the world *other than* God:

> I will no longer talk much with you,
> for the ruler of the world is coming.
> He has no power over me;
> but I do as the Father has commanded me,
> so that the world may know that I love the Father.
> (John 14:30-31)

Here Jesus seems to be personifying and identifying death as the devil *and* as the ruler of the world. Putting it all together, the devil is the ruler of the ordinary world wherein death stands at the end, while God is ruler of eternity and the eternal state of mind (which, as we shall see, is Heaven).

John 8:44 speaks of the devil as being "a murderer from the beginning," emphasizing its association with death which we have already seen, but also as having "nothing to do with the truth" and therefore being "a liar and the father of lies," which gives it its role as spinner of the grand illusion and deceiver of human beings. Because it is spoken of as ruler of the world, we get the sense that the entire world as we know it is subject to this great deception, even to the point of thinking of *oneself* as part of the illusion.

In the Pauline Letter to the Ephesians, we see this deceptive aspect brought out by the attribution to the devil of "wiles" (6:11). There are also a couple of mentions in the Pastoral Letters 1 and 2 Timothy such as 1 Tim. 3:6-7 wherein "the devil" is associated with ensnaring humans with "condemnation" and "reproach," stressing its original adversarial character.

The Letter of James equates the adjectives "earthly" and "unspiritual" with "devilish" (3:13), and offers the helpful suggestion: "Resist the devil and he will flee from you" (4:7). 1 Peter 5:8 speaks of it as an "adversary" to human beings, seeking to consume them. 1 John 3:10 mentions that it is specifically *love* that makes us "children of God" rather than "children of the devil."

The Book of Revelation characteristically offers striking imagery which in this case echoes the prophecy in Luke 10:18:

> And the great dragon was thrown down, that ancient serpent, who is called the Devil and Satan, the deceiver of the whole world—he was thrown down to the earth, and his angels were thrown down with him.
>
> (Rev. 12:9)

The devil's numbered days are alluded to in 12:12 ("he knows that his time is short!") and then 20:2 speaks of "the Devil and Satan" as being finally bound (perhaps ironic in light of the devil's binding, limiting function we have just seen). It is in the apocalyptic literature that the devil or Satan is most vividly portrayed. In the end, however, it and the world it rules and death itself are all burned up in a lake of fire (Rev. 20:10, 14), which represents our ultimate forgetting of them and all their (once deceptively and only seeming real) effects. The devil's greatest illusion, in other words, was to convince us of its own existence.

Jesus assures his students that the ruler of this world, whether the devil or death, will never touch them (as in Luke 9:27). 4 Ezra 6:26 stated similarly: "And they shall see the men who were taken up, who from their birth have not tasted death; and the heart of the earth's inhabitants shall be changed and converted to a different spirit." Once again, it is this psychological and internal change in "the heart of the earth's inhabitants" that is most significant.

The final battle which never occurs in the Book of Revelation is in the end as illusory as the dream-time world in which it is said to occur. The lake of fire represents the final forgetting of the supposed resistance to good. The beast that is consumed in the lake of fire is a composite of all the world systems, and its presence in the story harkens back to older Middle Eastern mythology wherein we all live in the belly of the beast Leviathan without really knowing (and so, therefore, are surrounded by illusion).

## Hell as a State of Mind

We have misinterpreted both hell and Heaven by conceiving of them as places rather than states of mind and being. By the time of the New Testament, people in that region of the Middle East thought of themselves as living within a threefold cosmos wherein earth was situated in the middle with Heaven above and hell below, with rampant movement between the three spheres. Earth and all her inhabitants could be buffeted by the spirits from either Heaven or hell, above or below, seemingly at will. The distinctions between the realms or states of reality were not as great as they now, in our modern world, seem. Each was only a thought away.

Therefore there are some indications in the Bible that Heaven and hell are meant to be experienced as internal states rather than external. That is, they can be experienced at any time, and in fact are often experienced in one aspect or another even as we *approach* their divergent and opposite states of mind and being.

Rather than above or below, we might think of these distinct realms as being poles on a continuum of experience, upon which we human beings find ourselves somewhere in the midrange. It is from Heaven that we originally come and to which we ultimately shall return, but we tend to bounce back and forth on the scale until we make a final choice or "judgment" on the matter.

What we think of as hell is actually a composite of various apocalyptic images. There *is* no conception of hell as we think of it in the Old Testament. The word with which older English translations such as the King James Version (KJV) translated "hell" was actually in Hebrew "*Sheol*," which meant simply "the grave." The confusion may stem back even earlier, to classical Jewish scholars' Greek translation (the Septuagint) in the centuries after Alexander the Great, wherein "*Sheol*" was translated as "Hades," giving it connotations of classical mythology and other Greek conceptions of hell such as Tartarus. But *Sheol* referred simply to being buried underground, after which time consciousness was assumed to be gone, and if there were inclinations of its seeping into caves of the underworld, these are only very slight in the Hebrew version.

Not one of us human beings *know* what happens to us individually after death. The speculations range from thinking nothing happens—all cognition and therefore all higher life stops—to thinking that consciousness is morphed into a much more spacious, even infinite superconsciousness of Being. That is, it is liberated to become automatically like God in terms of its omniscience. All higher life, in this latter conception, participates and shares in the life of God.

By the time the New Testament comes along, those centuries of reading "Hades" and thinking of elements of "Tartarus," coupled with Zoroastrian and Egyptian images of fire, had made *Sheol* seem like a place unto itself where dead souls go but do not necessarily stay. So fluid are the boundaries between the realms that there are rivers leading to and from the underworld and winds as of chariots sweeping us into the higher spheres and back down again.

As we have seen in regard to the devil, there is no systematic understanding of the term or concept "hell" in the Bible, as it was still under construction at the time of the New. It was itself in a transitional stage even as great theologians such as Origen and Augustine attempted to nail it down centuries later. It remained in a transitional stage as the great poets Dante and Milton creatively and somewhat humorously interpreted it. Due to their vivid imaginations, we think of the punitive aspects of fire, for instance, over its otherwise almost universally-conceived purifying character.

The ancient Hebrew conceptions are actually much more nuanced and subtle than we tend to think. Therefore, just in the Book of Psalms, we go from death as deprivation of consciousness to Sheol as a state of existential anguish as if just the very thought of death were enough to give Sheol its tortuous aspects. For the lack of consciousness interpretation, consider the following verse:

> For in death there is no remembrance of thee;
> in Sheol who can give thee praise?
> (Ps. 6:5)

Here we see that even God was thought to be forgotten in this view of Sheol as death. There is yet hope for escaping this state of extreme deprivation, this anticipated nothingness:

> For thou dost not give me up to Sheol,
> or let thy godly one see the Pit.
> (Ps. 16:10)

This "Pit" is another name for Sheol that suggests death or the grave. Consciousness was apparently thought to be inextricably tied to the body, so that when the body dies, so does consciousness, including all notion of one's *self*. But again, just the thought or anticipation of such nothingness is enough to drive one into existential crisis:

> the cords of Sheol entangled me,
> the snares of death confronted me.
> (Ps. 18:5)

Here is another instance of the equation of Sheol with torment, but it is the torment leading up to death that is spoken of:

> For my soul is full of troubles,
> and my life draws near to Sheol.
> (Ps. 88:3)

The existential crisis continues with the following passages, spoken from the heart and from experienced anguish:

> What man can live and never see death?
> Who can deliver his soul from the power of Sheol?
> (Ps. 89:48)

And here the anguish is identified directly:

> The snares of death encompassed me;
> the pangs of Sheol laid hold on me;
> I suffered distress and anguish.
> (Ps. 116:3)

The equation of Sheol with both death and the suffering that leads to death is evident in these passages. But the hope for divine rescue from such a cold, impersonal fate is spoken of with certainty here:

> Like sheep they are appointed for Sheol;
> Death shall be their shepherd;
> straight to the grave they descend,
> and their form shall waste away;
> Sheol shall be their home.

> But God will ransom my soul from the power of Sheol,
> for he will receive me. [Selah]
> 
> (Ps. 49:14-15)

The rescue is specifically from death and thought of death. It is a change of mind from one way of looking at the world (as inevitably tending towards death) to another (as inevitably tending towards life). Therefore this rescue, this salvation from death, can be immediate, and therefore we need not wait for death to have deathlessness demonstrated to us. It can be overcome long before we reach it. Ultimately, it will be specifically because of God's steadfast love, which informs and universalizes His justice, that rescue from the existential pit of Sheol is made possible:

> For great is thy steadfast love toward me;
> thou hast delivered my soul from the depths of Sheol.
> 
> (Ps. 86:13)

In the Book of Proverbs, a direct comparison is made between Sheol and an internal state:

> Sheol and Abaddon lie open before the LORD,
> how much more the hearts of men!
> 
> (Prov. 15:11)

Here the depths of Sheol have been equated with our own hearts, just as in the following passage it is identified with our obsessive surface desires, which tend to draw our minds away from Heaven:

> Sheol and Abaddon are never satisfied,
> and never satisfied are the eyes of man.
> (Prov. 27:20)

Such a comparison of Sheol to inner states might be a coincidence if written once, but seems more deliberate when mentioned twice. Jonah also equates (through the literary principle of parallelism) an inner distress with Sheol:

> I called to the LORD, out of my distress,
> and he answered me;
> out of the belly of Sheol I cried,
> and thou didst hear my voice.
> (Jonah 2:2)

Sheol, then, is in the Hebrew scriptures sometimes suggested to be an internal state of mind, specifically of distress. This leads to seeing and experiencing Heaven as an inner state as well, as we shall see in the next section. Prior to our concretized conceptions, these very different realms that comprised the tripartite cosmos were seen to lie side by side in the intertestamental ("Apocryphal") literature:

> Then the pit of torment shall appear, and opposite it shall be the place of rest; and the furnace of hell shall be disclosed, and opposite it the paradise of delight.
> (4 Ezra 7:36)

Here we see the association made clear between hell and the seemingly bottomless "pit of torment." The tormented state (as opposed to the state of "rest" and peace that is Heaven) is often experienced as being endless, when in reality it is not, such as when in the depths of depression one can see no light at the end of the tunnel. Hell is spoken of here as "the pit of torment," and that word "pit" harkens back to the Old Testament idea of a state wherein one feels trapped, characterized by death, as in Job 33:22.

There is a sense in 4 Ezra that hell is the human capacity "to suffer and not understand why" (4:12), which would mean that hell carries a certain ignorance or unconsciousness about it. Hell, in other words, is never *experienced* as "hell," but is instead always distorted, made to seem seemly, its full extent hidden from our awareness, covered over by seemingly natural concerns. This suggests that, difficult though it may be, it can be beneficial to discern the experience of hell from amid daily life, because then we will strive to avoid it by reaching (also unconsciously, but also consciously) for its polar opposite: the calm mind of Heaven.

Ezra says he wants to learn of "earthly things" (rather than otherworldly) when he asks "why we pass from the world like locusts, and our life is like a mist, and we are not worthy to obtain mercy" (4:24). Death is one of those "earthly things" we must work through for ourselves, or think through to its logical conclusion, whereby death itself seems "like a mist," something we socialized ourselves into believing without real subjectively-based proof. For death would be nothing without the experience (or taste) of death, and what if it is not experienced as death at all? Then all our time spent worrying about it would have been for naught.

4 Ezra takes the line of thought that there is a part of each of us that has been corrupted from the beginning of the world, and therefore needs purified:

> For a grain of evil seed was sown in Adam's heart from the beginning, and how much ungodliness it

> has produced until now, and will produce until the time of threshing comes!
> Consider now for yourself how much fruit of ungodliness a grain of evil seed has produced.
> (4 Ezra 4:30-31)

All evil comes from inside the human heart, which would mean that hell is inside the human breast. This idea is of course echoed and clarified in the New Testament teaching, wherein Jesus states that all evil comes from inside us.

Knowing this, that evil comes from inside the mind, that hell dwells there, we are given responsibility for it and some semblance of control over it.

> For out of the abundance of the heart the mouth speaks. The good man out of his good treasure brings forth good, and the evil man out of his evil treasure brings forth evil.
> (Matt. 12:34-35)

The same idea is psychologized or internalized in this pastoral letter:

> To the pure all things are pure, but to the corrupt and unbelieving nothing is pure; their very minds and consciences are corrupted.
> (Titus 1:15)

Here the Pauline tradition makes clear the idea that it is one's internal state of being (either "pure" or "corrupted") that determines how one sees the world. "To the pure all things are pure" tells us that the purity is *within ourselves* first, and only then projected onto the world. (The same would be true of corruption.) Here again perception, which we normally view as outside ourselves, is a function of our state of mind.

We have mentioned the idea that conflict within the mind is what causes the divisions we see within the world, and we have associated this with Satan's tragic flaw:

> And if Satan has risen up against himself and is divided, he cannot stand, but is coming to an end.
> (Mark 3:26)

It is this division that is the mark or true characteristic of hell. It feeds on conflict, having come originally from conflict in our mind. But, this being the case, it will eventually work its own demise. The seeds of its destruction are sown within it and unconsciously perpetuated by it, which is why it cannot last.

The New Testament tells of Jesus' descent into hell to free the captives (Eph. 4:8-10). Jesus thereby gives hope to those who believe they are entrapped, even by the seeming pit of hellish anguish. Jesus' own teaching was that anger and insult to a brother or sister, or any kind of judgment of them, set the condition of our own state of hell:

> But I say to you that every one who is angry with his brother shall be liable to judgment; whoever insults his brother shall be liable to the council, and whoever says, `You fool!' shall be liable to the hell of fire.
> (Matt. 5:22)

The condition of hell is set by how we view others, and this suggests that the condition of Heaven is set by viewing them quite differently. How we view others can cause us either great anguish or great peace.

We have seen in the First Letter of John how the love of God does not include even the merest *hint* of punishment. Justice itself would never involve punishment, only discipline (which has a teaching function), because true justice cannot involve partiality of any kind. It must be equally applied to be true. And if some get punished while others run free (who, for instance, have done the same crime), then there is justice for neither. Hell, therefore, *cannot* be a state of punishment, but must instead be a transitional stage from one state of mind (the earthly) to another (the Heavenly). The existential state, and when we are conscious of it, crisis, often stands between us and Heaven.

There is ample room therefore for us to think of hell in a psychological sense, as a tormented, anguished and loveless state of mind. Many people walk around in a state of existential frustration unconsciously, as if they lived in the belly of the beast, the monster Tiamut, in the very early Middle Eastern mythology without knowing it. To walk around in hell unconsciously is also not to know that God did not will this for them. Ultimately these well-intended unconscious or sleepwalking ones would come to doubt God's existence because they cannot believe that He would put them through this, not realizing that we do it to ourselves.

## The State of Heaven

If hell represents the state of mind that is alienated and estranged from others, broken within itself and conflicted with the reality around it, then Heaven is the state of congruence wherein internal consistency leads to a vision of all things working together for the good of the whole. It is the more holistic vision, whereas hell presents us with the chaotic vision wherein beings necessarily compete because they operate only out of self-interest. Hell is divided against itself, but Heaven is a state wherein self-interest is fully integrated with the interests of others.

In the tripartite universe imagined by most in the intertestamental period, that period after the Old Testament was completed but before the New was begun, Heaven existed above the realm associated with earthly life, while hell took a place below it. Though often currently conceived as places to go after one dies, Heaven and hell were at that time described as influences upon the human being, impinging from above or below. We might think of them respectively as superconscious and lower unconscious impingements affecting our current state of mind. The human being was therefore buffeted by cosmic influences from above or below at all times.

Earth, situated in the middle between these two states in the tripartite vision of the cosmos popular at the time, has permeable boundaries so that either Heaven or hell might influence the minds of its inhabitants. 4 Ezra, the apocryphal and intertestamental book we've studied in regard to the nature of hell, describes the changeover from one state to the other:

But think of your own case, and inquire concerning the glory of those who are like yourself, because it is for you that paradise is opened, the tree of life is planted, the age to come is prepared, plenty is provided, a city is built, rest is appointed, goodness is established and wisdom perfected beforehand. The root of evil is sealed up from you, illness is banished from you, and death is hidden; hell has fled and corruption has been forgotten; sorrows have passed away, and in the end the treasure of immortality is made manifest.

(4 Ezra 8:51-54)

Here, Heaven ("paradise") is the state wherein "sorrows have passed away, and in the end the treasure of immortality is made manifest." It is the state that arises after hell "is sealed up from you, illness banished from you, and death is hidden." Both are spoken of as places, but they are described as states with primarily psychological effects. These states of mind correspond with the two states of mind presented as possible in Genesis: the original, blissful state and the state of fallenness, "corruption," "illness," and "death."

That Heaven can be seen as the original, blissful state of mind and being is indicated by its association with "the tree of life." The Book of Revelation describes a similar return to the original beginning, a return to the paradisiacal state of Adam and Eve. This is affirmed by the fact that in the end the Tree of Life makes a return appearance, "with its twelve kinds of fruit, yielding its fruit each month." Here, the tree of life gains a new function in existence: "and the leaves of the tree were for the healing of the nations" (Revelation 22:2).

In this vision and experience of Heaven, no longer is anything "accursed" (Rev. 22:3). The supposed curse on reality brought about by the fall (which had included sorrow, toil, pain, and death) has been lifted. In one way or another, whether conceived theologically or psychologically or both, hell begins to fade and is forgotten in direct proportion to how the mind begins to recall and resemble Heaven. This is what it means that the New Jerusalem, eternal city, descends from the sky. It is the old world reinterpreted and replaced by a new vision, so that it now shines with perpetual light.

Anyone who shares this vision sees the gates of Heaven flung open wide for everyone to enter (when they are ready):

> The Spirit and the Bride say, 'Come.'
> And let him who hears say, 'Come.'
> And let him who is thirsty come,
> let him who desires take the water of life without price.
> (Revelation 22:17)

And people were indeed meant to share this vision. In the end, many would come to share the culminating experience of Heaven with which the vision comes. And all are invited: any who happen to hear, any who desire the change of mind it brings.

Note that throughout the Book of Revelation (as in most apocalyptic literature from this era) the seer, John—not the same John of the Gospel and the Epistles—is always lifted from his temporal context to see his visions. In other words, his visions are all born of experience. And so his writing is peppered with references to this transcendent experience, such as: "I was in the Spirit on the Lord's day" (Rev. 1:10) and "At once I was in the Spirit, and lo, a throne stood in heaven, with one seated on the throne!" (Rev. 4:1-2). This throne vision in chapter 4 is his vision of Heaven, which includes all manner of precious stones, flashes of lightning and peals of thunder, and many thrones surrounding the main throne of God. The seer receives his visions by actually sharing and experiencing God's eternal viewpoint.

This trance aspect of the apocalyptic myth is what is most missed in our attempts to arrive at wholly conceptual and in the end speculative metaphysical explanations. The trance aspect would have pointed to the idea that the visions therein described are meant to be shared *now*, in the present moment, and *not only* in the future. In this very popular form of writing of the time period and culture, we can see as the drama unfolds and from the words that are used that the impact on its hearers would have been what we would describe as packing much psychological depth.

It was specifically the trance itself that was meant to be imparted and shared with the hearers of the vision through the reporting or reading of the vision. Within the trance was the experience and the culmination of the vision of the events described.

In the Book of Revelation, also, the Heaven-sent climax of the New Jerusalem is seen to descend from the sky:

> And in the Spirit he carried me away to a great, high mountain, and showed me the holy city Jerusalem coming down out of heaven from God, having the glory of God, its radiance like a most rare jewel, like a jasper, clear as crystal.
> (Rev. 21:10-11)

Here we see that Heaven above sends an intermediary reality basically by superimposing itself upon our earthly reality. The description here, with the precious jewels and the glory of God, harkens back to both the throne room vision in chapter 4 and to the original creation.

The Book of Revelation sums up Jesus' message interestingly: "Behold, the dwelling of God is with men. He will dwell with them, and they shall be his people" (Revelation 21:3). Now this is interpreted differently depending on whether we prioritize "God" or "men," divine reality or ordinary reality. The fact that the two will eventually meet means to me that human beings will rise to God's reality, rather than God lowering Himself to our current level. And yet in the visions and dreamlike imagery employed by the apocalyptic literature, it does not matter *how* they get together so much as that eventually they *do*.

We have seen that Jesus himself talked about a "new world" coming as the new context for the new self of which he also speaks. He describes this as not so much a future event as it is a new perception of reality. If we can equate the kingdom of God with Heaven in much of Jesus' teaching, which I think we can, then the following saying confirms the idea that Heaven is a state of mind and being that is located specifically within:

> The kingdom of God is not coming with signs to be observed; nor will they say, `Lo, here it is!' or `There!' for behold, *the kingdom of God is within you.*
> (Luke 17:20-21, my italics)

A more direct statement one could not have. The context explains everything: We should not look outside ourselves for Heaven, but rather inside. It is not a place we *go* so much as it is a state of mind we *enter*. Therefore it is something we can experience now, and do not have to wait for. However, once we do enter it, we do see it begin to spread itself out upon the earth. It becomes a reality unto itself, for many, that which began in the mind and heart but that has spread out from there to all the world.

To say that our Father *is* "in Heaven," which Jesus does constantly (e.g., Matt. 5:45), means that He inhabits a state of Mind and Being that is transcendent of our ordinary states of mind and being that help us get by in this world. It is transcendent of effort, standing as it does at the end of all our effort, reminiscent of the day of rest that stands at the beginning of every week. This state in which God abides is flawless and unmixed, perfectly joyous, and ever-present. This is how God can be here among us, and yet be entirely unrecognized by us until we share His state of mind and being.

Jesus speaks of "treasures in Heaven" and of there being no corruption and no loss there (Matt. 6:20). These treasures are eternal and enduring states of mind and being that we will not need to try to achieve or remember. They will seem natural to us, and they arise naturally as we make the changeover from the corrupted state of mind and being to the flawless and perfect. Once realized, they remain with us; these treasures endure, and remind us how we endure.

Heaven is not a state that we constructed for ourselves. It comes from beyond us, and yet we as human beings are its gatekeepers in effect, for we are the ones who decide whether to accept it or not, and when. Therefore much of Jesus' teaching about Heaven is in regard to sparking our desire for it (as in Matt. 6:33: "seek first his kingdom and his righteousness, and all these things shall be yours as well"), evoking our motivation for it, and accepting its principles as applicable here in our earthly lives.

One of these principles is Jesus' urging us to live in the moment, to *be* in the present without concerning ourselves with past or future (as in Matt. 6:34). To say we need not *be-*

*come* anything, but only *be* in the present, is to affirm that we already exist in a state without lack. It is to affirm that the higher and more original part of the mind already subsists in Heaven. The problem, as always, is that we do not yet realize this, and this creates the myriad of ancillary problems such as "anxiety" (Matt. 6:28), which further cloud the state of Heaven.

We have forgotten the true nature of God, and this has caused us to forget His true character. All He has are enduring traits, attributes, His Mind being entirely consistent and His every thought eternal. We have forgotten not only the fact that He cares, but also the extent to which He does care. It is so great that there is nothing we can do to make Him stop caring. However, we are free to forget and to deny it.

In other words, we assume that because we believe *we* have evil intentions at times, that He must as well, but this thought is driven into unconsciousness because it makes no sense, and so we fear Him (irrationally) instead of letting our hearts leap to Him. This is what Jesus means by saying:

> If you then, who are evil, know how to give good gifts to your children, how much more will your Father who is in heaven give good things to those who ask him!
> (Matt. 7:11)

The fact that God is "in Heaven" means that He inhabits a realm of pure good. There is no darkness in Him, no ulterior motive except our true and persistent happiness. If we could want this same state for ourselves, we could by extension want it for others, which is good because it is by wanting it for others that we receive and keep it for ourselves. In the end we will know how we are one with them, and that what is given to one is given to all (for this is God's sense of perfect justice).

It is by "doing the will of the Heavenly Father" that we enter the state of Heaven (as in Matt. 7:21). And this "doing the will" of the Father is the product of becoming like Him, in the sense of reflecting His love, which in this world means being kind, patient, and understanding. It means being helpful rather than harmful.

> Truly, I say to you, unless you turn and become like children, you will never enter the kingdom of heaven. Whoever humbles himself like this child, he is the greatest in the kingdom of heaven.
> (Matt. 18:3-4)

In other words, *all* is great in that state of Heaven. The parts are not comparable to one another because they are not essentially different from one another. Each is greatest, and in this sense they are all equal and the same. All rise to the greatest common denominator, and they do this naturally, without really needing to try. It is only because we currently exist in a state of denial that we currently feel we must try so hard, and strive for something we do not already have. And it is only for this reason that we cannot already see the greatness that exists both outside (in others) and within ourselves.

We may not realize it, but there is part of us and of everyone that already is there in Heaven, contemplating the Most Holy Countenance:

> See that you do not despise one of these little ones; for I tell you that in heaven their angels always behold the face of my Father who is in heaven.
> (Matt. 18:10)

This greater part of ourselves is here symbolized as being our angels in Heaven. Luke 10:20 expresses this same idea slightly differently, where he says that we may "rejoice" that our "names are written in heaven." The most essential part of us is already there. It is only our conceptual mind, which is forever striving to make itself, that doubts this. Our original mind already knows, and knows *for us*. The Gospel of John expresses a similar idea via the words of John the Baptist:

> He who comes from above is above all; he who is of the earth belongs to the earth, and of the earth he speaks; he who comes from heaven is above all.
> (John 3:31)

Only in terms of earthly existence is the one who comes from Heaven above all; in Heaven itself, he is equal to all. This verse is therefore applicable to each of us because there is a part of us that is above and part that is below (on earth). But the part that comes from and *remains* above is the greater part. It is this part with which we need eventually to re-identify.

Paul describes his own personal experience of Heaven in 2 Corinthians chapter 12. There he says he will attempt to describe his most personal "visions and revelations of the Lord" (12:1). He begins by testifying that he was "caught up to the third heaven" 12:2), yet of course he entered Heaven in mind and experience without ever leaving the earth.

Paul says of this experience: "I was caught up into Paradise—whether in the body or out of the body I do not know" (12:3). What is important is not whether his body was in Paradise with him, but rather the experience itself was important. The body became, as it were, an afterthought. It was still there obviously, for he returned to it later, but it was not the predominant reality in Paul's mind during the course of this experience.

Paul says that while in this state, he "heard things that cannot be told, which man may not utter" (12:4). His experience was beyond words and transcendent of ordinary human concepts. It came with its own way of thinking and self-understanding. Perhaps this is why he does not elaborate on it any more than what is described here. But no doubt it influenced his theology and his view of God's will for humankind.

This is reminiscent of Jesus' making a distinction in John's Gospel between "earthly things" and "heavenly things" (John 3:12). He states in this regard that: "No one has ascended into heaven but he who descended from heaven, the Son of man" (3:13). Putting this together with Paul's account of his experience, if Paul indeed ascended into Heaven as he believes he has, then it was "the Son of man" within him that truly ascended. This is the new being, the Heavenly being within each of us that is able to experience Heaven at any time. No doubt such an experience as this is what gave Paul his certainty in the new but eternal identity we shall ultimately enjoy from God:

> For we know that if the earthly tent we live in is destroyed, we have a building from God, a house not made with hands, eternal in the heavens. Here indeed we groan, and long to put on our heavenly dwelling.
>
> (2 Cor. 5:1-2)

Note that "our heavenly dwelling" is described here as a kind of cloak we put around ourselves, yet it is also described as our true Heavenly identity. It is the eternal part of ourselves that *can* ascend to Heaven, and in truth already abides there. How easy it is to think we are worthy if we are already in some sense there!

# 10

# The Grandeur of Being

**Being Human**

In this chapter we return to one of our themes: the inherent greatness of God's creation. There is in truth no end to its greatness, because God's creation is without end. It has no limits, no boundary to set it off against any opposite, including supposed evil. There is therefore *no room* for evil in God's creation.

Evil, then, *must* be illusion. What we think to be evil, in other words, *does not exist*. Yet our minds are powerful, so powerful that what the mind believes tends to become its reality. One might say, therefore, that God's creation is creative, setting realities into motion. But none of these is really, objectively real, unless it is shared fully by the Mind of God.

Evil is something we fear, and believe to be true, though it never quite comes to fruition. It is the fear behind and before it specifically that keeps it going. As long as we don't look too fully into it, it remains "there," vague and nebulous and unexamined. This mere thought of a thought, this unexamined notion is why we are afraid to look too deeply into ourselves. Yet we ourselves, as we *are*, behind the illusion, could potentially be great evidence who prove in ourselves the greatness of God's creation, seen properly, or as "very good," as it was in the beginning.

The Psalmist asks of human beings in general:

[W]hat is man that thou art mindful of him,
and the son of man that thou dost care for him?
(Psalms 8:4)

This is one question that every philosopher, every theologian, every *person* must eventually ask. It is based simply on appreciation for being itself, and for the thought process inherent in *human* being in particular. It is appreciation and it is tribute, rolled into one. And it is a giant step in the recovery of our true selves and the restoration of our sense of true being.

One need not even posit a God to ask such a question. One may indeed ask it of the Universe. Who are we? Why are we here? What does it mean that we have being? Upon what basis do we have being? And, corollary to this, how do we as presently constituted participate in such cosmic being?

The answer to the last question is "Fully," but this means so much more than we think it does. At every level, from the most cosmic to the most mundane, we participate in being. Therefore we participate in God and we have and can know from within ourselves "eternal life."

Our presupposition, then, that we knew what it meant to be human, has been proven false. It is being re-examined as we speak and as we live, and increasingly jettisoned by stages and left to the past to be swallowed up and forgotten. We had only limited ourselves by such thinking and presupposing, by having accepted any categorical reality as human, or any human reality as categorical.

The Psalm answers its own question:

> Yet thou hast made him little less than God,
> and dost crown him with glory and honor.
> (Psalms 8:5)

This is what is spoken in the Bible about being human. The human being is defined as "little less than God," which would render us to have much greater significance than we ever would have conceived in the past. The human being is crowned "with glory and honor," and may in fact be spoken of as the "crown" of creation, the part most like God. So much like God are we that we are said to share something of His "glory and honor."

Such is the greatness and grandeur of the human being that we are spoken of in the same breath as God. We are compared to Him and likened to Him. We are not far from Him, as we imagine ourselves to be. We are in fact still *in* His Mind. That is where we live and move and have our being. That is our true context, our true world or, better, our true reality.

Infinite Mind is in some way mindful of us. We are more than objects, more than playthings to Whatever put us here. We are essential to *its* happiness, having been created for close relationship with it. We may not realize this now, but that does not make it any less true.

If this is the truth, whether conceived as a personal relationship or a universal one, then why did we hide it from ourselves? We might as well ask why we *do* hide it, because it is not as if we are not still doing so. Is there really a good answer to this question as to why we hide our own greatness of being from ourselves? Would not the very underlying assumption of the question, its premise and foundation, be an irrational one?

The idea that we once shared the grandeur and dignity of such promise, but let it go, denied it, refused to acknowledge it, means that *we were not in our right mind* when we did so. We were not thinking clearly at all when we denied such a thing to ourselves out of hand. And we are not in our right mind insofar as we continue to disbelieve it.

We are the ones who must have hidden the splendid truth about ourselves, for God would not have hidden it from us. There is no one else who could have hidden it from ourselves *except* ourselves, and there is no one else who *can* experience it again. So much depends on us! The entire cosmic drama, as we have seen from the last couple of chapters, plays out within the grand scale of the human mind and heart.

Our own being is much greater than we can imagine at present. We live within a diminished reality of our own making, our own interpretation, but this is only temporary, being illusion. This diminished and reductionistic reality is not even close to the truth about ourselves, and yet it seems true to us simply because we believe it. Again we see the principle displayed that belief determines perception.

Let us examine the evidence for Jesus' similarly great esteem for the human being. As great as we tend to see *him* as being, he sees *us* as being even greater. We cannot even imagine how God sees us. Their vision of us is greater than ours of them. But Jesus himself asks us to share this vision about ourselves, and to see others as ourselves.

Once on a Sabbath day, the disciples were plucking grain as they walked through a field. When some religious authorities who saw this accused Jesus of allowing his disciples to sin by working on the Sabbath, Jesus said:

> The Sabbath was made for man,
> not man for the Sabbath;
> so the Son of man is lord even of the Sabbath.
> (Mark 2:27-28)

Jesus is saying that the religious and cosmic law (represented here by keeping the Sabbath) was made for the benefit of human beings, not human beings for the benefit of the religious and cosmic law. In other words, *we* take precedence. Who we are from the inside, our worth even apart from what we currently conceive to be our worth, is what matters most. The Creator of the Universe has made *us* His top priority, not the law. The law was made for us, not us for the law.

So much for legalism. Jesus stressed instead a most grand vision of humanism, over and over upholding the value of the human being for us to see and marvel upon (see, for example, Matt. 6:26; 10:31; 12:12; Luke 12:7 and 12:24). Jesus' emphatic proclamations about the great "value" of the human being strongly suggest that it is God Himself who placed such value within us. It is we ourselves whom God most values—much more than we tend to value ourselves or anything else.

The law is nowhere near as important as the human being in Jesus' teaching. He is saying that God is actually more *humane* than that. A corollary to Jesus' argument about humans taking precedence over the law is given by Luke 6:9 wherein Jesus says to his protestors: "I ask you, is it lawful on the sabbath to do good or to do harm, to save life or to destroy it?" Here he is prioritizing the *well-being* of the individual human being over the law. The one he was about to heal was of much greater significance than any necessarily oppressive, coercive, and simply limiting law. Once again we see Jesus attempting to redress the imbalance he detected among those who placed the law before the human beings for whom it was meant.

It is the conceptual mind that does this, needing something to hang itself upon. Needing a sense of control it feels it does not have, it seeks to control others in lieu of controlling itself. But this haphazard attempt to resolve the issue only reinforces its lack of internal control, producing a vicious cycle whereby one no longer knows what one is doing to oneself, but is doing it by habit and therefore unconsciously.

What we often fail to see about the law is that it is perfectly *natural*: its consequences are built into it. It is not a burden, but instead a way of living more freely, and a vision of what this will look like. Think of every "shall" and "shall not" as a prophecy rather than a command, as what *will be* rather than what *should be*, as already fulfilled rather than awaiting our input, and you will understand the *visionary* nature of the law, how it frees and even magnifies our minds rather than limiting them.

The law is therefore not a command (or set of commands) that comes from above, but instead a new way of viewing oneself or understanding oneself, both in relation to God and to others. (In the traditional ten commandments, the first four emphasize our relationship to God, while the latter six stress our relationship to others.) We will explore further ramifications of this new way of viewing the law a bit later.

Our value is in fact infinite if the Father and all His thoughts are infinite. Jesus is trying in these passages to convince human beings of their natural and Godlike grandeur. Insofar as we exalt the Father, therefore, we exalt ourselves, His creation. There should exist no great gulf between the two. The Father cannot love anything unlike Himself, for His holy Mind cannot *conceive* of anything unlike Himself, which means that for this reason alone we *must* be like Him. And in fact, as we have seen, Jesus distills the law down to love and being like God, loving and thinking of ourselves as His children, who are like Him, even to the point of sharing His perfection and completion.

**Glorification**

Jesus tells his disciples that belief is a prerequisite for seeing the glory of God:

> Did I not tell you that if you would believe you would see the glory of God?
> (John 11:40)

To believe, it says here, is eventually to "see the glory of God." This is where belief leads, and so again we see that belief determines perception. But this leads to the question: Does belief cause the glory of God, or does it cause it simply to be seen? If the latter, then the glory of God is already there, waiting to be seen. Belief allows us to see it. It opens our eyes because it opens our minds.

When the Prophet Ezekiel saw the glory of God, it appeared to him as light radiating out from the center of God's Being, so that "there was brightness round about him." Ezekiel continues:

> Like the appearance of the bow that is in the cloud on the day of rain, so was the appearance of the brightness round about. Such was the appearance of the likeness of the glory of the LORD. And when I saw it, I fell upon my face, and I heard the voice of one speaking.
> (Ezekiel 1:27-28)

Ezekiel describes this otherworldly glory in a very concrete fashion. To him it seemed to resemble a rainbow. Yet it was so magnificent and so transcendent that it made him fall upon his face and to hear a supernatural voice speaking. And so we know that this was no ordinary rainbow that he saw.

Early attempts to describe the glory of God make it seem mysterious and somewhat hazy, as for instance appearing as light emanating from the midst of that cloud (compare Exod. 24:16-17; Num. 16:42). Early on we see the glory of God to be attached rather concretely to certain objects, as for instance it was once attached to the burning bush (Exod. 3:2-4) and the ark of the covenant (e.g., 1 Sam. 4:22), the vessel in which God's presence was thought to be carried. But it eventually comes to be associated with all of creation, as in this hymn of Isaiah:

> Holy, holy, holy is the LORD of hosts;
> the whole earth is full of his glory.
> (Isa. 6:3)

Glory here is spread out evenly upon all the earth. It is not attached to anything particular, but instead to *everything* ("the whole earth"). The second Isaiah describes the revelation of God's glory as a universal experience that occurs to *everyone*:

> And the glory of the LORD shall be revealed,
> and all flesh shall see it together,
> for the mouth of the LORD has spoken.
> (Isa. 40:5)

This is not only the culmination of the Hebrew Bible, it is also the culminating event of all humankind. It will make us one to see it all together. Whatever we believed to get to this point would no longer matter: it would matter only that we did believe and that we did indeed get to this point. We can see it early, of course, before everyone sees it together. But once we see it, we cannot unsee it. It will remain within our range of experience forever.

The second Isaiah (comprising chapters 40-55 of the Book of Isaiah) introduces a strong sense of universality into the Bible. God is the God of all people, who are called His sons and daughters:

> I will say to the north, Give up,
> and to the south, Do not withhold;
> bring my sons from afar
> and my daughters from the end of the earth,
> every one who is called by my name,
> whom I created for my glory,
> whom I formed and made.
> (Isa. 43:6-7)

All life, all creation is included here. The glory of God, which we can know or experience on a very personal level, is universalized here. It belongs to all that God created, and is in fact a necessary feature of all life.

The Johannine Jesus speaks of a similar universalization of the very personal experience of glory:

> He will glorify me, for he will take what is mine and declare it to you. All that the Father has is mine; therefore I said that he will take what is mine and declare it to you.
> (John 16:14-15)

Here Jesus states that his own personal experience will be passed along to others, in this case his disciples. He states first that he has everything because the Father has shared everything with him, including all His glory, before going on to say that all of this will be passed along to His children in general. It is as if the glory of God were *meant* to be shared among His entire creation, and Jesus was among the first to realize this.

Jesus' sharing of his own glory, which is God's glory, with all humankind would result eventually in Isaiah's aforementioned culminating vision in which all the sons and daughters of God will see His glory together. They would see it in themselves and in the creation around them, just as Jesus himself had done. Like Isaiah, Jesus envisions this glory as ultimately joining and unifying humankind. We shall soon see that when Jesus prays to His Father for oneness in John 17:22-24, he specifically mentions that "the glory" that God has given him would now be shared among all who so believed.

The Johannine vision of the sharing of the glory of God among all creation is foreshadowed early on in the book:

> And from his fulness have we all received, grace upon grace.
> (John 1:16)

Here we might equate glory with "fulness" in that it is universalized (something we have "all received"). Paradoxically, this universal glory comes from our having experienced it very personally, and this having been built up "grace upon grace" in our daily experience. Each experience of grace accumulates until there results the culminating vision of glory.

Paul speaks similarly, saying: "we rejoice in our hope of sharing the glory of God" (Romans 5:2). God's purpose in creating us *must* have been to *share* His glory. Otherwise, how could we as lesser beings know Him at all? Our mind would not be powerful enough, nor capacious enough, to understand Him. In Paul's estimation, we have been *predestined* for glory (e.g., Ro. 8:30; 9:23), which means that we must be destined first to believe, then to see, and then to know this glory once again.

The Pauline tradition speaks of "the mystery hidden for ages and generations but now made manifest to his saints" (Col. 1:26). It elaborates further upon "the glory of this mystery, which is Christ in you, the hope of glory" (Col. 1:26-27). That is, the glory within us ("in you") *is* the Christ.

All of us, having a share in the glory of God, also have a share the being of Christ. We are all entitled to proclaim of ourselves that we are legitimate aspects of God's perfect creation, but in order to do this, we must see all others as likewise constituted. The justice of God demands this, though not in an authoritarian sense; it simply means that of His glory we have all received an equal share. What is true of God's grace is also true of His glory.

Paul speaks very clearly of a *process* of increasing glorification whereby:

> we are being changed into his likeness from one degree of glory to another.
> (2 Corinthians 3:18)

As with Jesus, we become like God in order to commune with God, but this happens for us in stages. The change spoken of here is "from one degree of glory to another," incremental and gradual, involving stages of increasing glory and increasingly glorified states of mind. One might envision these increasing states and stages of increasing glory as being like a ladder or a stairway, and one might further envision that each of these states involves an unfolding of our own essential reality.

Paul states of Jesus that:

> Through him we have obtained access to this grace in which we stand, and we rejoice in our hope of sharing the glory of God.
> (Rom. 5:2)

Jesus had come to share this glory. Note that here again the fullness of the state of glory follows upon the heels of the grace we already experience. The sharing of the glory of God was the highest state, the state to which we aspire and for which "we rejoice in our hope."

This is precisely why the Pauline tradition states:

> When Christ who is our life appears, then you also will appear with him in glory.
> (Colossians 3:4)

It is through *our own* increasing glorification that we will be empowered clearly to see, to know, and indeed to be one with God and with "Christ who is our life." What this means is that a person needs to become as glorified as Christ in order to see him as he really is. The steps to this involve sharing his outlook and way of thinking, until, as Paul says, we realize that: "we have the mind of Christ" (1 Corinthians 2:16).

**'You Are The Light of the World'**

Light is an image for the being we truly and eternally are, and also for our understanding of that being. Therefore Jesus tells us how it represents our own eternal being:

> You are the light of the world. A city built on a hill cannot be hid. No one after lighting a lamp puts it under a bushel basket, but on the lampstand, and it gives light to all in the house. In the same way, let your light shine before others, so that they may see your good works and give glory to your Father in heaven.
> (Matthew 5:14-16, NRSV)

Jesus calls *us* the light of the world. This would represent a new category for human beings, and a new way of envisioning ourselves. Jesus' teaching seems to encourage, over and over, a new way of imagining ourselves, a new way of thinking about ourselves, as being more like God, as if this were the point of his teaching.

In this section, we will examine the abstract image of light found throughout the Bible, and how this relates to our own true self. The first light we see comes at the very beginning in Genesis 1:3 ("And God said, 'Let there be light'; and there was light"), wherein light is the very first of God's creations. This is bookended in Revelation wherein the descending city of God needs no physical sun because "the glory of God is its light" (Revelation 21:23). Light is therefore the first of God's creations and it is key to the culminating vision of the Bible itself.

Candles and especially lamps become symbols of God's leading, guiding, and final deliverance (ex., Exod. 25:37; 35). The candles and lamps were meant to signify the ancient Israelites' escape from captivity, slavery, and oppression in Egypt, and they remain important symbols in Judaism to this day. The important thing was that this memory of God be perpetuated and kept going in the present, which meant that the symbols of light also had to be perpetuated:

> Command the people of Israel to bring you pure oil from beaten olives for the lamp, that a light may be kept burning continually.
> (Lev. 24:2)

Light (of any kind or form) was a symbol of God, a remembrance of Him, transforming our darkness to light:

> Yea, thou art my lamp, O LORD,
> and my God lightens my darkness.
> (2 Sam. 22:29)

When the author says "God lightens *my* darkness," the darkness he (or she) is talking about is his own individual, psychologically *experienced* darkness. It is one's existential *sense* of darkness that is shone away by the light of God.

This psychological effect of light (as symbolic of God) continues in the Psalms:

> The LORD is my light and my salvation;
> whom shall I fear?
> (Ps. 27:1)

For with thee is the fountain of life;
in thy light do we see light.
(Ps. 36:9)

He will bring forth your vindication as the light,
and your right as the noonday.
(Ps. 37:6)

Oh send out thy light and thy truth;
let them lead me,
let them bring me to thy holy hill
and to thy dwelling!
(Ps. 43:3)

Note the multiplicity of possessive pronouns in the above passages: *"my* lamp," *"my* God," *"my* darkness," *"my* light," *"my* salvation," all very personal and existential, coupled with those referring to God: *"thy* light," *"thy* truth," *"thy* holy hill," *"thy* dwelling!" Encounter of the most intimate sort, being to being, is symbolized by this ever-present image of light.

Also psychologically significant is the symbol of light as a reminder of God's "steadfast love" (Ps. 136:7). This, we have seen, is a theme that runs throughout the Bible. It of course contains a great feeling sense as well as a cognitive sense, this idea of light as a constant reminder of God's perpetual, enduring, and "steadfast love."

It is said of God that:

even the darkness is not dark to thee,
the night is bright as the day;
for darkness is as light with thee.
(Ps. 139:12)

That is, God precedes the darkness and so no darkness exists in His Mind. As origin and source of light, God takes precedence over any kind of darkness, whether material or psychological. For Him, in this sense, "darkness is as light" and in this sense it does not exist for Him. Such an idea is reminiscent of John's saying later (in the New Testament) that "God is light and in him is no darkness at all" (1 John 1:5).

In sum, the Book of Psalms virtually radiates with images of light, speaking of the light of God's countenance (e.g., Psalms 4:6), the radiance of His Being, and also calling God "the light of life" (Ps. 56:13) who shines away our former darkness (or lack of understanding). The paradox as regards understanding is that we need the light of God in order to see the light of God, or as Psalms 36:9 puts it: "in thy light do we see light." Once again, as with the attainment (or realization) of glory, there is a process involved:

> The unfolding of thy words gives light;
> it imparts understanding to the simple.
> (Ps. 119:130)

Understanding unfolds over time. It comes with experience, much more than with words and concepts, which can be useful but cannot by themselves lead one into light. Understanding the words gives us conceptual understanding, but our experience of the meaning within ourselves gives us the understanding of God.

To continue with the Hebrew Bible (or what is commonly referred to as the Old Testament), we find in Proverbs the psychologically-charged association of "the path of the righteous" with "the light of dawn":

> But the path of the righteous is like the light of dawn,
> which shines brighter and brighter until full day.
> (Prov. 4:18)

There are stages here, but each of them is like light upon light, increasing in intensity until the bright radiance of "full day." We will attempt (in the section on "the Way") to lay out "the path of the righteous," a basic ethics, but here we are first trying to uncover its association with our inner selves.

The theme of light continues into the Prophets, such as when Isaiah proclaims a general resurrection:

> Thy dead shall live, their bodies shall rise.
> O dwellers in the dust, awake and sing for joy!
> For thy dew is a dew of light,
> and on the land of the shades thou wilt let it fall.
> (Isa. 26:19)

Tiny, perpetually-oppressed Israel in fact will be seen ultimately to be "a light to the nations" (Isa. 42:6) because they reflect the original light of God in both life and righteousness. It must not have seemed that way during the exile, when many of the people were removed from their homes and brought to foreign lands, but each of the exiled prophets believed that great ideas and images had no real boundaries. This idea of Israel as light to the nations speaks clearly of a universalization of the ideas which had originally been held by that tiny, seemingly-insignificant nation.

> I will give you as a light to the nations,
> that my salvation may reach to the end of the earth.
> (Isa. 49:6)

Such would be their vindication, their victory over exile, their validation in the eyes of the world. The ideas that held them together even through exile would eventually be seen as holding the world and all of life together. The idea of God as light (and of we as light with Him) would spread throughout the world and to every being in it.

Another idea, related to light, is that of God's sense of justice as spreading to all people: "my justice for a light to the peoples" (Isa. 51:4). This is later related to the helping of those who are oppressed in one's midst:

> if you pour yourself out for the hungry
> and satisfy the desire of the afflicted,
> then shall your light rise in the darkness
> and your gloom be as the noonday.
> (Isa. 58:10)

Again, this is highly psychological. The helping of others leads to a lifting of depression, or the "gloom" of meaninglessness. Practically speaking, it is by helping others that we help ourselves.

In the New Testament, the image of light plays a part at Jesus' birth, with the star followed by the wise men from the east (Matt. 2:2, 9). Light is also prominent in Jesus' transfiguration, when he appeared to the disciples to be suffused by an unearthly light (Matt. 17:2). Jesus also speaks of light in terms of a kind of superconscious awareness:

> For there is nothing hid, except to be made manifest; nor is anything secret, except to come to light.
> (Mark 4:22)

Light is full, superconscious awareness. It exists within us, but for most of us it is just a potential within our mind. It lies dormant, and therefore has gone dark by our own choice not to lend it our attention. Yet the light is still great within us, even in potential, a point which Jesus makes thusly:

> If then the light in you is darkness, how great is the darkness!
> (Matt. 6:23)

As great as the darkness we fear is hidden deep in our unconscious, the light will prove to be far greater. And the darkness itself will be shone away once the fullness of light emerges in us.

The Gospel of John says of Jesus:

> The true light that enlightens every man was coming into the world.
> (John 1:9)

Here again is that universalizing tendency we had seen blossoming with Isaiah. "The true light" will "enlighten" "every man," that is, everyone. This statement literally means that *all* people will find some measure of spiritual enlightenment. Jesus would be like a starter flame for all of our internal lamps.

In John's Gospel we also have Jesus proclaiming himself to be "the light of the world," saying that "he who follows me will not walk in darkness, but will have the light of life" (John 8:12). Later in that gospel, Jesus refers to those who follow him as "sons of light" (John 12:36). Something of Jesus' light will spark something of our own light, so that we ourselves might know ourselves to be "sons [and daughters] of light." Jesus, it seems, is an example and manifestation of what will be proved true of each and every person. For just as he had known himself to be light, so would he cause us to know ourselves as light.

Later in the New Testament we find light accompanying the angel that visited Peter in his jail cell (Acts 12:7). Paul is converted to Christianity in a striking experience that comes with sudden blinding light (Acts 22:3-11). There is also the tradition that speaks of the transformation of believers into "sons of light" and "children of light" (Eph. 5:8). John's first letter (e.g., 2:10), we have seen, equates light with love.

Paul speaks similarly as Jesus, saying that "the Lord" "will bring to light the things now hidden in darkness and will disclose the purposes of the heart" (1 Cor. 4:5). Again light symbolizes self-awareness, including transcendent self-awareness. There is a darkness within ourselves that we fear, but we fear it in large part *because* we keep it dark. We do not let it come to light so that we might examine it. Rather, we let it operate in the darkness because of our fear of it. And so it seems to take over and engulf us, when in reality this darkness is literally *nothing*—nothing except a feared delusion, a mistaken thought in our mind.

Therefore Paul speaks of the remedying "light of the knowledge of the glory of God" (2 Cor. 4:6), where again light means "knowledge" and spiritual awareness. Paul appropriately cautions those who "have a zeal for God, but it is not enlightened" (Rom. 10:2). We *need* grounding in experience, it seems. Our salvation should be firsthand, not secondhand; it should impact us on a *personal* and *psychological* level. Even the laws contained in the Bible were meant to enlighten, for: "the commandment of the Lord is pure, enlightening the eyes" (Ps. 19:8). Ephesians 1:18 speaks of "having the eyes of your hearts enlightened, that you may know what is the hope to which he has called you." These "eyes of [our] hearts" are kind of internal eyes that see quite clearly the internal things of spirit, just as well as the physical eyes see the physical world.

Finally, the Book of Revelation ends with a return of the original, first-created light (as found in Genesis), wherein sun and moon are no longer necessary because "the glory of God is its light" (Rev. 21:23). All of these references to light and enlightenment go to show that light is said to have a real psychologically-transformative capacity for human beings. The source documents of Christianity and Judaism lay great emphasis on on the psychological and spiritual experience of enlightenment. As Jesus had taught, when we see all things as reflecting light, then we will know that all this light comes from *us*:

> The eye is the lamp of the body. So, if your eye is sound, your whole body will be full of light; but if your eye is not sound, your whole body will be full of darkness. If then the light in you is darkness, how great is the darkness!
> (Matt. 6:22-23)

In the end we will find that all the light we have ever seen is *our own* light reflected in our perception and therefore in all the world.

# 11

# From Metaphysics to Praxis

**Oneness**

In this chapter we will be studying some of the more esoteric and metaphysical ideas in Christianity. The topics will include the idea of Oneness, the notion of an all-inclusive Son or collective Christ, what is described in the Bible as mutual indwelling, and the concept of predestination. The reason they remain esoteric is because they are difficult to understand in ordinary conceptual terms. Yet our examination of these concepts reveals them to be experiences as well as concepts, which give us inroads to an understanding we did not know was available to us.

We begin with the Shema, opening line of the most popular Jewish prayer in practice, spoken morning and night by many, learned and memorized very early in life:

> Hear, O Israel: The LORD our God is one LORD;
> and you shall love the LORD your God with all your heart, and with all your soul, and with all your might.
> 
> (Deut. 6:4-5)

It seems fitting that this verse stands at the center of Jewish daily life. In the first place, it affirms the monotheism at the heart of the religion. Secondly, it begins the commandments. And thirdly, Jesus echoes it with one small addition (to love others as oneself) when he sums up of the Bible.

The early Christians (such as Paul in the following passages) use the idea that "God is one" as the basis for much of their thinking:

> Or is God the God of Jews only? Is he not the God of Gentiles also? Yes, of Gentiles also, since God is one.
> 
> (Rom. 3:29-30)

> Now an intermediary implies more than one; but God is one.
> 
> (Gal. 3:20)

> You believe that God is one; you do well. Even the demons believe — and shudder.
> 
> (James 2:19)

We have also seen that one of the great themes running throughout the Bible is that of God calling all beings to return to Him and to be reconciled to Him. Such an idea depends on the premise that "God is one," for it is saying that all beings ultimately gravitate back towards Him. They still have their original being in Him—the one God, from whose Universal Mind they derived their being. And so, the realization will return that they are all one in Him.

The idea that this God of oneness seeks to reconcile us to Himself eventually transcends mere covenantal or legal relationship. It is more than mere technical agreement, more than a contract between us and God: it is *reality*. It is the way things are and always will be.

We, in all our glorious multiplicity, in all our seemingly endless variety and in the different types and flavors of our manifestations, we, in spite of all this diversity, are all called to oneness. We are all called back to our Origin. We all have a sense, already, behind the clouds of confusion, a sense of the oneness which still stands as our original state and to which we are called to return.

Once we begin to *think* this way, then we begin to *see* this way. We do indeed find what we were looking for. We are looking for some essential similarity, some likeness, something that can join us together and make us feel as one. We are looking for the aspect of God in each particular person, because God is one.

If God is one, and we all come from God, then we all come from the same place, the same Universal Mind. And so all the distinctions that once seemed to separate us, are suddenly seen for the illusions they were. Our hyper-focus on our differences had led us to forget our unity, but our remembrance that God is one highlights the unity that already exists.

The Pauline tradition speaks of "one God and Father of us all, who is above all and through all and in all" (Eph. 4:6). There are a lot of prepositions here: God is "*above* all and *through* all and *in* all." This leaves no place where God is *not*. It leaves us also with no place to hide. He is already with us, but something keeps us from seeing, experiencing, and knowing this fact.

The oneness of God is indicative of the closeness of our true relationship. If God remains one, and we seem to make two, then the two must ultimately still hide the one. No matter how many twos there are, they must still from the Godly vantage point be one.

Psychologically speaking, we sometimes experience a sense of oneness with those we love. Therefore it is fitting that the ideas of oneness and love are analogues and they go together (as in the first passage we cited, from Deut. 6:4-5). This sheds new light on Jesus' emphasis on love in his extended sermons and his upholding of love as the essence of the Hebrew Bible. We love others *as* ourselves because love makes us one with them. The same care we take for ourselves extends out to those we love, and this, too, makes us one.

In the Gospel of John Jesus prays for oneness:

> The glory that you have given me I have given them, so that they may be one, as we are one, I in them and you in me, that they may become completely one, so that the world may know that you have sent me and have loved them even as you have loved me.
> (John 17:22-23, NRSV)

First, Jesus says that he shares his "glory" with his students. This glory was given to him, and so he gives it freely to others. He does this, he says, "so that they may be one, as we are one," referring to himself and God. That is, he prays that his disciples might experience the same oneness he experiences between himself and God, the closeness, the affection, perhaps even the identification. He prays "that they may become completely one." And, at the end, we see again that love accompanies and informs this sense of oneness.

Note that the oneness extends from Jesus' personal relationship with God ("*we* are one") to all other beings ("that *they* may be one"). It begins with *his* relationship with God but culminates in *our own* experience of oneness. That is, Jesus' relationship with God was seen to spread out to others and to include them within it. However this occurs, it immures to the entire world's benefit; it is the universal and common good, something as good for each individual as it is for all together.

That Jesus turns to us and offers the same relationship that he enjoyed with God—a transcendent relationship involving oneness of Being and the sharing of the glory thereof—means that we were *meant* for the same close and intimate relationship. God is as near to us as our heart, as close to us as our mind, and as intimate to us as our self.

Such was Jesus' faith in God that it gave him faith in all beings. We notice from his prayer for oneness that he not only believed in God; he also believed in *us*. Jesus puts himself on the same level with humanity because of humanity's inherent (but still unknown or unrealized) oneness with God. This is what made him the Christ that bridges the gap between these two very different worlds, with their opposing natures and characteristics. To accept him, therefore, is also to accept our own true being.

## The Collective Christ

We saw in the second chapter that we are called upon to treat others *as* ourselves (via the Golden Rule) and to love others *as* ourselves (via the Great Commandment). Both of these essential aspects of Jesus' teaching require us to think of others *as* ourselves, to think of them *as* us, as part of us. It is not mere sentiment or platitude that is called for here. We are asked to think of others *as ourselves* because it happens to be true. It is actually true that we are one, in a sense that we cannot currently comprehend. This is how God created us: as whole individuals who are yet part of a greater whole. The greatness of our own being lies in our being *one* with all other beings. We shall see in this section that this collective Being, comprised of all of us, is sometimes referred to as "Christ" and sometimes as "the Son of God."

"The Christ" (the Greek translation of the Hebrew word meaning "Messiah") was thought of in Judaism to be a political figure, a savior of the nation. But the Christ in the burgeoning Christian circles had to be redefined into a spiritual figure, a humble servant and teacher. Sometimes in the New Testament the term refers specifically to Jesus, but sometimes (especially in Paul's letters), the term refers to a collective Being composed of all people (or at least all believers).

In the synoptic gospels, Matt. 1:16 states that Jesus "is called Christ." In Matt. 16:16, Peter declares Jesus to be "the Christ, the Son of the living God," and in 16:20 Jesus is said to have sworn the disciples to secrecy regarding this. Pilate is said to refer to him as "Jesus who is called Christ" (Matt. 27:17, 22). In Mark 9:41, Jesus tells his students that they will "bear the name of Christ."

Paul uses the term "Christ" most often to refer to Jesus, as a title (either "Jesus Christ" or "Christ Jesus"). The title does not stress Jesus' humanity so much as Jesus' role as a cosmic intermediary, the bridge between humanity and God. We will be focusing on the few instances where Paul seems to use the term to refer to all believers, and not just to Jesus himself, such as here:

> [I]n Christ Jesus you are all sons of God.... There is neither Jew nor Greek, there is neither slave nor free, there is neither male nor female; for you are all one in Christ Jesus.
> (Gal. 3:26, 28)

In saying, "you are all one in Christ Jesus," Paul is removing the distinctions that normally exist between people and declaring them to be individual parts of a larger Entity, a greater Being, a more collective Whole, which is also called "Christ":

> For as in one body we have many members, and all the members do not have the same function, so we, though many, are one body in Christ, and individually members one of another.
> (Rom. 12:4-5)

A similar expression occurs in First Corinthians:

> For just as the body is one and has many members, and all the members of the body, though many, are one body, so it is with Christ.
> (1 Cor. 12:12)

In these passages, "Christ" includes many beings. All beings participate in some respect. This suggests that we have not only *individual* being but also *corporate* being, *collective* being, and that the sum of our individual beings is a being in its own right in relation to God. That is, as we join with one another in a kind of mutual respect, appreciation, and love of one another, a new Being and identity emerges in our mind that includes all of them.

The Christ, here, is an actual being and identity that is shared by "many." For Paul to say that the Christ is "one body" with "many members" is to say that the sum of our individual beings is a whole Being unto itself, which Paul calls "Christ." This is not just rhetorical flourish. It is more even than metaphysics. It is the source of a new practical ethics, this new way of thinking about ourselves and others, and the relationship thereof.

In addition to our individual identities, then, we have a collective identity we share "in Christ." And because we share it with Christ, who shares it with everyone, *we also* share it with everyone, and everyone shares it with us. This is the meaning of our being "individually members one of another." All those we share it with become part of us and we of them, not only on a metaphysical level but also on a very practical level.

And so it is that in the Pauline tradition Christ is "in all" (Eph. 1:23). He is one being in whom we all partake, one being we all together comprise. Indeed, "in Christ shall all be made alive" (1 Cor. 15:22). Our true life is in this collective identity we share, which enhances and is enhanced by our individuality.

> Therefore, if any one is in Christ, he is a new creation; the old has passed away, behold, the new has come.
> (2 Cor. 5:17)

Practically speaking also, if *anyone* seems to lag behind, then *we ourselves* will not be complete. Hence the impetus behind the spreading of forgiveness, love, and reconciliation, and the significance of trying to understand others as we would want to be understood. For the truth does not exist outside them, just as it does not exist outside ourselves. It exists in what we share, and where we join. The real truth lies within them and also in ourselves. We *need* one another to find it.

Paul says further that "he who is united to the Lord becomes one spirit with him" (1 Cor. 6:17). This again is no platitude, but rather a reality of which he speaks. Our joining with the Lord as "one spirit" is meant to enable real communion and interrelationship, even to the point of *sharing the same Being with him*, which to us seems to be a "new creation."

John expresses the same idea in slightly different wording when he refers to "the Son" as a kind of collective being. It is within this collective identification with the Son that we will each find our own eternal life.

> And this is the testimony, that God gave us eternal life, and this life is in his Son. He who has the Son has life; he who has not the Son of God has not life.
> (1 John 5:11-12)

Whatever individual sense of eternal life we have is therefore realized *through* this collective identity shared by all, called by John "the Son of God." The Son here is an umbrella term that includes all of creation and all life. John uses the term "the Son of God" or "the Son" in much the same way that Paul often uses "the Christ." The real life of each individual being exists in that life of the whole, and so it will be our identification with this whole that will convince us ultimately of our own eternal life.

John says further that the idea of the Son of God entered the world specifically for the purpose of our sharing his greater sense of life with us:

> In this the love of God was made manifest among us, that God sent his only Son into the world, so that we might live through him.
> (1 John 4:9)

Again here we live *through* the Son; that is, we derive our own sense of life through identification with the Son. The Son is the life we share and the life in which we all participate. From such statements as we have studied in this section, we might begin to surmise that the creation in God's Mind is *both* individual *and* collective.

## Mutual Indwelling

This understanding of the oneness of being is supported by those curious statements in the New Testament wherein it is said that one being lives in another as that being lives in the first being. There are many such statements, which reflect a kind of relationship we might call mutual indwelling, as for instance when Jesus states: "Believe me that I am in the Father and the Father in me" (John 14:11). God dwells in him, but he also dwells in God. Our rational minds have trouble thinking of such mutual indwelling because we tend to see the self as embodied and therefore individualized. We should instead think of the self as instead a *cognitive* or *spiritual* reality in order to understand such statements.

What is remarkable is that such statements of mutual indwelling are not reserved for Jesus alone; they apply to us as well. For instance, we have this saying of Jesus:

> In that day you will know that I am in my Father, and you in me, and I in you.
> (John 14:20)

Here the mutual indwelling involves three: the Father, Jesus, and ourselves. There is a sort of sequential effect described here, wherein Jesus states that just as he is "in" the Father, so are his students "in" him. He is saying that we can and will realize the same mutual indwelling with him as he has with God, ultimately to enjoy our own intimate relationship with God through him. Jesus will serve as our bridge to the same kind of intimate and very close relationship with God that he enjoyed.

The image of the vine is another significant representation of such willful oneness of being. For here we have an image whereby all of life is known to be interconnected, joined in the Son, all perfectly integrated into a greater whole. Jesus describes it as a mutual indwelling between himself and us:

> Abide in me, and I in you. As the branch cannot bear fruit by itself, unless it abides in the vine, neither can you, unless you abide in me.
> (John 15:4)

Jesus is saying here that oneness accomplishes things. If we think of ourselves as one with others, and others as one with ourselves, then and only then shall we "bear fruit." They have to participate in the same being, obviously, to know their pre-existing oneness with him. Should they think of themselves as part of him, as he does of them, a circuit will be closed and a new energy take hold. Because of this, they will be able to do anything, endure anything, accomplish anything. This sheds new light on Jesus' having said, many times, that he healed by the power of the faith of the person before him.

The Gospel of John has Jesus praying for this sense of oneness brought about by mutual indwelling. He prays:

> that they may all be one; even as thou, Father, art in me, and I in thee, that they also may be in us, so that the world may believe that thou hast sent me.
> (John 17:21)

For Jesus to pray for oneness in this way suggests that the oneness is important for both him and God. Note too that he does not reserve exclusively for himself oneness with God. His entire purpose is to share such closeness and intimacy with everyone ("the world"). We have seen, both recently and in our section on "the Sonship," that his intention seems to have been to share even his own Sonship with them. He is also saying here that the proof of *his* oneness with God lies in *our own* experience of the same relationship.

## Predestined in Love

We have put forward the idea that human beings do not need to *do* anything in order to be the children of God, but they do have to change their minds to *realize* they are children of God. It follows that if we will *ever* be the children of God, then we must be so *now*. We do not determine *whether* or not we are in fact children of our parents; we determine only whether we want to *acknowledge* this fact (and comport with it) or not. And we face such a decision only because we must have thrown away this knowledge at some point in the primordially distant past. And so, to decide that we are children of God is to decide to be true to our true selves.

If we are children of God now, then nothing on earth or in Heaven could change that fact. God could not change His Mind about it. So it must have been *we* who forgot this is the case, and this is why it is *we* who have to realize again it is the case. But though we can indeed forget, and this is the one limit on our free will, we cannot make it untrue. It is simply a matter of fact. Even if we forget, it would still be our underlying reality and would still represent our true identity.

This, then, would be the true basis of predestination. We misunderstood it as being a *dual* kind of predestination, whereby some were destined for Heaven and others for a much more dismal place. But what kind of God would this be, who divides His own children so? Jesus assures us that God knows how to treat His children *better* than we know how to treat our own (Matt. 7:9-11). Therefore, if *we* can love all our children just the same, then predestination must be the same for all, and any division or conflict experienced must be a product only of our split minds. The ultimate destination of every child of God must be the same, *and* the same as its point of true origination.

John expresses this idea without using the word *predestined*, saying: "Beloved, we are God's children now," though "it does not yet appear what we shall be" (1 John 3:2). In other words, though we *are* His children now, but we do not yet realize this fact fully. We are not yet immersed in the higher reality; we are not yet completely identified with it. Because of who God is, however, we are bound to realize this fact once again. John's point is that though we might already realize we are children of God by learning of our capacity specifically to love like God, the fullness of our true reality and identity as children of God still eludes us for a time.

Paul is the New Testament scribe who uses the word *predestined*, associating this idea with sonship:

> For those whom he foreknew he also predestined to be conformed to the image of his Son, in order that he might be the first-born among many brethren.
> (Romans 8:29)

Here we see Paul saying, basically, that God knew us *before* we were born, and He still knows us in this same way. If God's Mind does not really change then, as His children and as thoughts in His Mind, *we* do not really change. Only our minds can change, but again they cannot change the fundamental nature of our true being because they cannot change the *simple fact* of our point of origin. We can change only our *acknowledgment* as to this fact.

But our mind is powerful, and so even our *denial* of reality seems to have real effects. It has already deluded us into thinking that we cannot be who we eternally *must* be. And so the world we perceive around ourselves, *through* ourselves, seems foreign because it was dreamed up by some foreign entity—all of us who once were strangers to ourselves. The world we see only seems to reinforce this prior decision, this primordial denial, to the extent that we have become stuck in a world of illusion.

God's plan has always been for us to know ourselves as His children—in the same way that Jesus knew himself as Son. Our sonship, like his, was pre-determined. We have seen that it is spoken about in the same breath as Jesus' sonship. And so, Jesus is "first-born" not in a metaphysical sense but rather in a salvific sense: in the sense that he was, from Paul's purview, the first to realize.

This knowing of ourselves as sons and children of God is more than a conceptual knowledge: it is an existential knowledge, a *lived* knowledge about our real being. It cannot really be grasped by the conceptualizing mind, and it may be for this exact reason that it seems primordial to us. It precedes this life and follows this life, but yet it *seems* to have nothing to do with our present life. It seems more like a dream than reality, when in reality it is the other way around.

The Letter to the Ephesians couples the idea that God foreknew His children (*all* of them) with the idea that He must always have loved them. It is because of this eternal love that we are predestined to return to Him:

> He destined us in love to be his sons through Jesus Christ, according to the purpose of his will, to the praise of his glorious grace which he freely bestowed on us in the Beloved.
> (Ephesians 1:5-6)

We were, each and all, "destined ... in love to be his sons." It is the remembrance of this eternal love that eventually draws us back, that compels us, and that causes us to remember our eternal self. According to this way of thinking, Jesus' purpose, and the way he fulfills the will of God, is to lift us to our own sense of sonship. We, like him and with him, rise to our very own sense of Belovedness, of being loved "freely" and "to the praise of his glorious grace," and neither excluded nor included by anything we have done or said, but simply because we *are* and always will be His Beloved Children.

As Jesus makes clear in his teaching, God does not discriminate in His perception—indeed, "He is kind to the ungrateful and the selfish" (Luke 6:35). This is different than we, with our thoughts of vengeance and judgment, can currently accept. And so we cannot accept the universal truth of this statement:

> and I, when I am lifted up from the earth,
> will draw *all men* to myself.
> (John 12:32, my emphasis)

Were we to interpret the above statement literally, it would mean that universal salvation is not only possible, but inevitable. Other statements of total inclusion in the Bible include the statement that "Christ is all, and in all" (Col. 3:11) and the following prophecy, cited by Paul:

> for it is written, 'As I live, says the Lord, every knee shall bow to me,
> and every tongue shall give praise to God.'
> (Rom. 14:11)

Again, if we were to take all these literally, it would mean that all beings eventually will recognize Him as their

Source (each in their own way, perhaps) and every individual will ultimately return to Him. If God calls them, and if His Voice truly is compelling, then eventually everyone *must* listen. It is *predetermined* if the love with which they were created remains with them, hidden somewhere deep within their minds.

Our destination, we have seen again and again, depends on our true origin. If we began in the Mind of God, then this is where we must forever be. This is where we will find our true origin, even should we forget. And so we are asked to think like God and especially to love like God in order to know the ins and outs of our own eternal being.

The entire point of this idea of predestination is simply that the world has little bearing on who we really are, appearances to the contrary notwithstanding. The plan is much greater—infinitely greater—than we can currently fathom, for it involves a greatly expanded and much more inclusive sense of self that supersedes and even precedes our lifespan on earth. Is it a *necessary* doctrine, destined to be a required theological belief? Of course not, though it could be *helpful* in raising the way we normally think of ourselves.

## The All-Inclusive King

It helps just to think about metaphysical ideas in a less exclusive sense than we normally do. It helps to see them as pertaining to *all* beings rather than to one individual or group alone. It would help us to take a step back and look at the big picture, so that then we can see where we ourselves fit into it.

The most concrete idea we will be studying in this chapter is just one aspect of one figure in one of Jesus' parables, the cosmic King who can be found in every being:

> Then the King will say to those at his right hand, 'Come, O blessed of my Father, inherit the kingdom prepared for you from the foundation of the world; for I was hungry and you gave me food, I was thirsty and you gave me drink, I was a stranger and you welcomed me, I was naked and you clothed me, I was sick and you visited me, I was in prison and you came to me.'
> Then the righteous will answer him, 'Lord, when did we see thee hungry and feed thee, or thirsty and give thee drink? And when did we see thee a stranger and welcome thee, or naked and clothe thee? And when did we see thee sick or in prison and visit thee?' And the King will answer them, 'Truly, I say to you, as you did it to one of the least of these my brethren, you did it to me.'
> (Matt. 25:34-40)

In this beautiful story, the King identifies with all his subjects, even the least. The story is obviously trying to motivate its hearers to help those in need: those who are "hungry," "thirsty," "a stranger," "naked," "sick," or "in prison." It seems to be saying that progress in one's spiritual journey of realization depends on doing these things: on helping others.

If the King in this story is to be representative of Jesus, which most interpreters believe it is, then Jesus is saying that he can be found in all those who need help. Or we might think of this King as "the Christ" in each person we meet, or a fellow "Son of God." The King is representative of *both* all people *and* a cosmic being. The King (however we might think of him) sees himself as one with all the inhabitants of his kingdom, not only as equal to them but also as one with them.

The egalitarian King in this parable identifies with every being in his Kingdom, even those who suffer silently, and every being can be seen as representative of the King. Perhaps this is how we will all see it eventually: that all our fellow beings share the Christ, and that if we can see it in them, then He must be in ourselves as well. This would make the Christ which is in all individuals the essential truth that stands behind all appearances.

In many of Jesus' parables and sayings a similar reversal of expectations is found. Therefore this cosmic King fits in quite well with Jesus' idea that worldly rulers should not "lord it over" those subject to their rule (Mark 10:42). They should not allow authority to go to their heads, so to speak. Therefore in this parable the King refers to those within his kingdom as "brothers." And elsewhere Jesus refers to those adjudged least in this world to all be *equally great* in the kingdom he envisions (see Matt. 11:11). Jesus stresses that "whoever would be great among you must be your servant" (Mark 10:43) and that "the Son of man also came not to be served but to serve" (10:45).

From this thought of equality and oneness, an experience and new perception of universal appreciation should result. The more beings it includes within it, we might say, the more naturally it will be to include ourselves as well. We will thereby be allowing ourselves to experience the idea, therefore to *de-esotericize* it for ourselves, or demystify it by making it personally very real, first in our thoughts of others, then in our vision of the world, and then in our thoughts of ourselves.

# 12

# Living as a Child of God

**The Deepening of Religion**

In this section we will focus on the practical, practicable and ethical aspects of coming to think of ourselves as children of God. We shall also see how this practical ethical advice given throughout the New Testament matches up with and confirms its metaphysics.

Take for instance Jesus' advice on how to live as children of God:

> But love your enemies, and do good, and lend, expecting nothing in return; and your reward will be great, and you will be sons of the Most High; for he is kind to the ungrateful and the selfish.
> (Luke 6:35)

The change in how we relate to others in the world ("love your enemies, do good, and lend") seems to go hand in hand with a transformation in identity ("you will be sons of the Most High"). We are asked to act, essentially, as God Himself (who is "kind to the ungrateful and the selfish") would act and to think and feel as God Himself would do so—i.e., universally and infinitely. The nexus between practical ethics and a transformation of identity comes when the ethics to be followed have to do with becoming more like God.

We have seen that Jesus continually emphasized a change of mind over a change of behavior (e.g., Matt. 5:21-22), as if he were attempting to *deepen* the religious law by applying it to each individual mind. For Jesus, a change of behavior is not transformative enough for a child of God. That is not to say that such behavior is not a step in the right direction and a means of instructing others through example (e.g., Matt. 5:16). However, to be consistent, to be "perfect" (Matt. 5:48), our thoughts and feelings must also be right.

We have seen that Jesus urges us to treat others and love others as ourselves. Here we have the ethics and the transformation expressed in the same few words, if we were to take the "as ourselves" part literally, as if we really are treating and thinking of others as being "ourselves"—we a part of them and they of us. Again, the behavioral change is necessary but insufficient of itself: a transformation of mind and identity is necessary for consistency and true salvation.

The transformation involves not only ourselves but also our relationships, all the interconnections we have already made and have yet to make. It is in this way, mysteriously, often without words, that salvation *really* is spread. It is passed along almost unconsciously and quite naturally, simply by our decision to have begun to see others *as* ourselves, both they and we parts of a greater whole. Not only that, they and we are also *essential* parts—essential to one another and also to God.

No one is ever thrown away, their life discarded as if it were so much trash. That is not how God operates, let alone how He thinks and feels. No one goes unthought about, uncared for, at least not in Heaven where God abides. The same is true of *our* heart and *our* mind, where He also abides.

Through these simple ethics, our interconnection with the entire universe is made known. We have seen in the last chapter, in regard to the all-inclusive King in Matt. 25, that practically speaking we are asked to give to each according to their need. There are many ways in which we might be kind, and do good, and love, several of which are described in the parable. Thus, if we see someone hungry, we feed them; if we see they are strangers, we welcome them; if we find they are sick or imprisoned, we visit them. We look to their basic needs both physical and psychological.

With Paul, as with Jesus, the change in behavior goes hand in hand with a change in our conception as to the nature of human beings. Thus Paul seems to echo Jesus, but expresses the same thought in his own way:

> Repay no one evil for evil, but take thought for what is noble in the sight of all.
> (Romans 12:17)

If we appeal to the *noble* part of *all* we meet and see, then our faith in them, minuscule as it may sometimes seem, will ultimately be justified. After all, there are two sides to everyone, but only one can be entirely and eternally true. The cosmic battle between good and evil is not one that occurs between us and someone else: it all boils down to an internal struggle, a psychological conflict. Which side we choose to see we will see *from*, and therefore *see*. Therefore:

> Finally, brethren, whatever is true, whatever is honorable, whatever is just, whatever is pure, whatever is lovely, whatever is gracious, if there is any excel-

lence, if there is anything worthy of praise, think about these things.

(Phil. 4:8)

It sounds so simple: we should be looking for the good in others—the *absolute* good—because it can be found in every person and in every aspect of creation. It is by seeing it there that we will come to know God and come to remember our true selves. Therefore we look for whatever is "honorable," whatever is "just," "lovely," "gracious," excellent and praiseworthy in everything and everyone. This means setting our minds on the higher things, the honorable within all we see, so that we might know the same honor within ourselves.

It begins and ends with our inner state. Contrary to popular belief, the world *must* change to conform to our vision. Most generally, we have thought that *we* must change to conform to the world, but no longer. The world must take a secondary place to what is truly noble and praise-worthy about ourselves.

The absolute good we seek is already there; we need only to acknowledge and appreciate it in order to see it everywhere. We need only to distinguish it from the evil with which it has become intermixed in this world and in our mind, to see it everywhere instead of the evil world we had been seeing. This is our part in the last judgment, as we have seen.

In the same way we need only "approve what is excellent" in order to know *ourselves* as "pure and blameless" (Phil. 1:10). Paradoxically, there is a certain "humility" that comes from such vision of nobility (Phil. 2:3):

Have this mind among yourselves, which is yours in Christ Jesus, who, though he was in the form of

> God, did not count equality with God a thing to be grasped, but emptied himself, taking the form of a servant, being born in the likeness of men.
> (Phil. 2:5-7)

What this is saying is that, although we cannot conceptually "grasp" or understand divine equality with our current mindset, we can follow Jesus in "taking the form of a servant" to others. The awareness of divine equality will arise precisely and paradoxically from this. And so we have both Paul and Jesus arguing for a cognitive-behavioral approach whereby our new actions are accompanied by a new way of thinking which makes us consistent in those actions.

As with Jesus, we seek only to serve, to "help" (Phil. 4:3), because this reminds us of the great love of God *for us*. We receive not only an inner reward for helping, not simply a good feeling about ourselves, but we remember something about the absolute truth behind and beyond this world—the *metaphysics*. Now, of course, to "help" others in this world, we must cultivate in ourselves a spirit of patience and "forbearance" (Phil. 4:5). In daily life this means that we "Do all things without grumbling or questioning" (Phil. 2:14). Whatever it is we are called to do, in whatever way we are called to serve, we do so gladly because *we* would be glad. In fact we find that it is by making *others* glad that *we* are made glad—as if they really were part of us—and this corroborates our interconnection with them.

The Pauline tradition's ethics are similar:

> Let all bitterness and wrath and anger and clamor and slander be put away from you, with all malice, and be kind to one another, tenderhearted, forgiving one another, as God in Christ forgave you.

(Ephesians 4:31-32)

Here we have the things to avoid as well as the things to look for. Note that both the good and the evil come from within: either kindness or anger, forgiveness or bitterness. We will therefore see the world in the same way as we see ourselves, proving that perception and cognition, behavior and thought, are two sides of the same coin.

And so it is characteristic of the believer, who has "received Christ Jesus" to abound "in thanksgiving" (Colossians 2:6-7), to be grateful and appreciative in practically everything. This is the way to a joyous life, on earth as it is in Heaven.

We find in James, similar to what we found in Jesus and Paul, that service to others is a primary objective of religion:

> Religion that is pure and undefiled before God and the Father is this: to visit orphans and widows in their affliction, and to keep oneself unstained from the world.
> (James 1:27)

This of course is an echo of the original Mosaic law. And with service performed for the sake of others, says Peter, comes deeper feeling in ourselves:

> Having purified your souls by your obedience to the truth for a sincere love of the brethren, love one another earnestly from the heart.
> (1 Peter 1:22)

Love is increased in its giving. Service flows naturally from the pure springs of love. We serve God best by *becoming* His love, and we know Him best by knowing ourselves thusly. Once again, we know Him from the inside. Therefore it is said: "And above all these put on love, which binds everything together in perfect harmony" (Colossians 3:14), or let it be our guiding light. And, "Let love be genuine … Never flag in zeal, be aglow in the Spirit, serve the Lord" (Romans 12:9, 11).

## The Internalization of the Law and the Sacralization of Life

The original Mosaic law arose in the earliest stages of the ancient Israelites' societal formation so that there was no difference between religious law and civic law. Thus civic law was sanctified and divinely validated as a step up from social chaos. But these laws were never meant to restrict or burden the people, but rather to instruct and help them coalesce. In a psychological way, they were meant to set people free by showing them a vision of life lived as children of God.

In a sociological sense, these laws were intended to unite the various and diverse tribes into a functioning unit. Up until the time of their codification, the folklore of this little society reflects near-constant upheaval and wandering. Adam and Eve are not left to enjoy the fruits of the paradisal garden for long before they are exiled and on the run. Noah is carried off on the flood as if from one world to another, Abraham unsettles his family and seeks to re-establish elsewhere. It is all a blur of motion and constant change even up through Moses' time.

Moses, you will recall, was said to have led this long-suffering people out of centuries-long enslavement in Egypt through a transitional period of decades-long wandering in the wilderness. Moses' great task had been to "deliver them out of the hand of the Egyptians, and to bring them up out of that land to a good and broad land, a land flowing with milk and honey" (Exodus 3:8). In this promised land, this veritable paradise on earth, the wandering tribe(s) would finally *begin* to settle down.

The law that arrived on the heels of this settling would hold these people, however disparate they may once have seemed, together in a civic way, in a religious way, and in a psychological way as well. It allowed them to think of themselves as distinct from other societies but also orderly and organized within their own. It remained in their imagination because it reminded them of the wondrous things they believed God had done for them, how He had saved them from oppression and ordered the world and society for their benefit.

The law *begins* with an emphasis on the idea that "God is one," (Deut. 6:4) perhaps because these diverse tribes needed unification if they were to live and work together. For the most part, they had to meld with the indigenous population of the land they would settle in. Perhaps each tribe had customarily thought slightly differently (at least) about God, bringing its own traditions into the mix, emphasizing certain aspects that they most appreciated or grew up with. It was the idea that God is one that fired their imaginations, led and unified them all.

Beginning as a couple of handfuls of commandments inscribed on "tables of stone" (Exodus 24:12), the law almost immediately grew voluminous, as if it cannot help but to multiply, and a couple handfuls of rules grew into a legal code. It continued multiplying itself until by Jesus' time, nearly a thousand years later, it had grown burdensome rather than freeing. Jesus apparently saw it as more limiting than instructive, necessary perhaps for a past age but insufficient for the new age.

For Jesus, religion was more personal and individual than an industry with a top-heavy hierarchical power structure. He came from the outskirts, a more rural area than Jerusalem, and looked for the outliers. We have seen that he was not enamored of tradition for tradition's sake. It is the same with the sacred core of the law: once it began to limit individuals, as for instance to keep them from healing on the sabbath, it *had* to be rethought. It had to be deconstructed as law and reconsidered as something entirely different, less coercive and more natural, if it was to be fulfilled and kept.

Jesus deepened religion by envisioning it as more personal, more a product of mind and heart than any institution. It was as if he were going back to the pre-law days in terms of human freedom, yet building on what the law had added in the intervening years. It is as if religion goes from its beginning in individual experience to societal instruction and then back to individual experience again. The sense of the sacred, after all, is *always* individually experienced, written on the mind and heart, if it is to have any depth to it at all.

Jesus was, in effect, reinterpreting the law so that it conformed to the individual human being, rather than the other way around. He was adding pre-legalistic and highly personal vision and revelation to the legalistic mix. After all, even the legal code began with Moses' vision and revelation. All religion begins in individual experience and ends in individual experience, yet in the meantime, other individuals are brought closer or made more distant, depending on whether one emphasizes either the personally psychological or the behavioral. The behavioral, as a psychological perspective, is only barely psychological, one might say, because there is no *self* in it.

Jesus made it a point to be seen hanging out with just those people the law considered abhorrent. In this way he was being civilly and religiously disobedient, not simply to be disobedient, but rather to be *more than lawful*. He was showing that his own, individualistic standard was higher than the law's, and at the same time more befitting his Father in Heaven.

Religion is deepened as the law is internalized and the human being is sacralized (or made sacred). Jesus showed that the personal and individual vision is the more sacred than any institutional reality. Thus in his vision, those without worldly power nonetheless held the true power. Indeed, "the meek" would eventually "inherit the earth" (Matt. 5:5). They would take it over because true power lay in the living God *and* in them, not in anything outside them.

The law, like behaviorism, is for unconscious beings rather than conscious and aware ones. As such, it belongs to an earlier stage of religious and societal development. Quite often in the Gospels, we catch Jesus reversing and replacing the law of Moses, such as in this famous instance:

> You have heard that it was said, `An eye for an eye and a tooth for a tooth.' But I say to you, Do not resist one who is evil. But if any one strikes you on the right cheek, turn to him the other also; and if any one would sue you and take your coat, let him have your cloak as well; and if any one forces you to go one mile, go with him two miles. Give to him who begs from you, and do not refuse him who would borrow from you.
> (Matt. 5:38-42)

Some of these seem to be radical and impossible instructions until we realize that Jesus envisions here a world not of meekness for meekness' sake, but rather one of meekness for the sake of transcendent power. It is a complete reassessment of values that is called for, a total re-thinking of all that tradition has handed down to us. The law of retaliation—"an eye for an eye and a tooth for a tooth"—is hereby replaced with a more positive reciprocation: kindness for kindness and respect for respect in relation to others, extending out and expecting eventually to return to you what is extended.

At times in this world, the kindhearted person is taken advantage of, but to the soul that has found its own finely-calibrated inner sensitivity, kindness itself is a form of salvation. Every little scrap of kindness one can find in a mean and sometimes terrible world becomes magnified to such a person. Little kindnesses to them, such as just the mere presence of a pleasant person in one's fleeting interactions of the day, mean so much to them personally that their lives are transformed just by seeing them, even if their kindness is directed towards others rather than themselves. The smallest kindness thereby becomes amplified into the greatest love.

We can perpetuate meanness, or we can initiate kindness: those are our two choices. Such a way of thinking about Jesus' teaching strips the varnish of theology (or just limiting traditional interpretation) from it and exposes it to new possibilities. All things would tend toward one or the other side of these two extremes (cruel or kind) rather than the usual dichotomy which seeps into our interpretations: that of right or wrong. That is to say, Jesus' teaching is not so much about being right or wrong as it is about being like God or *not* being like God, of being wholly loving or only partially so.

*Reacting* continually to perceived wrongs is no way to go through life. For there are always wrongs to be perceived here in the world, but we need to realize that the way we perceive and react to them tends to perpetuate them. We unknowingly perpetuate the ripples of chaos. We link ourselves to self-wrought chains of vengefulness that go on to bind and consume us, or we simply allow someone other than ourselves to determine what is most important to us. We have lost ourselves, our conscious center, in the process.

As Jesus avers, again and again, we ourselves are more important to God than the law. The law was made for us, not we for it. We are important; we are essential; we are integral to the whole of His glorious creation. And so, even all that we once experienced in a negative light now takes on a positive interpretation. For instance, once we have experienced alienation and estrangement, we are compelled then to seek out the alienated and estranged, for we find we hold much in common with them. Perhaps it is simply their approachability that lets us know this. That is to say, we have joined with those who before seemed unlike us.

Recall that Jesus had said that the entire law could be summed up simply by treating others with respect (the Golden Rule) and by loving them (the Greatest Commandment). It follows that these are *the only things* one needs really to think about and do. One need not master the law so much as one needs to master the experience of *love*. For Jesus this entails helping one another:

> For which is the greater, one who sits at table, or one who serves? Is it not the one who sits at table? But I am among you as one who serves.
> (Luke 22:27)

This is the ultimate way of re-perceiving the world by re-conceiving its values. Jesus points to himself as an example in this. His mere desire to help, to teach, to join with others, to comfort them and even just to include them: these are what are most important. And so the servant exceeds the master in importance and the world is transformed in the process. As Jesus says elsewhere: "the last will be first, and the first last" (Matt. 20:16).

The compassion inherent in Jesus' teaching harkens back to the Old Testament ideas of helping the helpless (the widow and orphan in Exod. 22:22) and of not turning away a stranger (Exod. 22:21), but it amplifies and universalizes these into the core attitudes of his new ethics. He also, with his regular refrain of "You have heard it said..., but I say to you" (six times in the space of Matt. 5:22-44), showed that the law needed to be continually reassessed if it is to keep pace with the individual's development. No code of laws could ever keep pace with (or, God forbid, limit) the perfection to which we as God's children are headed.

In effect, then, Jesus goes a long way toward fulfilling Jeremiah's prophesied *internalization* of the law:

> But this is the covenant which I will make with the house of Israel after those days, says the LORD: I will put my law within them, and I will write it upon their hearts; and I will be their God, and they shall be my people. And no longer shall each man teach his neighbor and each his brother, saying, `Know the LORD,' for they shall all know me, from the least of them to the greatest, says the LORD; for I will forgive their iniquity, and I will remember their sin no more.
> (Jeremiah 31:33-34)

To say "I will write it (the law) upon their hearts" is to say that the essence of the law will become part of the person, part of one's character and motivation but also part of one's being. Jeremiah, speaking for God, is saying that this has always been the goal; that is, the *written* or codified law was never the real goal, though it was appropriate for a certain time and stage of their development. The law was simply one way of establishing sufficient societal order so that ultimately, in God's words, "they shall all know me, from the least to the greatest."

This is why, for Jesus, the *person* is always more important than the law (cf. Mark 2:27). It is the inner person with whom God has relationship. The written law is superficial in comparison, and yet there is this tendency in people to externalize, and make it about the law rather than the person. Simply by recognizing this tendency to uphold the law over the person is to rise to a position of objectivity so that one may notice its ill effects before they happen, therefore to reverse the process. The law is actually quite natural if seen psychologically rather than behaviorally.

Paul's attitude toward the law is similar. Following Jesus, Paul concludes that the law is fulfilled inwardly:

> But he is a Jew, which is one inwardly; and circumcision is that of the heart, in the spirit, and not in the letter; whose praise is not of men, but of God.
> (Romans 2:29, KJV)

Paul, having once been a fervid follower of the law himself ("as to the law a Pharisee" (Phil. 3:5)), in his New Testament letters argues vehemently and consistently *against* the written law, saying for instance that "the law brings wrath, but where there is no law there is no transgression" (Rom. 4:15). He writes that the very existence of the law "aroused" "sinful passions" in him and the conviction of "death" as well (Rom. 7:6). He goes so far as to call the law "a curse" from which Christ comes to redeem us (Gal. 3:13). He notes that "sin" finds "opportunity" in the commandments (Rom. 7:8). He very nearly says that the law is sin, but catches himself at the last moment, instead clarifying:

> What then shall we say? That the law is sin? By no means! Yet, if it had not been for the law, I should not have known sin. I should not have known what it is to covet if the law had not said, 'You shall not covet.'
>
> (Rom. 7:7)

Law produced or at least perpetuated an internal conflict, which Paul describes so movingly in Romans 7. In a sense, his remedy to this conflict was to conceive of his two very different natures as running on parallel but separate tracks, the mind and the flesh:

> For I delight in the law of God, in my inmost self, but I see in my members another law at war with the law of my mind and making me captive to the law of sin which dwells in my members.... Thanks be to God through Jesus Christ our Lord! So then, I of myself serve the law of God with my mind, but with my flesh I serve the law of sin.
>
> (Rom. 7:22-23, 25)

The law *was* good, but psychological freedom from the law was a far greater good. Thus the internalization of the law was a great relief to him from the now-oppressive law and its effect of internal splitting.

> [T]he law of the Spirit of life in Christ Jesus has set me free from the law of sin and death.
>
> (Rom. 8:2)

Christ ended the tyranny of the law, replacing its requirements with the inward qualities of love and faith:

> For Christ is the end of the law, that every one who has faith may be justified.
> (Rom. 10:4)

We are made right with God not through the law itself, but through our individualized transcendence of the law, our realization that we no longer really need it because our internal perfection exceeds it. Paul indicates in Romans 10:5 that there are many ways to behave rightly (or to "practice righteousness"), and that the law is an *imperfect* way of doing so because it does not dig down into the thought and motivation behind behavior. And so, in the end, Paul agrees with Jesus that love alone fulfills the law in a perfect way:

> Owe no one anything, except to love one another; for he who loves his neighbor has fulfilled the law.... Love does no wrong to a neighbor; therefore love is the fulfilling of the law.
> (Rom. 13:8, 10)

Paul's own thoughts on the law had changed; his entire paradigm had shifted upon hearing and experiencing this message from Jesus that love fulfills the law. Whereas he used to pride himself on living according to the written law as best he could, now he is free from all of that, and no longer needs to think of God nor himself in such legalistic terms. He emerges with a stance that is more rational, more natural, and eminently more practical:

> 'All things are lawful for me,' but not all things are helpful. 'All things are lawful for me,' but I will not be enslaved by anything.
>
> (1 Cor. 6:12)

The law has gone from being a matter of life and death, a concern of utmost importance for salvation to being a burden in comparison to the freedom brought by Jesus and the Spirit:

> But now we are discharged from the law, dead to that which held us captive, so that we serve not under the old written code but in the new life of the Spirit.
>
> (Rom. 7:6)

Law and Spirit are juxtaposed here, as if they mean two dichotomously different things. The law itself had been a form of captivity, but to live by the Spirit instead is to live freely, therefore more truly to live more truly "to God" (Gal. 2:19). The law was meant to transition humankind from the chaos of competing self-interests to an orderly life, but it was never meant to be an end in itself. It was only the structure by which a community might be first organized. Even when first codified, the law was most significant not for itself, but rather because it came from God. It was God's way of speaking to an entire people through the vision of Moses.

For Paul, as for Jesus, the true goal of religion is described as "sonship," or realizing one's true relationship to God:

> But when the time had fully come, God sent forth his Son, born of woman, born under the law, to re-

deem those who were under the law, so that we might receive adoption as sons.
(Gal. 4:4-5)

Living by the Spirit renders the law unnecessary, because one's motivations and values have changed:

> But if you are led by the Spirit you are not under the law.... But the fruit of the Spirit is love, joy, peace, patience, kindness, goodness, faithfulness, gentleness, self-control; against such there is no law.
> (Gal. 5:18, 22-23)

Here Paul gives some eminently practical advice, based on a different way of seeing religion, as a personal encounter that shows itself in all interpersonal encounters. The advice is that the things we should be looking for stand far beyond the law itself. The positive characteristics that we will draw to ourselves come from encounter with the Spirit and with God, from that nexus spilling out into our worldly relationships and onto all of creation.

The Christian, then, should take an attitude of respectful *transcendence* toward the traditional, written law. As Paul stated so eloquently, we should raise our thinking above the law, and allow our minds to transcend the law, even while we seek only to "give no offense" to those still under the law (e.g., 1 Cor. 10:32). To all appearances we are still following the law, but by doing so out of love rather than obligation, we find that it is endemic to ourselves and naturally aligned with our inner Guide. We personally need no longer think in terms of the external religious law at all, and certainly not as being necessary for salvation. The law itself, properly seen, was always simply a way to encourage this internal change of mind and heart that *inspired* the law. All we need to think about is whether and how we are loving, for this alone gladdens our heart, this alone makes us like God, and this alone saves and justifies, redeems and delivers.

## The Personal and Universal Symbolism of the Cross

What then of the Cross? Isn't that spoken of in the Bible as necessary for salvation? Is there not a propitiatory or substitutional understanding of Jesus' crucifixion whereby we are saved?

We have examined the resurrection as being key for salvation because it is symbolic of a new identity. And we have noted that the crucifixion is almost always coupled with the resurrection in Paul's writings. This is because they are two parts of the same process.

Examining the issue a little more closely, we find that Jesus very rarely mentions the cross, either in the Synoptics or in John. Common to Mark, Matthew and Luke is this passage, in which Jesus speaks of the cross in terms of universal participation:

> And he said to all, 'If any man would come after me, let him deny himself and take up his cross daily and follow me. For whoever would save his life will lose it; and whoever loses his life for my sake, he will save it. For what does it profit a man if he gains the whole world and loses or forfeits himself?'
> (Luke 9:23-25)

First note that this is not about Jesus' cross alone, but rather about crucifixion as a participatory and obviously-symbolic event. It is participatory in the sense that it is something that is undergone by many ("all"). Specifically, it represents our denial of one self—the self we currently think we are—in favor a much greater sense of self that is truly ours.

We detect a process here, whereby one first denies oneself in order to find a new self. (This requires a leap of faith of course.) The first part of the process, self-denial, is symbolized with crucifixion, while the resurrection describes the new self that arises when the old is denied. If traceable back to Jesus, this saying may tell us something of *how* he came to be who he came to be. It may give us a peek into his own particular process and his own inner world.

The only other saying about the "cross" attributed to Jesus, also common to the Synoptics, is the following: "and he who does not take his cross and follow me is not worthy of me" (Matt. 10:38). Again here we have Jesus mentioning the cross as a participatory event, coming to each person at different times, depending on when they undergo the process. These two sayings represent the only words spoken by Jesus about the cross itself.

In regard to the "crucifixion," we have Jesus speaking of it as part of some cosmic prophecy not found in the Hebrew scriptures: "and deliver him to the Gentiles to be mocked and scourged and crucified, and he will be raised on the third day" (Matt. 20:19). Here we have Jesus coupling his own self-prophesied crucifixion with an experience of resurrection, as if, again, they were two parts of the same process. We can easily imagine such sayings to have been ways to bolster any early Christians who were being persecuted in those earliest stages of the religion's development. But we can also imagine that Jesus *might* have intuited something about his own death and the significance his rising would have as continuation of the process.

The point is that it was not the cross that was most significant to his teaching. He hardly spoke of it at all, and when it is spoken, its significance pales in light of the resurrection. It was not the cross that allowed him universal, or present to anyone anywhere. It was instead the resurrection, or the fact that his disciples would commune with him even after his death, that liberated *them* from the shackles of limitation. It was thereby that he proved for their sake that death was indeed nothing, as we have seen in his teaching.

Paul makes his own case for the priority of the resurrection, its greater importance for the world:

> If, because of one man's trespass,
> death reigned through that one man,
> how much more will those who receive the abundance of grace and the free gift of righteousness reign in life through the one man Jesus Christ.
> (Romans 5:17)

Here the death of Jesus is not even mentioned in the exchange, though it might well have fit. Rather it is Adam's death, or more specifically his introduction of the concept and apparent reality of death into the world, that is highlighted here, coupled with Jesus' having done away with any such faulty and fearful thinking as thinking of death as real. Just prior, Paul had said that the resulting good is always greater than the extent of the evil that seems to have preceded it.

> But the free gift is not like the trespass. For if many died through one man's trespass, much more have the grace of God and the free gift in the grace of that one man Jesus Christ abounded for many.
> (Rom. 5:15)

In Paul's mind, Jesus came to end our inadequate understanding of life, always coupled with death, and replace it with "the free gift" of another life altogether, another *kind* of life, a life of reconciliation and oneness ("through the one man") rather than opposition to God, to one another, and to eternal life itself. We are walking this Adam-Jesus argument backwards, trying to find the foundation upon which it rests.

In his teaching as a whole, we can see Paul trying out various ways of understanding the cross of Christ, spoken of as something of a scandal elsewhere: a "folly to those who are perishing" (1 Cor. 1:18), a "stumbling-block" (Gal. 5:11). He felt the need to defend the cross itself against those in his native Judaism who believed that crucifixion was "a curse":

> Christ redeemed us from the curse of the law, having become a curse for us—for it is written: "Cursed be every one who hangs on a tree"—that in Christ Jesus the blessing of Abraham might come upon the Gentiles, that we might receive the promise of the Spirit through faith.
> (Galatians 3:13-14)

Paul can be seen actively searching for an adequate explanation of the cross, because the idea is so foreign to his former understanding. And so, throughout his letters he speaks of it using various metaphors, including reconciliation, deliverance and redemption (as from slavery), justification, and atonement. The ideas of propitiation and expiation whereby the cross has become almost exclusively associated, whereby it fulfills once and for all the ancient tradition of sacrifice, are only some of the ways in which Paul is striving to make sense of what would formerly have seemed senseless (or worse) to him.

Returning to our argument based on Romans 5, we see Paul's familiar formula that while the crucifixion is said to "reconcile," it is *the resurrection* that is said to "save":

> For if while we were enemies we were reconciled to God by the death of his Son, much more, now that we are reconciled, shall we be saved by his life.
> (Rom. 5:10)

The cross, again, is most significant as a symbol counteracting Adam's symbolic fall from Paradise, specifically a symbol of reconciliation and unity whereby the fall must have been a fall into disunity and separateness. And once again, the cross is most significant as a participatory event or experience in which all humanity participates. As Christians and as human beings, we must each reckon with the evil inside us in order finally to let it go, every mistaken thought, to forgive it in ourselves and wherever else we see it, and to transcend all of it as a whole for a powerful new being, connected with the whole of life and the Source of life.

It is the "life" of the Son that is salvific, or effective for salvation. His life, his resurrection, is important *because* we all share it. Tracing the argument back, we find that Paul was trying to find a way to say with his Adam and Jesus metaphor that "sin is not counted where there is no law":

> Therefore as sin came into the world through one man and death through sin, and so death spread to all men because all men sinned—sin indeed was in the world before the law was given, but sin is not counted where there is no law.
> (Rom. 5:12-13)

St. Augustine would, centuries later, see this as evidence for the idea of original sin, but we can see here how it is really an argument for original and natural innocence, except that the law interfered, reinforcing the ancient sense of guilt rather than doing away with it. Sacrifice, too, had been an inadequate way of trying to deal with the pesky and persistent sense of guilt.

Thus for Paul it was to be a cross of joining, not exclusion, and because Jesus' trials are our trials, by virtue of our having been associated with "the one man," so is his rising above them *our* rising above them. Because we participate in him and his life, not only in his death but also his new life, his life is now our life. "It is no longer I who live," says Paul, "but Christ who lives in me" (Galatians 2:20). He has given himself over to the Universal Being within him, and has been granted a new identity because of his participation. This understanding of the cross was transformative for the individual, leading to a new knowledge of God, ourselves, and the world. It was to represent, not as it would seem on the surface, the inhumanity of draconian punishment, but rather the cross would come to represent for them the love of God for them and for all creation. The lesson for the early Christians was the transformation of their minds to see not only the crucifixion but everything differently, as newly graced with the love of God.

Paul's understanding of the crucifixion always involves our inner participation, as if its significance lay within our experiential comprehension and understanding. The crucifixion and resurrection of Jesus occurs not only in human history but also, and more significantly within the human being, and within many different human beings at once. It prepares for the real saving event, the resurrection, by unifying, by including rather than separating or distinguishing out. He appeals to his hearers' sense of reason in making his argument for universal participation in Christ:

> I speak to you as sensible men; judge for yourselves what I say. The cup of blessing which we bless, is it not a participation in the blood of Christ? The bread which we break, is it not a participation in the body of Christ? Because there is one bread, we who are many are one body, for we all partake of the one bread.
> (1 Corinthians 10:15-17)

Oneness is the underlying point of the eucharist, which reflects the crucifixion and resurrection. We participate by being blessed along with him, which makes us one in Christ and alive in Christ. So therefore should believers learn to live in existence, "no longer for themselves," but universally for him who now lives for all: "And he died for all, that those who live might live no longer for themselves but for him who for their sake died and was raised" (2 Corinthians 5:15). Again, the crucifixion unifies because he died for all, but this is only preparation for the salvation of the resurrection.

In this way, the significance of both events become internalized and psychologized: his death means our self-surrender, while his life evokes our own risen life, even here in daily existence:

> For if we have been united with him in a death like his, we shall certainly be united with him in a resurrection like his. We know that our old self was crucified with him.... But if we have died with Christ, we believe that we shall also live with him....
> The death he died he died to sin, once for all,
> but the life he lives he lives to God.
> (Romans 6:5-6, 8, 10)

We can see here that our own participation in his death and his life goes well beyond the eucharist and into the intricacy of daily life, for the eucharist is a symbol of his dying/rising, which in turn is a symbol of our own experience. He died "once for all," but his life is eternal, timeless, universal, because it is always within reach to be experienced and participated in.

The Pauline tradition reiterates that we ourselves participate in the events of Jesus' life: "you were buried with him in baptism, in which you were also raised with him through faith in the working of God, who raised him from the dead" (Colossians 2:12). We have *already* been buried with him in our spiritual baptism, and the resurrection has already occurred as well: "you have been raised with Christ" (Colossians 3:1). In 3:2, believers are already made "alive together with Christ" and raised up with him.

The Letter to the Ephesians takes this one step farther, and says that we already exist in Heaven with him:

> But God, who is rich in mercy,
> out of the great love with which he loved us,
> even when we were dead through our trespasses,
> made us alive together with Christ
> (by grace you have been saved),
> and raised us up with him,
> and made us sit with him in the heavenly places
> in Christ Jesus....
>
> (Ephesians 2:4-6)

We already "sit with him in the heavenly places" because we are already risen, in our understanding and therefore in our mind and therefore in our being. It is specifically because of the love of God that this is so. All of this is spoken of as if it has already happened and simply awaits our participation.

Here again the crucifixion is associated with unification as well as transcendence of the law as a means for salvation, which had split us into two rather than unified us:

> For he is our peace,
> who has made us both one,
> and has broken down the dividing wall of hostility,
> by abolishing in his flesh the law of commandments and ordinances,
> that he might create in himself one new man
> in place of the two, so making peace,
> and might reconcile us both to God in one body through the cross,
> thereby bringing the hostility to an end.
> (Ephesians 2:14-16, my italics)

Jesus' crucifixion is here a symbol of his transcendence of the religious law as a means of salvation. And this is where all the expiatory, propitiatory, and substitutionary interpretations of the cross are pointing. It does not mean a regressive harkening back to animal sacrifice as being beneficial for salvation, let alone necessary. Nor does it mean a limiting reliance on the law of "commandments and ordinances," but rather it signifies a transcendence of duality of any kind, including *any* thought of separation between either religions or between God and humankind. Recall, too, that for Paul God's Will for all life, and therefore the ultimate purpose for our having been created, is reconciliation with Him.

Our bodies had also been walls, in a sense, closing us off from other beings and in this sense closing us off from life itself. The crucifixion is spoken of as a moment of universality, in which all dividing walls (including all formerly firm and fixed categories in the mind) were broken down. The wall which once separated law from experience has been crossed over as the law is passed over, just as the the division between people into potential friends and enemies had been obliterated by Jesus' teaching to "love your enemies." Just so, the barriers that once seemed to close us off to others, including God, are crossed over, and we are already saved.

The cross should not be used to bolster any older view of salvation, like sacrifice or law, but rather should support Jesus' teaching to love, because it can be seen as his manifestation of this love (as in John 15:13: "Greater love has no man than this, that a man lay down his life for his friends"). In the end, he showed his students that only life is real, death being nothing except an illusion in our mind. Paul and others would interpret his death and resurrection as symbolic of their own spiritual transformation. We died with him, to alienation and estrangement, and have already risen again with him to all-encompassing transcendence, but we are not yet consistent in it. On the whole, however, the crucifixion/resurrection has given us access to a new *kind* of life.

## The Call to Freedom

From all of this, it follows that there are two basic ways of interpreting scripture. All the different ways of viewing the Bible fall under two major categories. It can be seen as repressive or liberating, as telling us what *not to do* or as inspiring us to *rise above* what limits us. This kind of choice goes back at least to Paul's differentiation between the letter of the law versus the spirit that comes from God:

> for the written code kills, but the Spirit gives life.
> (2 Cor. 3:5-6)

The Spirit provides all we need. It gives us more than the written law can possibly give us. Salvation is life, but life is much more than salvation. That is to say, salvation, which comes through a transformation of our minds, leads to a new kind of life, but is not itself that life. Life itself is to much more than "the written code," or any of the symbols that lead us to it.

We have just seen that Paul refers to the religious law in highly pejorative terms, as for instance "the dispensation of death" (2 Cor. 3:7) as contrasted with the "greater splendor" of "the dispensation of the Spirit" (3:8). He is contrasting the burden of following every regulation of the law with receiving direct guidance from the Spirit, the law having been commanded from outside us (and therefore coercive) while the Spirit is internal to us. The Word of God, therefore, is alive in believers' hearts, "written not with ink but with the Spirit of the living God, not on tablets of stone but on tablets of human hearts" (2 Cor. 3:3). The Word is active and alive, moving and dynamic rather than static and fixed. It is universal while at the same time being very personal to us. This, we might say, is what makes it inspired: It does not lay flat like dried ink on a page. Rather, it comes to life within ourselves.

Each of the two mutually exclusive ways of interpreting scripture (as in 2 Cor. 3:6: legalistic versus spiritual, the not free versus the free) reflects a completely different view of who *we* are, who *God* is, and who the people around us *are* to us. Most interpretations contain a mixture of these two basic elements. This new spiritual state of being, of course, is in our minds. It is there almost like a memory, except that its remembering involves full *participation* in the present. It is part of us, and we are part of it, yet we wander the earth as if unaware.

The legalism in our mindset had blinded us to the rich vein of freedom running throughout the Bible from the very beginning. In Genesis we find God's declaration of the freedom of His creation: "You may freely eat of every tree of the garden" (Gen. 2:16). It runs through Exodus where a return to freedom (from slavery and wandering) *is* the story. Deuteronomy picks up the thread even in its codification of laws, wherein it is said that a person benefits from giving freely and happily to others (as for instance in 15:10).

The theme of freedom becomes individualized again in the Writings, where in Psalms the cry for freedom is the cry of the individual to God: "Draw near to me, redeem me, set me free" (Ps. 69:18). Because it is for freedom—which is always a state of mind as well as freedom from someone else's legalism—and because as a state of mind it is very personal, we call such a cry *existential*. It pertains to existence itself, the fact of one's existence and how it relates to all other existence.

Happily, mercifully, we are told later in Psalms that our sense of oppression has already been lifted like a low-lying fog is dissipated by the rising sun: "I relieved your shoulder of the burden; your hands were freed from the basket" (Ps. 81:6). We read further that God's will, specifically for us, is "to hear the groans of the prisoners, to set free those who were doomed to die" (Ps. 102:20). All human beings *were* once doomed to die—but no longer. Now we are free to help others, thereby to lift ourselves, simply because our cries were heard. Our groans turned out *not* to have been in vain, but the response we receive from the Spirit of God *depends* on our participation.

We read further in the Psalms that God intends for His vast bounty—all that He has to give, which is everything—to be spread out to the whole of creation, for "He has distributed freely, he has given to the poor; his righteousness endures for ever" (Ps. 112:9), and then:

> Out of my distress I called on the Lord;
> the Lord answered me and set me free.
> (Ps. 118:5)

It is specifically from psychological "distress" that we are set free, whatever form it takes or *seems* to take. Even the smallest hint of distress makes life itself seem oppressive, but we are never meant to stop at such distress, or to be bound to the dark pit of despair, only to go *through* it to what lies on the other side. We acknowledge it, then let it go. Every human being endures great distress at some point or another, and this all boils down to some kind of limitation or some sense of lack.

Our past psychological distress was necessary only to lift us from this habit of accommodation with limitation. For we are very accomplished in the art of adjustment, so accomplished that we have adjusted even to a notion of death that has not yet been tested, and will never be tasted as we fear. As children of God, Godly beings, we should instead think this way: If death *seems* a reality to us, then our mind must already be in the wrong place, however prettified its surroundings might otherwise seem. Therefore let us set our minds to what we can know now: serving, helping, which we find to be natural to us, which occurs by our being more ourselves, and to transcending rather than conforming to limits of any kind, including the thought of death. Every such limit is acknowledged only to be finally let go, only as a tool toward the letting go.

The prophet Isaiah expresses the same yearning for freedom. It speaks of freedom as our natural inclination, given to us by God:

> I have aroused him in righteousness,
> and I will make straight all his ways;
> he shall build my city
> and set my exiles free,
> not for price or reward,
> says the LORD of hosts.
> (Isa. 45:13)

We are meant to release people from the limiting and self-constrictive ways of thinking of the world, thereby to release ourselves.

> Is not this the fast that I choose:
> to loose the bonds of wickedness,
> to undo the thongs of the yoke,
> to let the oppressed go free,
> and to break every yoke?
> (Isa. 58:6)

Our spiritual practice, though it may seem specific to us (here it involves "fasting" as a change of mind and direction), spreads out to others without our even trying. Our focus is on getting our own mind right, but our own individual freedom of mind *is* what frees the captives. We must "break every yoke" in our mind first, or set it free from every self-imposed binding, limitation and oppression, so others might be helped by its natural extension—others whose joy, we realize, is our own. Thus will we get there together, or not at all.

The voice of God in the Prophets is the voice of the individual heart and mind striving for a more total freedom, a more all-encompassing freedom. There is a hint of despair in this voice, only because of the acknowledgment that the world is not perfect, and that the mind therefore needs to change. Once the despair, our despair, is used for the general release from despair found in transcendence, it can be let go.

It has been a sub-theme of this book that the most personal way of thinking becomes the most universally applicable because we all share the same basic, internal psychological structure. Thus do we hear: "I will let the souls that you hunt go free like birds" (Ezek. 13:20). Moreover:

> I will heal their faithlessness;
> I will love them freely,
> for my anger has turned from them.
> (Hosea 14:4)

And again: "I will set your captives free from the waterless pit" (Zech. 9:11). We glean from all these passages that the intention of God for us, and ours for all, is for freedom. The voice of God whispers of increasing freedom, not wanting to intrude upon our tragi-comic debate as to *how* to restrict ourselves further. God is infinitely patient. A different view of God and humankind is not only foreseen but proclaimed with these prophets. They speak of the present more than the future, because the nature of the present is what *makes* the future.

Jesus, we have seen, speaks of how "the sons are free" (Matt. 17:26). In the Gospel of John he declares:

> So if the Son makes you free, you will be free indeed.
> (John 8:36)

We cannot be truly free without knowing our true nature as sons or children of God. It is this that draws us together, whatever our religion, whatever our way of conceiving of or imagining of *how* we are children of God. It is simply a fact, but the very idea of this fact has the power to join us all. The Johannine Jesus had said:

> you will know the truth, and the truth will
> make you free.
> (John 8:32)

It is simply by knowing the truth that we shall be made free. It is by knowing the facts, which involves seeing clearly, which involves both ourselves and others, that we are made utterly free. Pragmatically speaking, then, the only way that we ourselves can continually enjoy total freedom is if everyone shares it also with us. Such freedom, like all freedom, contains great responsibility. The better we know ourselves and others, the better we exercise it.

For early Christians, freedom from the old modes of salvation was made possible with the coming of Jesus:

> Let it be known to you therefore, brethren, that through this man forgiveness of sins is proclaimed to you, and by him every one that believes is freed from everything from which you could not be freed by the law of Moses.
> (Acts 13:38-39)

This freedom must have seemed total to them. It is expressed as freedom "from everything." Such is the perspective of the mind of the child of God. It knows complete freedom.

Paul, too, sees the call to freedom as equivalent to the call to sonship. We have seen that Paul speaks of our being "free from the law of sin and death" (Rom. 8:2), but he also speaks of freedom for the entire creation:

> because the creation itself will be set free from its bondage to decay and obtain the glorious liberty of the children of God.
> (Rom. 8:21)

In Paul's understanding, creation has been bound, imprisoned, subject to decay. It is imprisoned in large part by its own fleeting nature, by the seeming inevitability of its death and the death of all it knows (if it knows only the world). Death pertains only to the world of form, assures Paul, who speaks from his own Heavenly experience. Jesus as first-born Son was thought to bring with him, as gifts for us (but gifts that already belong to us), "the glorious liberty of the children of God."

Because it seems part of existence itself, part of the world, the problem is unconscious to us at first. It seems natural for things to grow old, decay, and finally die. Jesus showed that the more natural course was God's and it was characterized by eternal life. By identifying the insidious nature of the problem, we bring it to conscious awareness, where willful re-decision in favor of eternal life becomes possible.

Toward this end, we are given a Spirit—or, in modern psychological terms, we are made aware of the presence of Spirit—which has an eternal nature and which therefore allows us to distinguish between self-imprisonment and spiritual freedom:

> Now the Lord is the Spirit, and where the Spirit of the Lord is, there is freedom.
> (2 Cor. 3:17)

The emphasis in all these passages is towards increasing freedom and at the same time increasing joy. This freedom shows us who we really are (i.e., children of God) because it comes from who we really are, and it is this the Spirit reminds us of. Once we have tasted such freedom, we will no longer want to re-incarcerate ourselves.

> For freedom Christ has set us free; stand fast therefore, and do not submit again to a yoke of slavery.... For you were called to freedom, brethren; only do not use your freedom as an opportunity for the flesh, but through love be servants of one another.
> (Gal. 5:1, 13)

With inner guidance we are still responsible; we still decide. And with inner guidance we are offered the natural respect of our given position, our truth, as children of God. We had not known ourselves (or what God has given us) well enough to know God; yet we ourselves are living proof.

# Conclusion

There is more psychology in the Bible than we could ever have imagined. In fact one might say that all of its messages combine to form one basic, personal *psychological* understanding, more so than they form one consistent metaphysical, philosophical, or theological system. It is with the psychology and *internal* experience of the ancient authors and scribes that we can find most agreement. This agreement is very basic, common to all, and therefore inclusive of all people, including ourselves.

Without us, in fact, the Bible has no meaning. It has no meaning to one who does not see himself or herself interwoven among its pages. And this must come naturally to each individual; it cannot be forced nor coerced in any way. We are respected enough by the Universe that we are eventually led upon a path of reason and persuasion whereby, with a little digging, a little motivated study, we can find what has been hidden from our eyes.

To find the meaning of the Bible is to have found ourselves, and vice versa. There is a two-stage, alternating, dialectical process afoot whereby any enhanced understanding on one end results in deeper understanding on the other. The same process occurs in any relationship, whereby a deeper understanding of oneself leads to a better understanding of the other, and this in turn to a deeper understanding of oneself. The interconnection strengthens with each step.

It is like this with us and God. He has created it whereby as we know ourselves, we know Him, and as we know Him, we know ourselves. He has not drawn the same lines of classification we have drawn, nor does He allow Himself to be limited by them. He is all about the truth, and for Him the truth consists of Himself and all His creation. It is all the same category to Him.

The pendulum motion of the dialectic like clockwork still runs, as if to reinforce the fact that it is always us *plus* others, *never* either *alone*. Yet we can always increase our appreciation of one by appreciating the other. What works for God also works for others: we know them better the better we know ourselves, and we know ourselves as we know them.

Such was Jesus' message, the main idea of his teaching. It was all about the relationship, and because it was *him* teaching, he could place himself on the necessary equal footing. We did not realize that this applied to us as well, though it seems clear from his words that he meant it to be so. He did not see himself as special as we have made him. The theology that arose quickly in his wake did place him on an ineffable pedestal, however, and in the process distorted his teaching.

Paul did not mean for this to happen. By emphasizing faith as the little we need to do in order to receive God's grace, he did not mean to obfuscate Jesus' teaching nor the great logic with which he presented it. We can tell this from the way much of his writing seems to accord with and confirm Jesus' teaching. Paul's was a most creative mind, and so he searched for ways to express the same things in his own words, with his own images. This might even be thought of as the duty of every Christian: to come to understand everything via the same images with which one seeks to teach it. And as each individual expresses it in his or her own particular and diversified way, we come to fathom the commonality within all these various understandings, which commonality comes directly from the *depth* of the individual to whom it comes.

Understanding needs to be as broad as it is deep. It needs to be as applicable to all others as it is to our inner depths. In fact the more to whom we see it as applicable, the deeper our understanding will be of *ourselves*. There is no getting around this fact; even Paul's emphasis on faith and grace seems to support it. To speak colloquially: there but for the grace of God go we. If *we* needed grace to such an extent, then so do all others, and if this grace *came* to us from our simple faith in its existence which is also its dynamism, then so will it come ultimately to every other. Thereby are we *assured* that we have it ourselves.

Every life contains within it all life, because life is an infinitely generalizable idea, and the meaning of any particular part of it involves all of it together. No wedge exists between our deepest self and all of life unless we have put it there through our presupposing and our preconceiving. It is all of this ultimately that must be bracketed, not just the theology. Any preconception is susceptible to the light of truth entering in and shining it away as if it were nothing, and in the end we find that truly it was. Only truth were ever true, and the thing we did not understand was that we were essential parts of it all along, though this was not how we thought of ourselves (nor of others).

Who really knows what we shall be? God knows, and if He wills, so do we. What greater grace is there than for us to know the same truth God knows and by which He created all that is true? What greater purpose for faith itself than that it transforms itself into knowledge even as it transforms the one who has it?

Taking Paul to his logical extreme, we can say that *no one* has faith whom it was not given to them by grace to have. Positively stated, the faith of *every* believer is as much a gift as one's life. It is all a question as to when we are ready to accept all that we already have. But we do not even make ourselves ready. We simply are, or we are not. When we are, we will know.

Enlightenment, like revelation, is not even so much *enhanced* awareness as simply *accepted* awareness, whereby one *allows* the truth to be: that one is an essential and integral part of the truth that has been sought since before the world's foundations were lain. It contains a connotation of enhanced *appreciation* for the whole from which one has sprung and to which one forever belongs: the whole of knowledge inextricably intertwined with the whole of life. One is oneself part of this highest, most all-encompassing truth, and this indeed changes everything, including *oneself* insofar as one's conception of oneself was based on mere assumption.

There is no one and will never be anyone who can take your own rightful place. This is why your place is reserved for you and only you. *You* are the meaning; *you* are the life. *You* reveal God because *you* are His creation. What *you* think and what *you* feel is *all* that the cosmos itself can think and feel. If not for *you*, the physical universe would be a vast, empty space, devoid of mind, devoid of love.

So God blesses you and blesses the world with you. It is through you that we know of God's true creation and the infinity thereof, more depth than duration, yet extending to every aspect, making every aspect forever like itself. You are, each individually and even more so all together, the reason that love itself exists. And so all of creation—all that is—bows to you even as you greet it with appreciation and admiration.

# Index

absolute, (good) 250, (truth) 251
abstract, 29, 217
Adam, 101, 124-132, 138, 139, 190, 195, 254, 169, 270, 271
alienation, 62, 74, 121, 127f, 194, 259, 276
amnesia, 55, 126
anger, 49, 63, 67ff, 71ff, 192, 241, 251f, 260, 281
  (*see also* wrath)
anxiety, anxious, 49, 69, 147
apocalyptic literature, 158, 168ff, 178, 182, 184, 196ff
apocryphal literature, 189, 194
appreciation, 19, 54f, 65, 80, 81, 87, 88, 90, 165, 206, 233, 246, 250, 252, 255, 286
ascension, 143, 203
Augustine, 185, 271
awareness (see also consciousness), 18ff, 29, 66, 74, 82ff, 89ff, 94, 98, 103, 129, 139, 153, 175, 179, 190, 223f, 251, 257, 284, 286

baptism, 20, 110f, 172f, 274
  (*see also* John the Baptist)
Beatitudes, 37, 39, 257
beatific state, 126
behavior, 41, 43, 68f, 135, 138, 248, 249, 251, 252, 256, 257, 261, 263
behaviorism, behavioral, 43, 69, 248, 251, 256, 257, 261
being, 13, 17, 18f, 24, 34, 36, 40, 43f, 46, 57, 61f, 63, 64ff, 69ff, 83, 84, 88, 90f, 93ff, 96ff, 101ff, 105ff, 114ff, 117ff, 121f, 124-150, 152, 153f, 172, 174f, 178ff, 184, 191. 194f, 198ff, 205-216, 217, 219, 222, 227, 229ff, 233ff, 239ff, 244ff, 257f, 260, 271f, 274, 275, 278, 280
  (*see also* human beings)
order of being, 22
and mutual indwelling, 236-238
collective being, 231-235
and seeing, 17, 25, 29, 44f, 99, 141, 144, 153ff, 211, 250, 282
Being of God, 30, 46, 47, 54, 59ff, 67f, 71, 87, 96, 98, 111, 117, 133, 160f, 185, 211, 220, 234, 258, 272,
belief, 12f, 22, 35, 60, 73, 75-80, 102, 148, 167, 208, 211, 243, 250
  belief in Jesus, 22
  belief system, 12, 13
Bible, 9-14, 23, 35, 37, 47, 75, 83, 94, 133, 139. 145. 167, 168, 177, 179, 184, 185, 207, 213, 217, 219, 225, 226, 227, 242, 267, 277, 278, 285
  Hebrew Bible, 41, 80, 133, 135, 177, 212, 221, 229
body, 99f, 133, 138, 146, 149, 186, 202, 225, 232
  one body/body of Christ, 91, 103, 232f, 273
books of the Bible, 10f, 168, 178 (*see also* the individual books of the Bible by name)
  "this book," 9, 21, 145, 170, 214, 281

calibration, 161, 166
categories, categorization, 20, 48, 54, 206, 217, 275, 277
children, 21, 30f, 59, 60, 61, 70, 200, 201,
children of God (*see also* sons of God), 38, 39, 47, 53, 56, 59, 60, 62, 68, 70, 73, 103, 105-109, 110-114, 148f, 182, 224, 239-243, 247, 260, 280, 282ff
  children of light, 224
Christ, 103, 108, 136, 151, 164, 216, 230, (definition) 231, 232, 233, 242, 245, 250, 252,

261, 262, 263, 269, 270, 272, 273, 274, 284
Christ in you, 215
Christ is all and in all, 233, 242
Christianity, 145, 167, 224, 225, 226, 291
Christology, 23ff, 26f
Chronicles, First Book of, 177
cognitive, 27, 63, 137, 138, 140, 185, 219, 236, 251, 252
Colossians, Letter to, 102, 136, 215, 216, 242, 252, 253, 274
collective being/collective Christ, 103, 161, 226, 231-234, 235,
commandments (*see also* Greatest Commandment), 34, 43-45, 210, 225, 227, 255, 261, 275
communion, 117, 120, 215, 234, 269
concepts, conceptualization, 9, 10, 13, 14, 29, 31, 33, 116, 137, 142, 143, 145, 147, 159, 160, 163, 167, 170, 178, 184, 185f, 189, 197, 202, 203, 209, 220, 226, 241, 249, 251, 269
consciousness, conscious awareness, 94, 105, 154, 185f, 190, 193, 257, 258
contemplation, 123, 133, 165, 201
Corinthians, First Letter, 8, 101, 103, 113, 116, 118, 151, 154, 161, 165, 174, 175, 216, 224, 232, 233, 234, 264, 265, 270, 273
Corinthians, Second Letter, 102, 114, 136, 154, 157, 202, 203, 215, 224, 234, 273, 277, 278, 284
corruption, 84, 178, 190ff, 195, 199
counselor, 112
creation(s), 34, 52, 56, 62, 64f, 67, 68, 77, 78, 83, 101ff, 105f, 107f, 115, 124-132, 137f, 149, 151, 156, 158, 161, 171, 178, 185, 198, 200, 205f, 207, 209, 210, 212, 213ff, 217, 231, 234f, 243, 250, 259, 265, 272, 275, 278, 279, 283, 286
cross, crucifixion, 267-276
culmination, culminating point, 14, 36, 97, 108, 121, 124, 149, 158, 168, 169, 196, 197, 212, 214, 217, 229

Daniel, Book of, 168
Dante, 185
darkness, 26, 64, 71, 80, 152, 156, 164, 175, 200, 218-225. 279
David, 107, 174, 177
death, 97, 108, 127, 130, 137f, 146-152, 162f, 178f, 181f, 185-188, 190, 195f, 261f, 164, 268-273, 276f, 279f, 283
delusion, 62, 65, 195, 146, 175, 224, 240
depths, 116f, 122, 188, 190
depression, 49, 63, 190, 222
desire, 30, 45, 50, 81-86, 128, 175, 188, 196, 199, 222, 259
Deuteronomy, Book of, 43, 95, 278
devil (see also Satan), 24, 125, 177-182, 185

Ecclesiastes, Book of, 32, 94, 121
effort, 10, 20, 86, 199
emptiness, empty, 119-123, 251
end of the world, 145, 153-158, 167, 177
enemies, 46f, 105, 247, 271, 276
Ephesians, Letter to, 74, 89, 114, 152, 181, 192, 224, 225, 228, 233, 241, 252, 274, 275
equal, equality, 40, 106, 111, 149, 168, 193, 201, 202, 215, 245, 246, 251
eschatology, 158, 171
estrangement, 62, 128, 129, 194, 259, 276

eternal, eternity, 18, 29-33, 46, 55, 61, 62, 66, 80, 87-100, 102, 103, 105, 106, 114, 115, 117, 121, 122, 126, 132, 137, 138, 143-155, 158f, 162f, 166, 167, 171, 174, 176, 178, 181, 196, 197, 199, 200, 203, 217, 240, 241ff, 249, 274, 284
eternal life, 55, 87-100, 102, 103, 107, 113, 127, 137, 143f, 146, 148f, 153, 162f, 206, 234f, 270, 274, 284
eucharist, 273-274
existential, 48, 127, 128, 129, 138, 186, 187, 188, 193, 218, 219, 241, 278
Exodus, Book of, 59, 171, 212, 218, 254, 255, 260, 278
Ezekiel, Book of, 211, 281
Ezra, Book of IV, 182, 189, 190f, 194f

faith, 10, 78-80, 89, 90, 91, 108, 133, 151, 230, 237, 249, 263, 265, 268, 270, 274, 281
fall from original being, 66, 94, 124-132, 134, 138, 195, 196, 271
fear, 63-66, 67-74, 94, 97, 126, 128, 139, 149, 150, 163, 165ff, 200, 205, 219, 223, 224, 269, 280
fire, 21, 156, 167, 168-176, 182f, 185f, 192, 255
flesh, 99ff, 103, 141, 177, 179, 212, 262, 275, 284
forgiveness, 34, 46-52, 71ff, 89f, 98, 110, 134f, 154, 162, 234, 251f, 260, 271, 283
foundation, 9, 14, 30, 32, 66, 108, 116, 131, 156, 173f, 207, 244, 270
free, freedom, 13, 19, 22, 32, 44f, 51, 60, 77, 83, 91, 106ff, 132, 137, 139, 142, 149, 192, 210, 229, 241f, 254ff, 262ff, 269
    free gift, 87, 137, 269, 277-184
    free will, 239
Freud, Sigmund 10, 47
full, fullness 8, 9, 17ff, 27, 32, 36, 43, 54, 60, 63, 64ff, 74, 79, 80, 83, 91, 100, 103, 108, 116, 117f, 119ff, 122, 123, 126, 132, 136, 139, 142

Galatians, Letter to, 44f, 80, 108, 227, 232, 261, 264, 265, 270, 272, 284
Garden of Eden, 128, 132, 133, 254, 278
Genesis, Book of, 59, 103, 124-129, 131ff, 195, 217, 225, 268, 278
Golden Rule, 41-42, 43f, 46, 231, 259
glorification of believer, 102, 195. 207, 211-216, 220, 229f, 259
glory of God, 151, 171, 197f, 211-217, 224f, 230
grace, 30, 72, 89, 91, 125, 214ff, 241f, 249f, 269, 272, 274
Greatest Commandment, 43-45, 46, 96, 231, 259
guilt, 48-51, 57, 58, 63, 68, 69, 71, 73, 74, 128, 129, 134f, 138f, 163, 271f

hallucination, 136, 156
healing, 20, 37, 51m 78f, 80, 85, 89f, 195, 209, 237, 256, 281
heart, 14, 34, 35f, 38, 39, 43, 48, 57, 61, 64, 69, 71, 76, 82, 84f, 89, 95, 96, 108, 114, 120, 121, 122, 132, 135f, 144, 149, 164, 172, 174, 175, 182, 187, 188, 190, 191, 199, 200, 208, 224f, 226f, 230, 249, 251, 252, 256, 258, 260f, 266, 277, 281
Heaven, heavenly, 9, 17, 21, 24ff, 31, 37, 38, 46, 47, 53, 56, 57, 67, 70, 81, 84, 101, 107, 110, 129, 136f, 142f, 145, 155, 169, 170, 171, 177, 180, 181, 184, 188f, 190, 192f, 194-204, 217, 239, 249, 252, 256, 274, 283
human beings, 10f, 19, 21, 23, 29, 33ff, 40ff, 50ff, 54, 60, 71, 90, 101ff, 105ff, 113, 115, 124ff, 136, 157, 178, 180f, 185, 194, 198f, 205-216, 217, 225, 239, 249, 256f, 271f, 279
help, 13, 20, 25, 37, 39, 40, 50, 79, 83, 84, 85, 90, 91, 111, 113, 181, 199,

201, 222, 243, 244f, 251, 254, 255, 259f, 264, 279, 280, 281 (*see also* service)
hell, 9, 139, 145, 166, 174, 177, 184-193, 194f, 196
Hellenistic, 177
hidden, hiding, 30, 32, 38, 47, 48, 49, 51, 56, 64, 65f, 69, 79, 81, 82, 83, 84, 88f, 94, 116, 122, 128f, 131f, 154, 163, 164, 170, 175, 179, 190, 195, 207f, 215, 217, 222ff, 228, 243, 285f
Holy Spirit, 29, 30, 90, 110-114, 115, 117, 173

identity, identification, 10, 11, 25, 28, 34, 36, 39, 44, 55, 57, 59, 61, 62, 87f, 95, 99, 100, 101f, 105, 107, 108, 109, 115, 124, 126, 135, 138, 139, 140, 143, 144, 148, 149, 171, 178, 180, 181, 187, 188, 202, 203, 229, 233ff, 239, 240, 244, 245, 247f, 267, 272, 284
illusion, illusory, 62, 72, 108, 130ff, 139, 146, 171, 173, 175f, 181ff, 205, 208, 228, 241, 276
innocence, 50, 71, 162, 271
interpretation, 9f, 15, 26, 31, 64, 79, 100, 101, 126, 132, 137, 138f, 145f, 148, 149, 153ff, 158, 184, 185f, 196, 198, 208, 242, 245, 256, 258f, 265, 275f, 277f
intertestamental period, 156, 168, 178, 189, 194
intuition, 13, 268
Isaiah, Book of, 67, 71, 73, 85, 95, 111, 121, 133, 134f, 136, 212, 213, 214, 221, 222, 223, 280
Israel, 34, 37, 169, 177, 218, 221, 226, 260
  ancient Israelites, 133, 171, 218, 254

Jeremiah, Book of, 34, 135, 172, 260
Job, Book of, 41, 177, 190
John, First Letter of, 45, 59-62, 63-64, 67, 68, 71, 106, 166, 182, 193, 196, 220, 234f, 240

John, Gospel of, 21, 23-28, 56, 87, 97ff, 98, 99, 100, 103, 107, 112, 115, 116, 140-143, 147f, 150, 157, 160, 161, 169, 180f, 196, 202, 203, 211, 213, 214, 223f, 229, 236, 237, 242, 267, 276, 282
John the Baptist, 20, 173, 202
judgment, 13, 23, 38, 39, 51, 68, 69, 71, 72, 97, 147, 148, 150, 155, 157, 160-167, 192, 242, 245, 272
  last judgment/final judgment, 155, 160-167, 168, 170, 184, 250
justice, 111, 165, 168, 188, 193, 201, 215, 222, 249
justification, 249, 263, 266

kindness, 91, 252, 257f, 258, 265
kingdom of God/Heaven, 21, 29, 37, 38, 81-86, 101, 111, 140, 154, 155f, 157, 179, 198, 199, 201, 244, 245, 245
Kings, Book of 2, 171
KJV, 3, 78, 184, 261
knowledge, 8, 9, 10, 11, 14, 19, 21, 25, 26, 29, 31, 33, 34, 35, 40. 47, 48, 50, 53f, 57, 59, 60, 61ff, 66, 68, 70, 72, 79, 80, 81, 83, 84, 85, 86, 88, 95, 97, 101, 102, 103, 105-109, 110, 112, 114, 115-118, 119-123, 128, 129, 130, 132, 135, 141ff, 146, 147, 149, 150, 154, 156, 158, 160, 161, 162, 163, 165f, 167, 176, 181, 182, 183, 185, 191, 193, 200, 202, 203, 206, 210, 212, 213, 215, 216, 224f, 226, 228, 229, 230, 236, 237, 239, 240, 241, 243, 249, 250, 253, 258, 259, 260f, 262, 272, 273, 280, 282, 282, 284, 286, 287
  eternal knowledge, 31, 33
  foundational knowledge, 32
  "knowledge of good and evil," 128ff, 170, 249
  revealed knowledge, 83

law, 34f, 41, 43ff, 55, 96, 139, 165, 171, 209f, 225, 248, 252, 254-266, 270, 271, 275, 276, 277, 278, 283

natural law, 34, 35, 165, 171
"the law and the prophets," 41, 43, 45
legalism, 209, 227, 255, 256, 263, 278
Leviathan, 183
light, 26, 49, 51, 64f, 65f, 68, 71, 72, 90, 147, 152, 154, 156, 162, 164, 171, 174, 175, 196, 211f, 217-225, 253
limitation, 29, 54, 67f, 75ff, 83, 100, 116, 129, 130, 147, 149, 150, 180, 182, 205, 206, 209f, 239, 255, 258, 260, 269, 275, 277, 279ff, 286
love
    as Greatest Commandment, 43-45, 46
    "God is love," 59-62, 63, 164
    of enemies, 46f, 105, 247, 271, 276
    love vs. fear, 63-66
Luke, Gospel of, 20, 21, 24, 27, 30, 31, 40, 47, 51, 53, 55, 56, 57, 58, 59, 78, 88, 96, 97, 105, 106, 117, 135, 146, 149, 154, 157, 162, 172, 173, 178, 180, 182, 198, 202, 209, 242, 247, 259, 267

Mark, Gospel of, 20, 21, 22, 24, 37, 40, 55, 75, 76, 82, 146, 154, 179, 180, 192, 208, 223, 231, 245, 261, 267
Matthew, Gospel of, 20, 21, 24, 29, 30, 32, 35, 36, 37, 38, 39, 40, 41, 43, 46, 47, 48, 49, 50, 53, 54, 55, 56, 57, 59, 66, 68, 70, 77, 78, 79, 81, 84, 85, 88, 89, 90, 97, 106, 110, 111, 112, 116, 119, 146, 147, 152, 153, 155, 156, 166, 169, 170, 179, 180, 191, 192, 199, 200, 201, 209, 217, 222, 223, 225, 231, 239, 244, 245, 248, 249, 257, 259, 260, 267, 268, 282
Milton, 185
mind, 9, 10, 12, 13, 18, 25, 27, 29, 32, 33, 35, 36, 40, 43, 48, 51, 53, 54, 56, 58, 60, 61, 62, 63, 65, 68, 69, 71, 72, 73, 75, 76, 77, 78, 79, 82, 83, 85, 88, 90, 94, 95, 96, 99, 100, 101, 102, 112, 115, 120, 121, 122, 126, 127, 130, 132, 137, 138, 139, 140, 142, 144, 147, 148, 149, 150, 151, 153, 155, 156, 157, 158, 159. 165. 167, 168, 170, 171, 174, 176, 178, 179, 180, 181, 184, 188, 190, 191, 192f, 194ff. 198ff, 202, 203, 205, 208, 209, 210, 211, 215, 216, 223, 224, 230, 233, 239, 240, 241, 243, 248f, 250, 251, 256, 262, 265, 269, 272, 274f, 276, 277, 278, 280, 281, 283, 286
Mind of God, 61, 62, 64, 95, 120, 121, 130, 132, 199, 206. 207, 210, 220, 227f, 235, 239, 240, 243
Moses, 73, 143, 171, 254, 256, 257, 264, 283
    Mosaic law, 252, 254
mystery, 13, 81, 151, 212, 215, 248
mythology, 10, 24, 47, 94, 97, 124, 125, 127, 168, 178, 179, 183, 185, 193, 197

natural, 18, 19, 20, 21, 25, 34, 35, 39, 45, 49, 65, 68, 69, 70, 77, 81, 82, 83, 84, 85, 86, 88, 114, 122, 126, 133, 134, 161, 165, 167, 171, 180, 190, 199, 201, 210, 246, 248, 253, 256, 261, 265, 271, 280, 281, 283, 284, 285
natural law, 34f, 165, 171
New Jerusalem, 196, 197
noble, 249f
NRSV, 3, 217, 229
Numbers, Book of, 212

oneness, 22f, 27, 42, 43-45, 82ff, 90f, 96, 106, 111, 119, 152, 163, 166, 172, 173, 200f, 202, 212, 214, 216, 226-230, 231-235, 236-238, 244-246, 248, 269f, 272f, 275, 286
    of God, 64f, 150, 255
Origen, 185
origin, original creation/life/being, 61f, 88, 89, 90, 91, 94, 99-104, 107, 117, 121, 124-132, 133f,

137, 141f, 143, 144, 153, 166, 195, 198, 200, 202, 220, 221, 225, 227, 228, 240, 243, 271
original sin, 271

parables, 36, 57, 73, 81, 82, 83, 84, 88, 143, 169, 180, 244f, 249
paradoxical, 26, 53, 91, 121, 122, 137, 158, 214, 220, 250f
parallel, 31, 60, 90, 101, 103, 262
parallelism, 189
Philippians, Letter to, 80, 122, 250, 251, 261
philosophy, 10, 11f, 13, 29, 33, 28, 93, 127, 206, 285
point of culmination (*see* culminating point)
point of origin, 100, 102, 104, 133, 141, 142, 153, 240
praise-worthy, 21, 29, 78, 186, 241, 242, 250, 261
prayer, 46, 53, 110, 112, 119-123, 214, 226, 229, 230, 237
predestination, 177, 215, 226, 239-243
pre-existence, 32, 56, 116, 117, 129, 237
presumption, presuppositions, 24, 27, 79, 129, 148, 206, 286
prodigal son, 55ff, 73, 135
proof, 22, 190, 238, 284
prophets, prophecy, 34, 41, 43, 67, 91, 107, 111, 134, 171, 172, 180, 182, 210, 211, 242, 260, 268, 280, 281, 282
prove, 18, 32, 57, 66, 76, 79, 84, 94, 153, 158, 205, 206, 223, 224, 252, 269
Proverbs, Book of, 41, 174, 188, 189, 220, 221
Psalms, Book of, 41, 59, 120, 133, 134, 174, 186, 187, 206, 207, 218, 219, 220, 224, 278, 279
psyche, 10
psychology, psychological, 9-14, 21, 33, 37, 46, 47, 48, 63, 68f, 94, 97, 126, 135, 145f, 147, 155f, 167, 169, 179, 182, 191, 193, 195, 196, 197, 218ff, 222, 224f, 229, 249, 254f, 256, 261, 262, 273, 279, 281, 284, 285
punishment, 63f, 67, 69, 139, 176, 186, 193, 272

reality, 14, 19, 29-32, 33, 34, 36, 37, 40, 52, 55, 66, 67, 76, 77, 78, 79, 80, 82, 83, 87, 90, 100, 102, 103, 106, 107, 108, 116, 121, 125, 127, 130, 131, 132, 137, 138, 140, 141, 143, 145, 146, 147, 149, 150, 152, 154, 157, 158, 159, 160, 162, 167, 169, 170, 172, 174, 184, 189, 194, 195, 197, 198, 199, 203, 205, 206, 207, 208, 216, 224, 228, 234, 236, 239, 240, 241, 257, 269, 280
realization, 10, 13, 25, 29, 30, 31, 32, 33, 46, 49, 50, 51, 55, 56, 60, 61, 71, 72, 74, 75. 77. 82. 83. 86, 89, 91, 94, 97, 98, 99, 102, 105, 107, 109, 110, 111, 112, 113, 114, 116, 117, 121, 122, 123, 127, 130, 133, 138, 144, 152, 155, 157, 158, 162, 164, 165, 166, 170, 175, 193, 199, 200, 201, 207, 214, 216, 220, 227, 230, 234, 236, 239, 240, 241, 245, 257, 258, 263, 264, 281
reason, 9, 10, 12,13, 51, 65, 70, 71, 72, 73, 74, 76, 79, 80, 88, 94, 98, 104, 110, 117, 126, 137, 145, 151, 160, 161, 165, 201, 210, 226, 241, 272, 286, 289
recognition, 21, 33, 85, 88, 89, 90, 127, 132, 151, 165, 199, 242, 261
reconciliation, 54, 136, 139, 227, 234, 270, 271, 275
redemption, 108, 134, 261, 264, 266, 270, 278
relationship, 10, 11, 21, 22, 30, 34, 41, 46, 50, 52, 53, 54f, 56, 57, 58, 71, 80, 90, 96, 113, 115, 132, 136, 160, 207, 210, 227f, 228, 229, 230, 233, 234, 236, 248, 261, 264, 265, 285
religion, 10, 11, 12, 20, 41, 43, 50, 111, 208, 209, 227, 247, 248, 252, 254, 255ff, 264f, 268, 275, 277, 282

repentance, 57
resurrection, 106, 145-152, 153, 158, 163, 221, 267-276
reunion, 58
revelation, 11, 34, 64, 66, 83, 108, 111, 116, 157, 182, 195, 196, 197, 202, 212, 225, 256, 286
Revelation, Book of, 123, 169, 170, 182, 183, 195, 196, 197, 198, 217, 225
reversal, the great, 37-40, 137, 154, 245
righteousness, 38, 59, 69, 72, 199, 220, 221, 244, 263, 269, 279, 280

salvation, 18, 89, 90, 133-139, 157, 188, 218f, 221, 224, 241, 242, 248, 258, 264, 265, 267, 271, 273, 275, 276, 277, 282
gifts of salvation, 89ff
Samuel, First Book of, 172, 212
Samuel, Second Book of, 218
Satan, the, 125, 177-183, 192
scripture, the scriptures, 43, 93, 97f, 171, 189, 268, 277, 278
self, the new/true/eternal self, 10, 23-28, 61, 90, 96, 100, 101, 110, 117, 119, 132, 140, 149, 159, 164f, 166, 171, 186, 198, 203, 217, 224, 230, 236, 242, 243, 256, 262, 267f
"old self," false/self-limiting self, 23f, 26, 27, 65, 67, 68, 74, 90, 93, 95, 101, 117, 119, 138, 158f, 161, 173, 179, 186
self-interest(s), 39, 42, 153, 194, 264
selflessness, 23-28, 61, 121
separate, separation, 10, 18, 44, 62, 128f, 130, 133, 164, 166, 228, 262, 271, 275f
service, 45, 57, 91. 111, 231, 245, 251, 252f, 259, 280, 284
Sheol, 174, 184-189
sin, 30, 34, 51, 57, 59, 71, 72, 74, 89f, 99, 134, 138, 139, 208, 260, 261f, 262, 271, 283
sons/daughters of God, 19, 38f, 46, 47, 53, 103, 105-109, 110-114, 148f, 213, 214, 232, 241, 247, 265, 282

sonship, 19, 55, 105-109, 110-114, 117, 162, 238, 240, 241, 242, 283
stages, 13, 34, 36, 141, 155, 157, 185, 193, 206, 215f, 221, 254, 257, 260, 268
states of mind and being, 13, 19, 25, 52, 72, 83, 94, 96, 102, 107, 108, 124, 126f, 128, 129, 130, 133f, 137f, 139, 142, 145, 149, 153, 158, 161, 165, 166, 169, 178, 180, 181, 184-193, 194f, 198ff, 200f, 203, 216, 228, 250, 278
subjective, 10, 14, 35, 36, 80, 116, 144, 149, 167, 190, 286
supernatural, 25, 212

temptation, 87, 129, 178f
theme(s), 11, 24, 46, 102, 106, 134, 136, 139, 158, 205, 219, 221, 227, 278
theology, 9-14, 17, 22, 23, 24, 29, 33, 185, 196, 203, 206, 243, 258, 285
throne vision, 196ff
timelessness, 93, 96, 137, 158f, 274
tradition, 10, 36, 107, 167, 168, 210, 224, 255, 257, 258, 265, 270
transcendence, 12, 13, 19, 22, 26, 27, 28, 53f, 98, 116, 117, 130, 169, 196, 199, 203, 212, 224, 227, 230, 257, 263, 265, 271, 275, 276, 276, 280, 281
transformation, 29, 31, 52, 61, 68, 74, 75-79, 102, 103, 120, 151, 154f, 169, 218, 224, 247, 248, 258, 259, 272, 276, 277
transfiguration, 222
tripartite cosmos, 189, 194

unconscious, 33, 46-52, 66, 69, 71, 74, 81, 94, 112, 117, 127, 129, 161, 170, 174, 190, 192, 193, 194, 200, 210, 223, 248, 257, 283
understanding, 8, 9-14, 20, 21, 24, 27, 30f, 32, 36, 37, 47, 50, 60, 83, 85, 113, 114, 118, 122, 131, 137, 140, 142, 143, 144, 145f, 147, 150, 155, 160, 167, 177, 185, 190, 201, 210, 215, 217, 220, 226, 234, 236,

251, 267, 269, 270, 272, 274, 283, 285, 286, 289
unification, 111, 214, 255, 272, 273, 275
unity, 10, 228, 234, 254, 271, 273
Universe, the, 206, 209, 272, 285
    Universal Mind, 227, 228
universal, universality, 12, 23-27, 55, 60, 106, 107, 111, 121, 150. 159. 188, 207, 212, 213, 214, 221, 223, 230, 242, 246, 247, 249, 260, 267, 268, 272f, 274, 275, 278, 281, 286

value, values, 11, 35, 40, 84f, 87, 89, 179, 209, 210, 257, 259, 265
vine, 237
vision, 52, 100, 110, 123, 153, 154, 155, 158, 194, 195ff, 198, 208, 209, 210, 214, 217, 246, 250, 254, 256, 257, 264

well-being, 58, 209
words, 9, 14, 25, 29f, 32f, 35f, 41, 44, 48, 53, 97, 99, 137, 148, 150, 162, 180, 184, 190, 197, 202, 203, 220, 231, 234, 248, 261, 268
Word of God, 33, 35f, 119ff, 144, 261, 277

Zechariah, Book of, 175
Zoroastrianism, 156, 168, 170, 178, 185

**Also by Michael Roden:**

*A Church Not Made with Hands: Christianity as Spiritual Experience*

*Jesus and Ourselves: An Alternative Understanding of Christianity*

*Paradise Re-Envisioned*

*Songs of the Morning*

*Love is the Reason*

For more information, see:

*michaelroden.com*

*infinitepassionpublishing.com*